CLARENDON LIBRARY OF LOGIC AND PHILOSOPHY

General Editor: L. Jonathan Cohen

THE NATURE OF
NECESSITY

THE NATURE OF NECESSITY

—

ALVIN PLANTINGA

OXFORD

AT THE CLARENDON PRESS

1974

Oxford University Press, Ely House, London W. 1

GLASGOW NEW YORK TORONTO MELBOURNE WELLINGTON
CAPE TOWN IBADAN NAIROBI DAR ES SALAAM LUSAKA ADDIS ABABA
DELHI BOMBAY CALCUTTA MADRAS KARACHI LAHORE DACCA
KUALA LUMPUR SINGAPORE HONG KONG TOKYO

ISBN 0 19 824404 5

© *Oxford University Press 1974*

*Printed in Great Britain
at the University Press, Oxford
by Vivian Ridler
Printer to the University*

TO MY PARENTS

CORNELIUS AND LETTIE PLANTINGA

PREFACE

ALTHOUGH the notion of necessity has had a long and distinguished career in Western thought, it has not, on the whole, been treated kindly by twentieth-century philosophy. The dominant traditions (both Anglo-American and Continental) have for the most part made a determined effort to dispense with necessity, or to explain it away in favour of linguistic, psychological, or sociological surrogates.

I think this is a mistake; and in the present book I take the idea of necessity seriously and at face value. In the first chapter I try to locate and fix the idea in question—the idea of broadly logical necessity—and to distinguish it from others in the neighbourhood. I also distinguish *de dicto* necessity—a matter of a proposition's being necessarily true—from *de re* necessity, which involves an object's having a property essentially or necessarily. In Chapters II and III, I consider and reject some objections to modality *de re* and argue that it can be explained by way of modality *de dicto*. Chapter IV introduces and explains the idea of possible worlds; this notion, I believe, permits a genuine advance in our grasp of matters modal. The question of Chapter V is whether an object has an essence: a property essential to it and essentially unique to it; the answer is indeed it has. Chapter VI examines the so-called problem of transworld identity, widely thought to afflict the view that the same object exists in more than one possible world; it concludes that this problem is more appearance than reality. In Chapters VII and VIII, I explore one aspect of the venerable problem of not-being. Some possible worlds contain objects that do not in fact exist: must we conclude that there are some things that do not exist? Can we think and talk about what does not exist? The answer is we must not and cannot. Chapters IX and X consider the bearing of some of the foregoing ideas on two traditional concerns of natural theology: the problem of evil and the ontological argument for the existence of God. I argue that these ideas enable us to resolve the former and find a sound formulation of the latter. Finally, in the appendix,

I examine and partly concur with Quine's claim that quantified modal logic presupposes what he calls Aristotelian Essentialism —the view that objects typically have both accidental and essential properties.

My thanks to *Nous* for permission to reprint a few paragraphs of "*De Re et De Dicto*" (1969) and "What George Could Not Have Been" (1971) in Chapters II and III; to *The Philosophical Review* for permission to reprint a few paragraphs of "World and Essence" (1970) in Chapter IV; and to New York University Press for permission to reprint a portion of "Transworld Identity or Worldbound Individuals?" (*Logic and Ontology*, ed. Milton Munitz, 1973) as part of Chapter VI.

I am also happy to record my gratitude to the Danforth Foundation and the Center for Advanced Study in the Behavioral Sciences; an E. Harris Harbison Award from the former and a fellowship from the latter enabled me to spend the year 1968–9 at the Center (a scholarly retreat than which none greater can be conceived), where I composed an early draft of the book. Similar thanks are due the Guggenheim Foundation for a fellowship for the year 1971–2, which I spent at U.C.L.A.; there I completed most of the final draft. I am grateful to U.C.L.A. for working space and secretarial help; and to Calvin College for secretarial help as well as for a reduced teaching load for the years 1969–70 and 1970–1.

I am especially eager to express my indebtedness to a large number of colleagues—in particular, those at Calvin and U.C.L.A.—students, and friends for penetrating criticism, stimulating discussion, and wise advice. Special thanks for such benefits are due Roderick Chisholm, Peter De Vos, David Kaplan, David Lewis, Lawrence Powers, and Nicholas Wolterstorff.

CONTENTS

I

PRELIMINARY DISTINCTIONS AND REMARKS

1. *Necessity Circumscribed*

THE distinction between necessary and contingent truth is as easy to recognize as it is difficult to explain to the sceptic's satisfaction. Among true propositions[1] we find some, like

(1) the average annual rainfall in Los Angeles is about 12 inches

that are contingent, while others, like

(2) $7+5 = 12$

or

(3) If all men are mortal and Socrates is a man, then Socrates is mortal

that are necessary.

But what exactly do these words—'necessary' and 'contingent' —mean? What distinction do they mark? Just what is supposed to be the difference between necessary and contingent truths? We can hardly explain that p is necessary if and only if its denial is impossible; this is true but insufficiently enlightening. It would be a peculiar philosopher who had the relevant concept of impossibility well in hand but lacked that of necessity. Instead, we must give example and hope for the best. In the first place, truths of logic—truths of propositional logic and first order quantification theory, let us say—are necessary in the sense in question. Such truths are logically necessary in the narrow

---

[1] Necessity, truth, and allied properties are at bottom (as I see it) properties of propositions, not sentences. A sentence is true, on a given occasion of its use, if on that occasion it expresses a true proposition. My conception of proposition as non-linguistic entity expressed by but distinct from sentences parallels Moore's idea of proposition, Frege's of *Gedanke*, and Bolzano's of *Satz*. Some find propositions objectionable—on the grounds, apparently, that they lack 'a clear criterion of identity'. In so far as the alleged debility can be made tolerably clear, it is one that propositions share with electrons, mountains, wars—and sentences.

sense; (3) above would be an example. But the sense of necessity in question—call it 'broadly logical necessity' is wider than this. Truths of set theory, arithmetic and mathematics generally are necessary in this sense, as are a host of homelier items such as

No one is taller than himself
Red is a colour
If a thing is red, then it is coloured
No numbers are human beings

and

No prime minister is a prime number.

And of course there are many propositions debate about whose status has played an important role in philosophical discussion —for example

Every person is conscious at some time or other
Every human person has a body
No one has a private language
There never was a time when there was space but no material objects

and

There exists a being than which it is not possible that there be a greater.

So the sense of necessity in question is wider than that captured in first order logic. On the other hand, it is narrower than that of *causal* or *natural* necessity.

Voltaire once swam the Atlantic

for example, is surely implausible. Indeed, there is a clear sense in which it is impossible. Eighteenth-century intellectuals (as distinguished from dolphins) simply lacked the physical equipment for this kind of feat. Unlike Superman, furthermore, the rest of us are incapable of leaping tall buildings at a single bound, or (without auxiliary power of some kind) travelling faster than a speeding bullet. These things are impossible for us; but not in the broadly logical sense. Again, it may be necessary—causally necessary—that any two material objects attract each other with a force proportional to their mass and inversely proportional to the square of the distance between them; it is not necessary in the sense in question.

Another notion that must carefully be distinguished from necessity is what (for want of a better name) we might call 'unrevisability' or perhaps 'ungiveupability'. Some philosophers hold that *no* proposition—not even the austerest law of logic—is in principle immune from revision. The future development of science (though presumably not that of theology) could lead us rationally to abandon any belief we now hold, including the law of non-contradiction and *modus ponens* itself. So Quine:

... it becomes folly to seek a boundary between synthetic statements which hold contingently on experience, and analytic statements, which hold come what may. Any statement can be held come what may, if we make drastic enough adjustments elsewhere in the system. Even a statement very close to the periphery can be held true in the face of recalcitrant experience by pleading hallucination or by amending certain statements of the kind called logical laws. Conversely, by the same token, no statement is immune to revision. Revision even of the logical law of excluded middle has been proposed as a means of simplifying quantum mechanics; and what difference is there in principle between such a shift and the shift whereby Kepler superseded Ptolemy, or Einstein Newton, or Darwin Aristotle?[1]

Giving up a truth of logic—*modus ponens*, let us say—in order to simplify physical theory may strike us as like giving up a truth of arithmetic in order to simplify the Doctrine of the Trinity. In any event, Quine's point is that no statement is immune from revision; for each there are circumstances under which (perhaps with a reluctant wave) we should give it up, and do so quite properly.

Here Quine may or may not be right. But suppose we temporarily and irenically concede that every statement, *modus ponens* included, is subject to revision. Are we then obliged to follow those who conclude that there are no genuinely necessary propositions? No; for their conclusion displays confusion. To say of *modus ponens* that it (or its corresponding conditional) is a necessary truth is not, of course, to say that people will never give it up, as if necessity were a trait conferred by long term popular favour. I may be unprepared to give up the belief that I am a fine fellow in the face of even the most recalcitrant experience; it does not follow either that this belief is necessarily true or that

[1] W. V. O. Quine, "Two Dogmas of Empiricism", *From a Logical Point of View*, 2nd edn. (Cambridge, Mass.: Harvard University Press, 1961), p. 43.

I take it to be so. Nor would the unlikely event of everyone's sharing my truculence on this point make any difference. Just as obviously, a proposition might be necessarily true even if most people thought it false or held no opinion whatever on the matter.

So necessity has little or nothing to do with what people would *in fact* give up under various happy or unhappy circumstances. But it must also be distinguished from what cannot be *rationally* rejected. For clearly a proposition might be both necessary and such that on a given occasion the rational thing to do is to give up or deny it. Suppose I am a mathematical neophyte and have heard and accepted rumours to the effect that the Continuum Hypothesis has been shown to be independent of Zermelo–Frankel Set Theory. I relate this rumour to a habitually authoritative mathematician, who smiles indulgently and produces a subtly fallacious argument for the opposite conclusion—an argument which I still find compelling after careful study. I need not be irrational in believing him and accepting his argument, despite the fact that in this instance his usual accuracy has deserted him and he has told me what is necessarily false. To take a more homely example: I have computed the sum $97 + 342 + 781$ four times running and each time got the answer 1120; so I believe, naturally enough, that $97 + 342 + 781 = 1120$. The fact, however, is that I made the same mistake each time—carried a '1' instead of a '2' in the third column. But my belief may none the less be rational. I do not know whether circumstances could arise in which the reasonable thing to do would be to give up *modus ponens*; but if such circumstances could and did arise, it would not follow that *modus ponens* is not a necessary truth. Broadly logical necessity, therefore, must be distinguished from unrevisability as well as from causal necessity and logical necessity strictly so called.

It must also be distinguished from the *self-evident* and the *a priori*. The latter two are epistemological categories, and fairly vaporous ones at that. But consider the first. What does self-evidence come to? The answer is by no means easy. In so far as we can make rough and intuitive sense of this notion, however, to say that a proposition p is self-evident is to answer the question 'how do you know that p?' It is to claim that p is utterly obvious—obvious to anyone or nearly anyone who understands it. If p is self-evident, then on understanding it we simply see that it is true; our knowledge of *modus ponens* may be cited as of this sort. Now obviously many questions arise about this notion; but in so far as we do apprehend it, we see that many necessary propositions are not thus transparent. $97+342+781 = 1220$ is indeed necessary, but certainly not self-evident—not to most of us, at any rate.

Still, perhaps we could say that this truth is self-evident in an extended sense: it is a consequence of self-evident truths by argument forms whose corresponding conditionals are themselves self-evident. Could we add that all necessary truths are self-evident in this extended sense? Not with any show of plausibility. The Axiom of Choice and the Continuum Hypothesis are either necessarily true or necessarily false; there is little reason to think that either of these, or either of their denials, are deducible from self-evident propositions by self-evident steps. You may think it inappropriate to speak of truth in connection with such an item as, say, the Continuum Hypothesis. If so, I disagree; I think this proposition just as true or just as false as the commonest truths and falsities of arithmetic. But no matter; there are simpler and more obvious examples. Each of Goldbach's Conjecture and Fermat's Last Theorem, for example, is either necessarily true or necessarily false; but each may turn out to be such that neither it nor its denial is self-evident in the extended sense. That is to say, for all I know, and, so far as I know, for all *anyone* knows, this may be so. I do not mean to assert that this is *possibly* so, in the broadly logical sense; for (as could plausibly be argued) where S is the set of self-evident propositions and R that of self-evident argument forms, a proposition p *possibly* follows from S by R only if p *actually*, and, indeed, *necessarily* thus follows. And since I do not know whether Goldbach's Conjecture or Fermat's Theorem *do* follow from S by R, I am not prepared to say that it is *possible* that they do so. My point is only that the question whether, for example, Goldbach's conjecture is self-evident in the extended sense is distinct from the question whether it is a necessary truth. Later on (Chapter V, Section 2) we shall see that there are any number of propositions that are necessarily true but not self-evident, even in the extended sense.

So not all necessary propositions are self-evident. What about the converse? Are some contingent propositions self-evident? The question is vexed, and the answer not obvious. Is the proposition I express by saying '2+2 = 4 is self-evident for me now' self-evident for me now? Perhaps so, perhaps not. Perhaps the idea of self-evidence is not sharp enough to permit an answer. What is once more important is that a negative answer is not immediate and obvious; self-evidence must be distinguished, initially, at least, from necessity.

Not strictly to the point but worth mentioning is the fact that some propositions *seem* or *appear* to be self-evident although they are not necessarily true or, for that matter, true at all. Some of the best examples are furnished by the Russellian Paradoxes. It seems self-evident that for every condition or property P there is the set of just those things displaying P; it seems equally self-evident that there is such a condition or property as that of *being non self-membered*. But of course these (together with some other apparently self-evident propositions) self-evidently yield the conclusion that there is a set that is and is not a member of itself; and this is self-evidently false. Some may see in this the bankruptcy of self-evidence. It is not my purpose, in these introductory pages, to defend self-evidence or answer the question how we know the truth of such propositions as *modus ponens*. Still, the conclusion is hasty. Our embarrassment in the face of such paradoxes shows that a proposition may seem to be self-evident when in fact it is false. How does it follow that *modus ponens*, for example, is not self-evident, or that there is some other or better answer to the question of how we know that it is true? The senses sometimes deceive us; square towers sometimes appear round. It does not follow either that we do not know the truth of such propositions as *The Empire State Building is rectangular* or that we have some non-empirical method of determining its truth.

Finally, the distinction between the necessary and the contingent must not be confused with the alleged cleavage between the *a priori* and the *a posteriori*. The latter distinction, indeed, is shrouded in obscurity. But given the rough and intuitive understanding we have of the terms involved, it is clear that the distinction they mark, like that between what is self-evident and what is not (and unlike that between the necessary and contingent), is *epistemological*. Furthermore, the relation between what is known *a priori* and what is necessarily true is by no means simple and straightforward. It is immediately obvious that not all necessary truths are known *a priori*; for there are necessary truths—Fermat's last theorem or its denial, for example—that are not known at all, and *a fortiori* are not known *a priori*. Is it rather that every necessary truth that is known, is known *a priori*? This question divides itself: (*a*) is every necessary truth that is known, known *a priori* to everyone who knows it? and (*b*) is every necessary truth that is known to someone or other, known *a priori* to some one or other? The answer to (*a*) is clear. Having taken the trouble to understand the proof, you may know *a priori* that the Schroeder–Bernstein Theorem is a consequence of some standard formulation of set theory. If I know that you are properly reliable in these matters and take your word for it, then I may know that truth *a posteriori*—as I may if I've forgotten the proof but remember having verified that indeed there is one. To learn the value of the sine of 54 degrees, I consult a handy table of trigonometric functions: my knowledge of this item is then *a posteriori*. In the same way even such simple truths of arithmetic as that $75 + 36 = 111$ can be known *a posteriori*. So the answer to (*a*) is obvious. The answer to question (*b*) is perhaps not quite so clear; but in Chapter V (Section 2) I shall give some examples of truths that are necessary but probably not known *a priori* to any of us.[1]

So necessity cannot be identified with what is known *a priori*. Should we say instead that a proposition is necessary if and only if it is know*able a priori*? But by whom? We differ widely in our ability to apprehend necessary truths; and no doubt some are beyond the grasp of even the best of us. Is the idea, then, that a proposition is necessarily true, if and only if it is *possible*, in the broadly logical sense, that some person, human or divine, knows it *a priori*? Perhaps this is true. Indeed, perhaps every truth whatever is possibly known *a priori* to some person—to God if not to man. But suppose we avoid the turbid waters of speculative theology and restrict our question to *human* knowledge: must a contingent proposition, if known, be known *a posteriori*? The question is as vexed as the notion of *a priori* knowledge is obscure. What is known *a priori* is known independently, somehow or other, of experience. My knowledge of *modus ponens* or

[1] See also my "World and Essence", *Philosophical Review*, 79 (1970), 481.

that $7+5 = 12$ would be cited by way of example. But how about my knowledge that I do know that $7+5 = 12$? Is that independent of experience in the requisite fashion? Suppose

(4) I know that $7+5 = 12$;

cannot I know *a priori* that (4) is true? And this despite the contingency of (4)? Perhaps you will say that I know (4) only if I know

(4') I believe that $7+5 = 12$;

and perhaps you will add that knowledge of this last item must be *a posteriori*. But is this really true? On a strict construction of 'independent of experience' it may seem so; for surely I must have had *some* experience to know that I thus believe—if only that needed to acquire the relevant concepts. But on such a strict construction it may seem equally apparent that I know no truths at all *a priori*; even to know that $7+5 = 12$ I must have had some experience. There is no specific *sort* of experience I need, to know that $7+5 = 12$; and this (subject, of course, to all the difficulty of saying what counts as a *sort* here) is perhaps what distinguishes my knowledge of this truth as *a priori*. But the same thing holds for my knowledge of (4'). Belief is not (*pace* Hume) a special brilliance or vividness of idea or image; there is no specific sort of experience I must have to know that I believe that $7+5 = 12$. So perhaps I know *a priori* that I believe that $7+5 = 12$. If so, then I have *a priori* knowledge of a contingent truth. Similarly, perhaps my knowledge that I *exist* is *a priori*. For perhaps I know *a priori* that I believe that I exist; I also know *a priori* that if I believe that I exist, then indeed I do exist. But then nothing but exceptional obtuseness could prevent my knowing *a priori* that I exist, despite the contingency of that proposition.

It is fair to say, therefore, that I probably know some contingent truths *a priori*. At any rate it seems clearly *possible* that I do so. So necessity cannot be identified with what is knowable *a priori*.[1] Unrevisibility, self-evidence, and *a priori* knowledge are

[1] In "Naming and Necessity" (*Semantics of Natural Language*, ed. Davidson and Harmon, Dordrecht: D. Reidel, 1972, p. 253) Saul Kripke suggests that another kind of propositions is contingent but knowable *a priori*. Suppose, he says, that I fix the reference of the term 'one metre' as the length of a certain stick (call it S) at a time t. Then 'one metre' is not synonymous with the phrase 'the length of S at t' but is instead a proper name or 'rigid designator' of the length S actually has

difficult notions; but conceding that we do have a grasp—one that is perhaps halting and infirm—of these notions, we must also concede that the notion of necessary truth coincides with none of them.

2. *Modality* de dicto *and Modality* de re

I have spoken of necessity as a property or trait of *propositions* and tried to distinguish it from others sometimes confused with it. This is the idea of modality *de dicto*. An assertion of modality *de dicto*, for example

(5) necessarily nine is composite

predicates a modal property—in this instance *necessary truth*—of another *dictum* or proposition:

(6) nine is composite.

Much traditional philosophy, however, bids us distinguish this notion from another. We may attribute necessary truth to a proposition; but we may also ascribe to some object—the number 9, let us say—the *necessary* or *essential possession* of such a property as that of *being composite*. The distinction between modality *de dicto* and modality *de re* is apparently embraced by Aristotle, who observes (*Prior Analytics*, i. 9) that 'It happens sometimes that the conclusion is necessary when only one premiss is necessary; not, however, either premiss taken at random, but

at t. And under these conditions, he adds, my knowledge of the proposition *S is one metre long at t* is *a priori* despite the contingency of that proposition. "If he used stick S to fix the reference of the term 'one metre', then as a result of this kind of 'definition' (which is not an abbreviative or synonymous definition) he knows automatically without further investigation, that S is one metre long" (275). Here we may have doubts. Suppose I have never seen S and hold no views as to its length. I propose none the less to use 'one metre' as a rigid designator of the length, whatever it is, that S actually displays at t. After thus determining the reference of 'one metre', I know that the *sentence* 'S is one metre long at t' expresses a truth in my language; the truth it does express, however, is one I neither know nor believe. So my thus determining the reference of 'one metre' is not sufficient for my knowing *a priori* that S is one metre long.

What I do know *a priori* (or so it seems to me) is that if I use 'one metre' as a rigid designator of the length of S (and given the appropriate function of the phrase 'S is . . . long at t') then the sentence 'S is one metre long at t' expresses a truth in my language. This conditional, however, is necessary rather than contingent.

The issues here are complex and much more must be said; unfortunately "Naming and Necessity" came into my hands too late for the detailed consideration I should like to have given this and other issues it raises.

the major premiss.'¹ Here Aristotle means to sanction such inferences as

(7) Every human being is necessarily rational
(8) Every animal in this room is a human being

so

(9) Every animal in this room is necessarily rational;

he means to reject such inferences as:

(10) Every rational creature is in Australia
(11) Every human being is necessarily a rational creature

so

(12) Every human being is necessarily in Australia.

Now presumably Aristotle would accept as sound the inference of (9) from (7) and (8) (granted the truth of 8). If he is right, therefore, then (9) is not to be read as

(9′) It is necessarily true that every animal in this room is rational;

for (9′) is clearly false. Instead, (9) must be construed (if Aristotle is correct) as the claim that each animal in this room has a certain property—the property of being rational—*necessarily* or *essentially*. That is to say, (9) must be taken as an expression of modality *de re* rather than modality *de dicto*. And what this means is that (9) is not the assertion that a certain *dictum* or proposition—*every animal in this room is rational*—is necessarily true, but is instead the assertion that each *res* of a certain kind has a certain property essentially or necessarily—or, what comes to the same, the assertion that each such thing has the modal property of being essentially rational.

In *Summa Contra Gentiles*, St. Thomas considers the question whether God's foreknowledge of human action—a foreknowledge that consists, according to St. Thomas, in God's simply *seeing* the relevant action's taking place—is consistent with human freedom. In this connection he inquires into the truth of

(13) What is seen to be sitting is necessarily sitting.

For suppose at t_1 God sees that Theatetus is sitting at t_2. If (13)

¹ Quoted by William Kneale in "Modality *De Dicto* and *De Re*", in *Logic, Methodology, and Philosophy of Science*, ed. Nagel, Suppes, and Tarski (Stanford University Press, 1962), p. 623.

is true, then presumably Theatetus is *necessarily* sitting at t_2, in which case he was not free, at that time, to do anything *but* sit.

St. Thomas concludes that (13) is true taken *de dicto* but false taken *de re*; that is

(13') It is necessarily true that whatever is seen to be sitting is sitting

is true but

(13") Whatever is seen to be sitting has the property of sitting necessarily or essentially

is false. The deterministic argument, however, requires the truth of (13"); and hence that argument fails. Like Aristotle, then, Aquinas appears to believe that modal statements are of two kinds. Some predicate a modality of another statement (modality *de dicto*); but others predicate of an object the necessary or essential possession of a property; and these latter express modality *de re*.

But what is it, according to Aristotle and Aquinas, to say that a certain object has a certain property essentially or necessarily? That, presumably, the object in question could not conceivably have lacked the property in question; that under no possible circumstances could that object have failed to possess that property. Here, as in the case of modality *de dicto*, no mere definition is likely to be of much use; what we need instead is example and articulation. I am thinking of the number 5; what I am thinking of then, is prime. *Being prime*, furthermore, is a property that it could not conceivably have lacked. Of course, the proposition

(14) What I am thinking of is prime

is not necessarily true. This has no bearing on the question whether what I am thinking of could have failed to be prime; and indeed it could not. No doubt the number 5 could have lacked many properties that in fact it has: the property of numbering the fingers on a human hand would be an example. But that it should have lacked the property of being prime is quite impossible. And a statement of modality *de re* asserts of some object that it has some property essentially in this sense.

Aquinas points out that a given statement of modality *de dicto*

—(13′) for example—may be true when the corresponding statement of modality *de re*—(13″) in this instance—is false. We might add that in other such pairs the *de dicto* statement is false but the *de re* statement true; if I am thinking of the number 17, then

(15) What I am thinking of is essentially prime

is true, but

(15′) Necessarily, what I am thinking of is prime

is false.

The distinction between modality *de re* and modality *de dicto* is not confined to ancient and medieval philosophy. G. E. Moore discusses the idealistic doctrine of internal relations;[1] he concludes that it is false or confused or perhaps both. What is presently interesting is that he takes this doctrine to be the claim that all relational properties are *internal*—which claim, he thinks, is just the proposition that every object has each of its relational properties essentially in the above sense. The doctrine of internal relations, he says, "implies, in fact, quite generally, that any term which does in fact have a particular relational property, could not have existed without having that property. And in saying this it obviously flies in the face of common sense. It seems quite obvious that in the case of many relational properties which things have, the fact that they have them is a mere matter of fact; that the things in question might have existed without having them" (p. 289). Now Moore is prepared to concede that objects do have some of their relational properties essentially. Like Aristotle and Aquinas, therefore, Moore holds that some objects have some of their properties essentially and others non-essentially or accidently.

One final example: Norman Malcolm believes that the Analogical Argument for other minds requires the assumption that one must learn what, for example, *pain* is "from his own case". But, he says, "if I were to learn what pain is from perceiving my own pain then I should, necessarily, have learned that pain is something that exists only when I feel pain. For the pain that serves as my paradigm of pain (i.e. my own) has the property of existing only when I feel it. That property is essential, not accidental; it is nonsense to suppose that the pain I feel could

[1] In *Philosophical Studies* (London: Routledge & Kegan Paul Ltd., 1951), p. 276.

exist when I did not feel it."[1] This argument appears to require something like the following premiss:

(16) If I acquire my concept of *C* by experiencing objects and all the objects that serve as my paradigms have a property *P* essentially, then my concept of *C* is such that the proposition *Whatever is an instance of C has P* is necessarily true.

Is (16) true? I shall not enter that question here. But initially, at least, it looks as if Malcolm means to join Aristotle, Aquinas, and Moore in support of the thesis that objects typically have both essential and accidental properties; apparently he means to embrace the conception of modality *de re*.

There is a prima facie distinction, then, between modality *de dicto* and modality *de re*. This distinction, furthermore, has a long and distinguished history. Many contemporary philosophers who find the idea of modality *de dicto* tolerably clear, however, look utterly askance at that of modality *de re*, suspecting it a source of boundless confusion. Indeed, there is abroad the subtle suggestion that the idea of modality *de re* is not so much confused as vaguely immoral or frivolous—as if to accept or employ it is to be guilty of neglecting serious work in favour of sporting with Amaryllis in the shade. In the next chapter, therefore, we shall examine objections to modality *de re*.

[1] "Wittgenstein's *Philosophical Investigations*", *Philosophical Review*, 63, 1954. Reprinted in Malcolm's *Knowledge and Certainty* (Englewood Cliffs: Prentice–Hall Inc., 1963). The quoted passage is on p. 105 of the latter volume.

II

MODALITY *DE RE*: OBJECTIONS

1. *The Problem*

ONE who accepts the idea of modality *de re* typically holds that some objects—9, for example—have some of their properties—being composite, for example—*essentially* or *necessarily*.[1] That is to say, 9 has this property and could not conceivably have lacked it. And here the force of 'could have' is that broadly logical notion of possibility outlined in Chapter I. This is a notion of possibility broader than that of *causal* or *natural* possibility: it is causally impossible that David should have the attribute of travelling from Boston to Los Angeles at a velocity greater than the speed of light, but not impossible in the sense in question. On the other hand, this sense is narrower than that of logical possibility strictly so called. That someone should have the attribute of knowing that $7+5 = 13$ is impossible, and impossible in the sense in question; the resources of logic alone, however, do not suffice to demonstrate this impossibility. The claim that objects have some of their properties essentially or necessarily is part of what we may call *essentialism*. To this contention the essentialist, as I shall understand him, adds the claim that objects have accidental as well as essential properties. Socrates, for example, has self-identity essentially but is accidentally snubnosed; while he could not have been self-diverse, he could have been non-snubnosed. Still further, essentialism (as here understood) includes the idea that some properties are essential to some but not all objects; thus 9 but not 5 is essentially composite. So the essentialist holds that objects have both essential and accidental properties; and that some properties are had essentially by some but not all objects.

[1] In speaking of the view in question, I use the words 'necessarily' and 'essentially' as synonyms. Of course I neither assume nor suggest that these words are in fact synonyms as ordinarily employed. See R. Marcus, "Essential Attribution", *Journal of Philosophy*, 68 (April 1971), 193.

According to Quine, essentialism "is the doctrine that some of the attributes of a thing (quite independently of the language in which the thing is referred to, if at all) may be essential to the thing and others accidental".[1] I take the point to be this. When the essentialist says of something *x* that it has a certain property *P* essentially, he means to be predicating a property of *x*—a property distinct from *P*.[2] For every property *P* there is the property of having *P* essentially; and if *x* has *P* essentially, then *x* has the property *having P essentially*. This has two important consequences. In the first place, a proposition of the form *x has P essentially* entails that *something* has *P* essentially and is therefore properly subject to existential generalization. To say that 9 is essentially composite is to predicate a property—that of being essentially composite—of 9; hence

(1) 9 is essentially composite

entails

(2) There is at least one thing that is essentially composite.

A second consequence: if *x* has *P* essentially, then the same claim must be made for anything identical with *x*. If 9 is essentially composite, so is Paul's favourite number, that number being 9. This follows from the principle sometimes called 'Leibniz's Law' or 'The Indiscernibility of Identicals':

(3) For any property *P* and any objects *x* and *y*, if *x* is identical with *y*, then *x* has *P* if and only if *y* has *P*.

Like Caesar's wife Calpurnia, this principle is entirely above reproach.[3] But then, if an object *x* has a property *P* essentially, it has the property of having *P* essentially; by (3), therefore, anything identical with *x* shares that distinction with it. Accordingly, if an object has a property essentially, so does anything

---

[1] "Three Grades of Modal Involvement", in *The Ways of Paradox* (New York: Random House, 1966), p. 173.

[2] Alternatively, we might take it that what he asserts is a proposition predicating of *x* and *P* a special relation of *property-inherence*: that in which an object and a property stand if the former has the latter essentially. Such a proposition, presumably, will be equivalent to one predicating of *x* the property of having *P* essentially.

[3] Apparently Leibniz himself did not clearly distinguish (3) from:

(3′) Singular terms denoting the same object can replace each other in any context *salva veritate*

a 'principle' that does not hold for such excellent examples of language as English.

identical with it. *Having P essentially* is a property of an object *x*; it is not, for example, a three-termed relation involving *x*, *P*, and (say) some description of *x*.

The essentialist, therefore, holds that some objects have both accidental and essential properties—properties not everything has essentially. He adds that where *P* is a property, so is *having P essentially*. And many philosophers view these claims with suspicion, if not outright disdain. What are the objections to it?

2. *Essentialism and Set-theoretical Reduction*

Some who accept essentialism point, by way of illustration, to the fact that the number 9 has the property *being composite* essentially or necessarily. Gilbert Harman is unsympathetic to this notion.[1] Arguing that "the claim that numbers have such essential properties is incompatible with the familiar idea that number theory can be reduced to set theory in various ways" (p. 184) he taxes those who accept *de re* modality with putting forward this idea "less as an empirical hypothesis than as a metaphysical or religious doctrine" (p. 185); and he rhetorically asks "Why should we take them seriously?"

While I have no ready answer to this last question, I do feel that the theory of *de re* modality, taken as a religious doctrine, is a bit thin. It will never replace the Heidelburg Catechism, or even Supralapsarianism. What is presently interesting, however, is Harman's argument for the thesis that 9's being essentially composite *is* incompatible with this familiar idea. How does it go? According to the familiar idea, says Harman,

the natural numbers can be identified with any of various sequences of sets. Zero might be identified with the null set, and each succeeding natural number with the set whose only member is the set identified with the previous number. Or a natural number might be identified with the set of all natural numbers less than it. And there are an infinity of other possible identifications all of which allow the full development of number theory. (p. 184)

So far so good. That the natural numbers can be identified, in this fashion, with various distinct set theoretical structures is indeed a familiar idea. But of course there is no reason to stick thus unimaginatively to sets; we may, if we wish, identify

[1] "A nonessential Property", *Journal of Philosophy*, 67 (April 1970), 183.

President Nixon with zero and the remaining numbers with propositions about him: *Nixon is less than one foot tall, Nixon is less than two feet tall, . . .* All we need for such 'identification' is a countably infinite set of objects together with a relation[1] under which they form an infinite sequence or progression. Since practically any object you please is the tenth element in some progression, any object you please can be 'identified', in this fashion, with 9.

"But", continues Harman, "being a composite number is not an essential property of any set. Therefore," he says, "if numbers can be identified with sets and *de re* necessity is in question, no number is necessarily a composite number. Being a composite number is not an essential property of any number." (p. 184)

Here there may be less than meets the eye. How, exactly, are we to construe this argument? Taken at face value, it appears to involve an application of Leibniz's Law; perhaps we can outline it as follows:

(4) No set is essentially a composite number,

that is

(5) No set has the property of being essentially composite.

But

(6) Numbers can be identified with sets.

Therefore (given Leibniz's Law),

(7) No number has the property of being essentially composite.

Put thus baldly, this argument, obviously, is about as imperforate as an afghan knit by an elephant. We might as well argue that 9 does not have the property of being divisible by 3, since Nixon does not, and it can be identified with him.

The point is this. That number theory can be reduced to set theory in various ways is indeed, in Harman's words, a familiar idea. It is widely recognized and accepted as accurate and as part of the current lore about numbers and sets. And according to this familiar idea, a given number can be 'identified' with any of many distinct sets. But what this comes to (in so far as the idea in question *is* widely accepted) is only this: there are many

---

[1] Perhaps recursive; see Paul Benacerraf, "What Numbers could not be", *Philosophical Review*, 74 (1965), 51.

denumerable families of sets that form a progression under some (recursive) relation. Accordingly, for any number *n*, there are many distinct sets each of which is the *n*+1st element in some progression and can therefore play the role of *n* in some set theoretical development of number theory. But of course the fact that numbers can be identified in *this* sense with Nixon or with various distinct set theoretical objects does not suggest that any number is in fact *identical with* Nixon or some set; it is this latter, however, that is required for an application of Leibniz's Law.

3. *Essentialism and the Number of Apostles*

According to the essentialist, for each property *P* there is the property of having *P* essentially—a property an object has (if at all) in itself, regardless of how it may be described or referred to. If 9 is essentially composite, so is Paul's favourite number, that number being 9. The essentialist therefore rejects the idea that 9 *qua*, as they say, Paul's favourite number, has the property of being his favourite number essentially, but *qua* the successor of 8 has that property accidentally; this would be to say that *being essentially Paul's favourite number* is not a property at all but perhaps a relation involving 9, the property of being Paul's favourite number, and a designation of 9. He holds instead that such an item as *being essentially composite* is a property —in this case, one enjoyed by 9; hence it is a property of Paul's favourite number, if indeed Paul's favourite number is 9.

It is here that he makes his mistake, according to William Kneale.[1] For, says Kneale, an object does not have a property *P* essentially *just as an object* (to speak oracularly); instead it has *P* essentially (if at all) *relative to* certain ways of specifying or selecting it for attention—and perhaps accidentally, relative to other ways. When we say that *x* has *P* essentially or necessarily, this must be construed as "an elliptical statement of relative necessity" (p. 629); that is, as short for something like '*x* has *P* necessarily relative to *D*' where *D* is some description. Of course if *P* is a *truistic* property—one which, like *is red or is not red*, is had

---

[1] "Modality *De Dicto* and *De Re*", in *Logic, Methodology and Philosophy of Science*, ed. Nagel, Suppes, and Tarski (Stanford University Press, 1962), p. 622.

necessarily by every object relative to every way of describing it, then this reference to ways of selecting *x* may perhaps be suppressed without undue impropriety, so that we may say *simpliciter* that *P* is essential to *x*. In these cases, then, the reference to a description is otiose; but where *P* is not truistic such a reference is crucial, even if implicit. Fundamentally, therefore, Kneale holds that there is no such thing, for a property *P*, as the property of having *P* essentially; these are only three termed relations involving *P*, an object *x*, and the various ways of selecting *x* for attention.

But why so? The opposite view, he says, is based on the mistaken assumption that

properties may be said to belong to individuals necessarily or contingently, as the case may be, without regard to the ways in which the individuals are selected for attention. It is no doubt true to say that the number 12 is necessarily composite, but it is certainly not correct to say that the number of apostles is necessarily composite, unless the remark is to be understood as an elliptical statement of relative necessity. And again, it is no doubt correct to say that this at which I am pointing is contingently white, but it is certainly not correct to say that the white paper at which I am looking is contingently white, unless again, the remark is to be understood as elliptical. (p. 629)

Kneale's argument does not wear its structure upon its sleeve. How, exactly, does it go? What are the premises? The *conclusion*, pretty clearly, is that an object does not have a property necessarily *in itself* or just as an object; it has it necessarily or contingently, as the case may be, *relative to* certain descriptions of the object. There is no such thing as the property of being necessarily composite; and a proposition like

(8) the number 12 is necessarily composite

does not predicate a property of 12; instead it predicates a relation of 12, the property of being composite, and a 'way of selecting 12 for attention'. But why should we think so? How are we to construe the argument? Perhaps it has something like the following premises:

(9) 12 = the number of apostles
(8) The number 12 is necessarily composite
(10) If (8), then if there is such a property as *being necessarily composite*, 12 has it.

(11) The number of apostles is not necessarily composite.

(12) If (11), then if there is such a property as *being necessarily composite*, the number of the apostles lacks it.

It therefore follows that there is no such property as *being necessarily composite*; hence, it is false that for any property *P*, there is the property of having *P* essentially or necessarily; and hence the essentialist thesis is mistaken.

Now clearly Kneale's argument requires Leibniz's Law as an additional premiss—a principle the essentialist will be happy to concede. And if we add this premiss then the argument is apparently valid. But why should we accept (11)? Consider an analogous argument for the unwelcome conclusion that *necessary truth* or *being necessarily true* is not a property that a proposition has in itself or just as a proposition, but only relative to certain descriptions of it:

(13) The proposition that $7+5 = 12$ is necessarily true.

(14) The proposition I am thinking of is not necessarily true.

(15) The proposition that $7+5 = 12$ is identical with the proposition I am thinking of.

Therefore

(16) *Being necessarily true* is not a property.

This argument is feeble and unconvincing; if (15) is true then (14) must be false. But is not the very same comment appropriate to (11) and (9)? If (9) is true, then presumably (11) is false. And so the question becomes acute: why *does* Kneale take (11) to be true? The answer, I suspect, is that he reads (11) as

(11′) The proposition *the number of apostles is composite* is not necessarily true.

More generally, Kneale seems to think of sentences of the form '—— has . . . essentially' (where the first blank is filled by a singular term and the second by an expression denoting a property) as short for or a stylistic variant of the corresponding sentences of the form 'the proposition —— has . . . is necessarily true'; where 'α' ranges over singular terms and '*B*' over expressions denoting properties, Kneale apparently means to ascribe something like the following definitional schema to the essentialist:

D₁ ⌜α has *B* essentially⌝ = def. ⌜The proposition α *has B* is necessarily true⌝.

But this ascription is at best uncharitable as an account of what the essentialist means by his characteristic assertions. As noted above, the latter holds that a proposition like

(17) 12 is essentially composite

predicates a property of 12 and hence entails (by way of existential generalization)

(18) There is at least one object x such that x is essentially composite.

Applying D_1 (and making appropriate grammatical adjustments) we have

(19) There is at least one object x such that the proposition x is *composite* is necessarily true.

But of course (19) as it stands is grotesque; there is no such thing as the proposition x is *composite*; the words 'x is *composite*' do not express a proposition. The essentialist may be benighted, but he does not confound (18), which he accepts, with such a darkling hodge-podge as (19).

Fundamentally, however, to saddle the essentialist with D_1 is to ignore his claim that an item like (17) is a *de re* assertion that predicates a *property* of the number 12. If he accepts (17) then he will also hold that the number of apostles is essentially composite; and he will be utterly unshaken by the *de dicto* truth that

(11') *the number of apostles is composite* is not necessarily true.

A central feature of his programme, after all, is to distinguish such *de re* propositions as (17) from such *de dicto* items as (11'); and to ascribe D_1 to him is to ignore, not discredit, his claim that there is such a distinction to be drawn.

But perhaps we were being hasty. Suppose we look again at Kneale's argument. Perhaps he does not mean to ascribe D_1 to the essentialist: perhaps we are to understand his argument as follows. We have been told that 'x has P essentially' means that it is impossible or inconceivable that x should have lacked P; that there is no conceivable set of circumstances such that, should they have obtained, x would not have had P. Well, consider the number 12 and the number of apostles. Perhaps it *is* impossible that *the number 12* should have lacked the property of being composite; but it is certainly possible that *the number of apostles* should have lacked it; for clearly the number of apostles could have been 11, in which case it would not have been composite. Hence *being essentially composite* is not a property and the essentialist thesis fails.

How could the defender of essentialism respond? The relevant portion of the argument may perhaps be stated as follows:

(20) The number of apostles could have been 11.
(21) If the number of apostles had been 11, then the number of apostles would have been prime.

Hence

(22) It is possible that the number of apostles should have been prime

and therefore

(23) The number of apostles is not essentially composite.

But the essentialist has an easy retort. The argument is successful only if (23) is construed as the assertion *de re* that a certain number—12 as it happens—does not have the property of being essentially composite. Now (22) can be read *de dicto* as

(22a) The proposition *the number of apostles is prime* is possible;

it may also be read *de re*, that is as

(22b) The number that numbers the apostles (that is, the number that *as things in fact stand* numbers the apostles) could have been prime.

The latter entails (23); the former, of course, does not. Hence to preserve the argument we must take (22) as (22b). Now consider (20). The same *de re/de dicto* ambiguity is once again present. Read *de dicto* it makes the true (if unexciting) assertion that

(20a) The proposition *there are just 11 apostles* is possible.

Read *de re*, however—that is, as

(20b) The number that (as things in fact stand) numbers the apostles could have been 11

—it will be indignantly repudiated by the essentialist; for the number that numbers the apostles is 12 and accordingly could not have been 11. We must therefore take (20) as (20a).

This brings us to (21). If (20*a*) and (21) are to entail (22*b*), then (21) must be construed as

> (21*a*) If the proposition *the number of apostles is 11* had been true, then the number that (as things in fact stand) numbers the apostles would not have been composite.

But surely this is false. For what it says is that if there had been 11 apostles, then the number that in fact does number the apostles—the number 12—would not have been composite; and at best this is outrageous. No doubt any inclination to accept (21*a*) may be traced to an unremarked penchant for confusing it with

> (24) If the proposition *the number of apostles is 11* had been true, then the number that *would have* numbered the apostles would have been prime.

(24), of course, though true, is of no use to Kneale's argument. Accordingly, Kneale's objection to essentialism is at best inconclusive.

4. *Essentialism and the Mathematical Cyclist*

Let us therefore turn to a different but related complaint. Quine argues that talk of a difference between necessary and contingent attributes of an object is baffling:

> Perhaps I can evoke the appropriate sense of bewilderment as follows. Mathematicians may conceivably be said to be necessarily rational and not necessarily two-legged; and cyclists necessarily two-legged and not necessarily rational. But what of an individual who counts among his eccentricities both mathematics and cycling? Is this concrete individual necessarily rational and contingently two-legged or vice versa? Just insofar as we are talking referentially of the object, with no special bias towards a background grouping of mathematicians as against cyclists or vice versa, there is no semblance of sense in rating some of his attributes as necessary and others as contingent. Some of his attributes count as important and others as unimportant, yes, some as enduring and others as fleeting; but none as necessary or contingent.[1]

Noting the existence of a philosophical tradition in which this distinction *is* made, Quine adds that one attributes it to Aristotle

---

[1] *Word and Object* (M.I.T. Press, 1960), p. 199.

"subject to contradiction by scholars, such being the penalty for attributions to Aristotle". None the less, he says, the distinction is "surely indefensible".

Now this passage reveals that Quine has little enthusiasm for the distinction between essential and accidental attributes; but how exactly are we to understand him? Perhaps as follows. The essentialist, Quine thinks, will presumably accept

(25) Mathematicians are necessarily rational but not necessarily bipedal

and

(26) Cyclists are necessarily bipedal but not necessarily rational.

But now suppose that

(27) Paul K. Zwier is both a cyclist and a mathematician.

From these we may infer both

(28) Zwier is necessarily rational but not necessarily bipedal

and

(29) Zwier is necessarily bipedal but not necessarily rational

which appear to contradict each other twice over: (28) credits Zwier with the property of being necessarily rational while (29) denies him that property; (29) alleges that he has the property of being essentially bipedal, an allegation disputed by (28).

This argument is unsuccessful as a refutation of the essentialist, whatever its merits as an evocation of a sense of bewilderment. For consider the inference of (29) from (26) and (27). (29) is a conjunction, as are (26) and (27). And presumably its first conjunct

(30) Zwier is necessarily bipedal

is supposed to follow from the first conjuncts of (26) and (27), viz.

(31) Cyclists are necessarily bipedal

and

(32) Zwier is a cyclist.

But sensitive, as by now we are, to *de re/de dicto* ambiguity, we see that (31) can be read *de dicto* as

(31*a*) Necessarily, all cyclists are bipedal

or *de re* as

(31*b*) Every cyclist has the property of being necessarily bipedal.

And if (30) is to follow from (32) and (31), the latter must be seen as predicating of every cyclist the property (30) ascribes to Zwier; (31), that is, must be read as (31*b*). So taken, there is less than a ghost of a chance the essentialist will accept it. No doubt he will concede the necessary truth of

(33) All (well-formed) cyclists are bipedal

and thus the truth of (31*a*); he will accept no obligation to infer that such well-formed cyclists as Zwier are essentially bipedal. And the same comments apply, *mutatis mutandis*, to the inference of the second conjunct of (29) from those of (26) and (27). Accordingly, (26) is true but of no use to the argument if we read it *de dicto*; read *de re* it will be repudiated by the essentialist.

Taken as a refutation of the essentialist, therefore, this passage misses the mark; but perhaps we should emphasize its second half and take it instead as an expression of a sense of bewildered puzzlement as to what *de re* modality might conceivably be. Similar protestations may be found elsewhere in Quine's works:

An object, of itself and by whatever name or none, must be seen as having some of its traits necessarily and others contingently, despite the fact that the latter traits follow just as analytically from some ways of specifying the object as the former do from other ways of specifying it.

And

This means adapting an invidious attitude towards certain ways of specifying *x* . . . and favouring other ways . . . as somehow better revealing the 'essence' of the object.

But "such a philosophy", he says, "is as unreasonable by my lights as it is by Carnap's or Lewis's".[1]

Here Quine's central complaint is this: a given object, according to the essentialist, has *some* of its properties essentially and others accidentally, despite the fact that the latter follow from certain ways of specifying the object just as the former do from others. So far, fair enough. Snubnosedness (we may suppose) is not one of Socrates' essential attributes; none the less it follows

[1] *From A Logical Point Of View* (New York: Harper & Row, 1961), pp. 155–6.

(in the sense in question) from the description 'the snubnosed teacher of Plato'. As we construe him, furthermore, the essentialist holds that among the essential attributes of an object are certain non-truistic properties—properties which, unlike the property of being red or not red, do not follow from every description; so it will indeed be true, as Quine suggests, that ways of uniquely specifying an object are not all on the same footing. Those from which each of its essential properties follows must be awarded the accolade as best revealing the essence of the object.

But what, exactly, is "unreasonable" about this? And how, precisely, is it baffling? The real depth of Quine's objection, as I understand it, is this: he holds that 'A's are necessarily B's' must, if it means anything at all, mean something like 'necessarily, A's are B's'; for "necessity resides in the way we talk about things, not in the things we talk about" (*Ways of Paradox*, p. 174). And hence the bafflement in asking, of some specific individual who is both cyclist and mathematician, whether he is essentially rational and contingently 2-legged or vice versa. Perhaps the claim is, finally, that while we can make a certain rough sense of modality *de dicto*, we can understand modality *de re* only if we can explain it in terms of the former. I turn to such explanation in Chapter III.

III

MODALITY *DE RE*: EXPLANATIONS

1. *The Locus of Necessity*

ALTHOUGH the idea of modality *de re* is now more respectable than it was during the palmy days of positivism, there remains in many quarters a lack of hospitality to it, and perhaps a suspicion that those who accept it, while not exactly corrupt, display a certain lack of moral fibre. The objections explicitly offered are not impressive; they mostly involve furtive confusion of *de re* with *de dicto* modality. To reply to objections, however, is not necessarily to dispel this residual cloud of suspicion. The feeling persists that there must be something incoherent or unintelligible about *de re* modality—modality *de dicto* may be at any rate marginally acceptable, but modality *de re* makes sense only if explicable in terms of the former. One source of this feeling, as we saw at the end of the last chapter, is the notion, endorsed by Quine, that necessity resides in the way we speak of things, not in the things we speak of.

This sentiment is echoed by many, and raises many fascinating (if cloudy) issues—issues I must here forbear to enter. But what, even approximately, does this claim come to? That, presumably, the necessity of a given proposition—$7+5 = 12$, for example, or *modus ponens*, or *Socrates is not a number*—depends, somehow, on our behaviour—specifically, our linguistic behaviour. This seems implausible enough. It is surely hard to see how anything we could have done or said would have resulted in these propositions' being contingent. Of course we could have used the *sentences* involved to express different and contingent propositions; to think *this* the issue, however, is to fall victim to outrageous confusion. But suppose for the moment we concede that modality resides where Quine says it does. Is it any easier to see that the necessary truth of *modus ponens* depends upon our linguistic behaviour, than that the essential primeness of 5 so depends? Consider the facts that 9 is essentially composite and that *9 is composite* is necessarily true; is it harder to ascribe the former than the latter to linguistic behaviour? Suppose we agree for the moment that necessity resides in the way we talk about things; how does it follow that essentialist assertions are false, or senseless? How does it follow that they are more enigmatic than their *de dicto* counterparts?

Apart from these considerations of the locus of necessity, furthermore, it is by no means easy to see that *de re* modality is in principle more obscure than modality *de dicto*. An object x has a property P essentially just in case it is not possible that x should have lacked P; a proposition p is necessarily true just in case it is not possible that p should have lacked the property of being true. Seen from this perspective, modality *de dicto* is a special case of modality *de re*. And what is so special about this special case? What makes it clearer than the general case? Quine, indeed, points out that for any property P Socrates has, there is a description of Socrates from which P follows, suggesting that once we see this, we see that the essentialist's discriminations among an object's properties is arbitrary and unjustifiable. The idea of modality *de dicto*, however, involves the very same contrast. Consider any necessary proposition p—$7+5 = 12$, let us say. For any property P of this proposition, there will be a description of it entailing P. The description 'Kant's most famous example of necessary truth', for example, denotes it and entails the property *being used by Kant as an example*. Yet p will be necessarily true and only accidentally used as an example by Kant. Furthermore, for any true proposition p there is a description of p that entails truth; is it not therefore arbitrary and baseless to single out only *some* true propositions as *necessarily* true, denying that title to others?

So far, therefore, it is hard to see why modality *de re* and modality *de dicto* are not on all fours. Consider, indeed,

(1) Socrates could not have been a planet

and

(2) The proposition *Socrates is a planet* could not have been true.

Given that 'could have' in each case expresses broadly logical necessity, is the latter more limpid than the former? Is it harder to understand the former than the latter? I think not. Indeed we might ask whether these two express *equivalent* propositions, where a pair of propositions are equivalent if their biconditional is necessary in the broadly logical sense. The answer is not quite clear; it may plausibly be claimed that (1), as an expression of modality *de re*, predicates a property of Socrates and thereby entails (in that broadly logical sense) that Socrates exists, that there is such a thing as Socrates.[1] (2), on the other hand, is plausibly thought to be itself a necessary truth, in which case it entails no such mere contingencies as that there is such a thing as Socrates. So let us turn instead to

(3) Socrates could not have been a planet

or

(3′) Socrates is essentially a non-planet

and

(4) Socrates is a non-planet and the proposition *Socrates is a planet* is necessarily false.

If (3) and (3′) are contingent, then (for the same reason) so is the first conjunct of (4) and hence (4) itself. And (3′) and (4), as it seems to me, are indeed equivalent in the broadly logical sense.

2. *The Kernel Function*

I therefore do not see that modality *de re* is in principle more obscure than modality *de dicto*. Still there are those who do or think they do; it would be useful, if possible, to *explain* the *de re* by the *de dicto*. What might such an explanation come to? Perhaps the following would suffice: a general rule that led us from such propositions as (3′) to such propositions as (4)—a general rule, that is, that enables us to find, for any *de re* proposition, a *de dicto* equivalent. Or, alternatively, one that enables us to replace any sentence containing expressions of *de re* modality by an equivalent sentence all of whose modal terms express modality *de dicto*. Of course it would not do to say simply that an object *x* has a property *P* essentially just in case *x* has *P* and the proposition that *x* lacks *P* is necessarily false; for what, for given *x* and

---

[1] See below, Chapter VIII.

P, is the proposition that *x* lacks *P*? Let *x* be the object variously denoted by 'Socrates', 'the teacher of Plato' and 'the Greek philosopher who was married to Xantippe'; and let *P* be the property of being snubnosed. What would be *the* proposition that *x* lacks *P*? *Socrates is not snubnosed? The teacher of Plato is not snubnosed? The Greek philosopher married to Xantippe is not snubnosed?* These are different propositions (the second, unlike the first, entails that Plato had a teacher, while the third, unlike the first or second, entails that Xantippe was married). Each, however, predicates *P* of *x*; hence each seems to have as good a claim to the title '*the* proposition that *x* has *P*' as the other; hence initially none has a legitimate claim to it. We must pick out the one that has the right properties; once we have done so, we could, if we liked, call that one '*the* proposition that *x* has *P*'.

Our problem, then, in explaining the *de re* by the *de dicto* may be put as follows: suppose we are given an object *x* and a property *P*. Is it possible to state general directions for picking out some proposition—call it the *kernel* proposition with respect to *x* and *P*—whose *de dicto* modal properties determine whether *x* has *P* essentially? Perhaps we can begin by looking once more at the equivalence of (3') and (4). The former says of Socrates that he has essentially the property *being a non-planet*; the latter says that he *has* that property, and that a proposition predicating its complement of him is necessarily false. What we seek is a general means of locating, for given *x* and *P*, the appropriate proposition of this latter sort. Suppose we try

D₁ Where *x* is an object and *P* a property, the kernel proposition with respect to *x* and *P* (K(*x*, *P*)) is the proposition expressed by the result of replacing '*x*' and '*P*' in '*x* has the complement of *P*' by proper names of *x* and *P*,

adding that

D₂ *x* has *P* essentially if and only if *x* has *P* and K(*x*, *P*) is necessarily false.

Here several points call for comment.

A. By 'proper name' I mean to speak not of so-called 'logically proper names', whatever exactly these come to, but of proper names properly so called—such names as 'Socrates', 'Jim Whittaker', and 'Kareem Abdul-Jabbar'. These are to be contrasted with such items as 'the teacher of Plato', 'the first American to climb Everest', and 'the premier centre of professional basketball'.

B. D_1 suggests that *properties* do or can have proper names. That they *can* have proper names is clear; we could, if we wished, dub the property of being pink 'Sam', whereupon the sentence 'the Taj Mahal has Sam' would express the proposition *the Taj Mahal has the property of being pink*. That they typically *do* have proper names is perhaps not quite so obvious; is 'wisdom', for example, a proper name of wisdom? The answer may not be clear. In a way, the answer does not matter; for 'wisdom' enjoys the same semantic properties that a proper name of wisdom would have, even if it is not properly called a proper name of that property. For present purposes, therefore, I shall extend the use of 'proper name' and reckon such terms as 'masculinity', 'being composite', 'open-hearted friendliness', 'being more than seven feet tall', and the like, as proper names of the properties they denote; in this regard they contrast with such terms as 'Jabbar's most striking property' and 'David's most endearing property'.

C. There are, of course, many people named 'Aristotle'; among them, for example, we find both the Stagarite and the shipping tycoon; both the student of Plato and the husband of Jackie. When Plato remarks 'Aristotle is wise', therefore, what he asserts is not identical with what Jackie probably asserts with the same sentence. Some might be so unkind, indeed, as to claim that these two propositions differ in truth value. And this means that K (Aristotle, wisdom) is not well defined; *many* propositions are expressed by the result of replacing 'x' and 'P' in 'x has the complement of P' by proper names of Aristotle and wisdom. But an easy remedy is at hand. The kernel proposition with respect to x and P must be one of the propositions predicating of x the complement of P (if our x is the Stagarite, then Jackie's proposition does not meet this condition); a clause to this effect is easily added to D_2.

D. But what about objects that have no proper names? Of course there are such things; indefinitely many real numbers, for example, have never been named.[1] How can D_2 and D_3 help us find the *de dicto* equivalent of some proposition about an

[1] But see my *"De Re et De Dicto"*, *Nous*, 3 (1969), 253.

unnamed object? The largest shark in the Indian Ocean, for example? Worse, what about such *general* propositions as

(5) Every real number between zero and one has the property of being less than two essentially?

What is the *de dicto* explanation of (5) to look like? Our definitions direct us to

(6) Every real number r between zero and one is less than two and such that K(r, *being less than two*) is necessarily false.

Will (6) do the trick? It is plausible to suppose not, on the grounds that what we have so far gives no explanation of what the kernel of r and P for *unnamed r* might be.[1] If we think of D_1 as a function, perhaps we must concede that the function is defined only for *named* objects and properties. Hence it is not clear that we have any *de dicto* explanation at all for such a proposition as (5).

Again, however, an easy remedy (short of naming everything) is at hand.[2] Suppose we say that an object or property is *baptized* if it has a proper name. We may then revise D_1 to

D_3 For any object x and property P, if x and P are baptized, then K(x, P) is the proposition expressed by replacing 'x', and 'P' in 'x has the complement of P' by proper names of x and P; otherwise K(x, P) is the proposition that *would be* expressed by the result of the indicated replacement if x and P were baptized.

And accordingly a general proposition like

(7) If all men are essentially persons, then some things are essentially rational

goes into

(8) If, for every object x, x is a man only if x is a person and K(x, personhood) is necessarily false, then there are some things y such that y is rational and K(y, rationality) is necessarily false.

3. *Some Objections*

An object x has a property P, therefore, if and only if x has P and K(x, P) is necessarily false. Suppose we now consider some objections.

[1] See Richard Cartwright's "Some Remarks on Essentialism", *Journal of Philosophy*, LXV. 20 (1968), 623.

[2] But see "*De Re et De Dicto*", p. 253; and see pp. 248–56 for a fuller development of some of the ideas of this section.

A. *The Kernel Function and Kripke Semantics*

According to Professor Marcus,

If we take as our stock of eligible E-predicates those which have no quantifiers and no sentence parts, and are direct and general (N-predicates), then, as Parsons has shown, if

$$E_M (Ex) \ \Box Fx \ \& \ (Ex) \sim \Box Fx$$

is true where F is as above, then for any nonmodal sentences S, if S is not already a theorem, $\Box S$ is not entailed by E_m. Those, like Plantinga, who imagine that with sufficient cunning they can 'reduce' the essentialist's *de re* truths to *de dicto* truths have not been sufficiently attentive to these results.[1]

I plead not guilty. I *have* been attentive to these results—attentive enough to note that they are quite consistent with my suggestion that every *de re* proposition is equivalent, in that broadly logical sense, to a *de dicto* proposition. What Parsons[2] shows, among other things, is that in Kripke semantics a formula like

(9) $(Ex)\Box Fx \ \& \ (Ex) \sim \Box Fx$

(where F meets the conditions indicated by Professor Marcus) does not semantically imply a formula of the form $\Box S$, if S is not a theorem. That is, for any formulas A and S, if A is of the form of (9) (F meeting the conditions laid down by Professor Marcus) then $A \supset \Box S$ is not a valid formula of Kripke semantics unless S is. Parsons also shows that such formulas as (9) are not implied by formulas of the form $\Box S$ (where S lacks constants and lacks internal modalities). But how do these facts bear on my claim that every *de re* proposition is equivalent, in that broadly logical sense, to some *de dicto* proposition? A proposition of the form *x has P essentially* is equivalent, I have claimed, to the corresponding proposition of the form *x has P and* K(x, P) *is necessarily false*. Mrs. Marcus points out that formulas of the form of (9) do not imply formulas of the form $\Box S$ unless S is already a theorem. How is this relevant to my claim? Is the idea that I take some sentences of the form of (9)

(10) $(Ex)\Box x$ is prime and $(Ex) \sim \Box x$ is prime,

---

[1] "Essential Attribution", *Journal of Philosophy*, LXVIII. 7 (1971), 199.

[2] "Essentialism and Quantified Modal Logic", *Philosophical Review*, 78 (1969), 47-8. For a brief account of Kripke semantics, see below, Chapter VII, Section 2.

for example, to entail a sentence of the form $\Box S$? I do take such entailments to hold, but only where S is in fact necessary (or the entailing sentence impossible); presumably there is no objection to this. And how shall we apply the rider 'where S is not already a theorem'? I find it hard to see just how Professor Marcus's remarks bear on my suggestions.

The important point, however, lies in a different direction. According to D_2

(11) Socrates is essentially a non-number

is equivalent to

(12) Socrates is a non-number and $K(x, \textit{numberhood})$ is necessarily false;

and

(13) Some things are essentially persons and some things are not

is equivalent to

(14) There is an object x such that x is a person and $K(x, \textit{non-personhood})$ is necessarily false; and there is an object y such that either y is not a person or $K(y, \textit{non-personhood})$ is not necessarily false.

No doubt the relevant biconditionals ((11) iff (12) and (13) iff (14)) are not instances of formulas valid in Kripke semantics (indeed, I would not know how to represent them in the systems Kripke studies). But I never claimed this honour on their behalf; I said only that they were *necessarily true*—not valid in Kripke semantics. And of course there are any number of necessary truths that are not instances of formulas valid in Kripke semantics. Truths of arithmetic would be examples; the same holds for such items as *red is a colour*, *every well-formed cyclist is bipedal*, and *every proposition George knows is true*. I have argued that the *de re* can be explained by way of the *de dicto*; this argument involves no claims about validity in Kripke semantics.

B. *Identity and the Kernel Function*

Surely Socrates has the property *being identical with Socrates* essentially. D_2 and D_3 give the right result here; for Socrates *has* the property of being identical with Socrates, and K (Socrates, identity-with-Socrates), i.e.

(15) Socrates has the complement of identity-with-Socrates

i.e.

(16) Socrates is distinct from Socrates

is indeed necessarily false.

But what about Lew Alcindor and Kareem Abdul-Jabbar?[1] Lew Alcindor, clearly enough, has *identity with Lew Alcindor* essentially. Since Alcindor is identical with Jabbar, the latter, according to the essentialist, must also have this property essentially. But does he according to D_2 and D_3? Granted, he has *identity with Lew Alcindor*; but is K (Jabbar, identity with Alcindor), i.e.

(17) Kareem Abdul-Jabbar is distinct from Lew Alcindor

necessarily false, as it must be if our definitions are to be adequate?

Perhaps it is plausible to suppose not. In a similar context, Quine remarks that

We may tag the planet Venus, some fine evening with the proper name 'Hesperus'. We may tag the same planet again, some day before sunrise, with the proper name 'Phosphorus'. When at last we discover that we have tagged the same planet twice, our discovery is empirical. And not because the proper names were descriptions.[2]

But of course what this shows is not that the propositions *Hesperus is distinct from Phosphorus* and *Jabbar is distinct from Alcindor* are contingent rather than necessarily false; it shows at most that it is possible to discover their falsity *a posteriori*. ('At most', because perhaps what we discover here is only such contingent items as that we have tagged the same planet twice.) But this by no means implies that the propositions in question are not necessarily false.[3] Indeed I think they *are* necessarily false. Is it possible that Jabbar should have been distinct from Alcindor? I cannot see how. Of course Alcindor need not have been *named* 'Jabbar'; had he not, no doubt the sentence

(18) Lew Alcindor is distinct from Kareem Abdul-Jabbar

would not have expressed a false proposition. But it does not follow that what the proposition (18) *does* express—now that in

---

[1] For purposes of illustration I am supposing (contrary to fact) that when Alcindor changed his name, he retained his old name as well as gaining a new.
[2] "Reply to Professor Marcus", in *The Ways of Paradox* (New York: Random House, 1966), p. 180.
[3] See above, pp. 6–8.

fact he *is* named 'Jabbar'—would have been true. I shall say more about this matter in Chapter V, Sections 3 and 4; here I wish only to record my belief that such propositions as (18) are indeed necessarily false, just as, according to D_2 and D_3, they should be.

Of course our definitions are accurate only if (18) expresses *the very same proposition* as

(19) Kareem Abdul-Jabbar is distinct from Kareem Abdul-Jabbar.

More generally, our definitions presuppose the following. Take, for any pair (x, P), the class of sentences that result from the suggested substitutions into '*x* has the complement of *P*'; and consider those members of this class that express a proposition predicating the complement of *P* of *x*: these all express the same proposition.[1] I think this is true; but questions of propositional identity are said to be difficult, and the contrary opinion is not unreasonable. One who holds it (but takes the propositions expressed to be equivalent) need not give up hope; he can take $K(x, P)$ to be a *class* of propositions—the class of propositions expressed by the results of the indicated replacements; and he can add that *x* has *P* essentially just in case each member of this class is necessarily false.

c. *Circularity and the Kernel Function*

D_2 and D_3 are satisfactory only if

(20) When and only when an individual *x* has a property *P* essentially, any proposition that predicates *P* of *x* and is expressed by the result of replacing '*x*' and '*P*' in '*x* lacks *P*' by proper names of *x* and *P* will be necessarily false.

Joseph Camp presents what he takes to be a counter-example to this principle.[2] His example runs essentially as follows. We hear Harry talking about some object, but we do not know which. We ask him to tell us what he is talking about; he churlishly refuses, whereupon we decide to call this thing, whatever it is, 'George'. Now consider the proposition expressed by

(21) George lacks the property of being prime.

This proposition, says Camp, is not necessarily false, since it *could* be that George is a blackboard eraser—that is,

(22) George is a blackboard eraser

---

[1] I defend this claim in Chapter V, Section 3.
[2] "Plantinga on *De Dicto* and *De Re*", *Nous*, 5 (1971), 215.

is possibly true. But (22) entails (21), and hence by a familiar principle (21) is also possible. The fact is, however, that George is the number 7; George, therefore, is essentially prime. Accordingly, (20) is false.

But why suppose that (22) *is* possible? If George is a number, will it not be necessarily false? What leads Camp to think it possible? ". . . it *could* be", he says, "that George is a blackboard eraser, and it is necessarily true that all blackboard erasers lack primeness" (218). This seems accurate enough. In the envisaged circumstances, we might indeed say, "It could be that George is a blackboard eraser" or even "Possibly George is a blackboard eraser"; and if we did, we would be right. Does not this show, then, that (22) is possible in the broadly logical sense? No.

Unfamiliar with the ways of matrices, I might say, and say quite properly, "Possibly the determinant of the matrix $\begin{pmatrix} 2 & 0 & 1 \\ 1 & 3 & 2 \\ 1 & 4 & 3 \end{pmatrix}$ is greater than 3". But of course what I say does not imply that the proposition

the determinant of the matrix $\begin{pmatrix} 2 & 0 & 1 \\ 1 & 3 & 2 \\ 1 & 4 & 3 \end{pmatrix}$ is greater than 3

is possibly true in the broadly logical sense; I just mean that *for all I know* it is true. Similarly, were we to say, in Camp's circumstances, "Possibly George is an eraser", we would not mean (if we were careful) to assert that the proposition expressed by the sentence (22) (taking 'George' therein as a proper name of George) is not necessarily false; we would be saying only that for all we know it is true. We can see this more clearly, perhaps, if we imagine Harry's joining our conversation. After telling him that the subject of his earlier remarks has been named 'George' we ask him whether the proposition *George is a blackboard eraser* is logically possible. If he is willing to answer truthfully, he will say no.

But, says Camp,

the clincher is this: the proposition *George is a blackboard eraser* is a very simple proposition and it seems to me that the best available test for logical possibility in such a case is to try to conceive of a state of affairs or 'world' wherein the proposition would be true. And given the context in which we supposed ourselves to be using the name

'George' we could apply this test to the proposition expressed by
'George is a blackboard eraser' with no trouble at all. For instance
we might imagine Harry suffering a change of heart and showing us
a blackboard eraser, with the explanation that this is the thing he
was talking about. (p. 220)

Crucial to this argument is the claim that the proposition
expressed by (22) would be true in any world where Harry was
talking about a blackboard eraser (and presumably false in any
other). Camp apparently believes that (22) and

(23) the thing Harry was talking about is a blackboard eraser

(where the contained definite description is used *attributively* in
Donnellan's[1] sense) express the same or equivalent propositions.
But why so? On most occasions, certainly, a proper name such
as 'George' is not interchangeable with a definite description
like 'the thing Harry was thinking of'. Why think so here?
Perhaps the reason goes approximately as follows. All we know
about George is that it is the thing Harry was talking about.
George, we might say, is *given* to us as the thing Harry was
talking about; it was *introduced into our thought and discourse* under
that title, and that description affords our only means of *identi-*
fying it. Hence when we name it, the name we bestow abbreviates this description.

No doubt these ideas of identification and 'introduction into
discourse' are less than perfectly precise. Still we do have something of a grasp of them, and, given this grasp, I think it is clear
that the argument is far from conclusive. There is no reason to
suppose that we cannot give proper names to such things as the
thing Harry was speaking of, even if we know no more than that
about it. And when we do give a proper name to such an object,
that name is not an abbreviation for some description incorporating what we do know about the thing. Suppose you and
I know that someone was seated behind the screen at *t*; we
know nothing further about this person. Suppose we name him
'Paul'. It does not follow that

(24) Paul is not sitting behind the screen at *t*

expresses a necessarily false proposition. No doubt there would
be something self-defeating and absurd in our thus changing

    [1] See K. Donnellan, "Reference and Definite Descriptions", *Philosophical Review*,
75 (1966), 281–304.

our minds about Paul and asserting the proposition (24) expresses. All we know about Paul is that he is the person sitting behind the screen; so if we did assert (24) perhaps we should be unable to give a coherent answer to the questions Who is Paul? To whom are you referring? Who is it that you say was not sitting behind the screen at t? Perhaps our only means of answering these questions is to identify Paul as the man behind the screen at t; if we say that Paul was not then behind the screen, perhaps we fall into a kind of incoherence or absurdity. But none of this shows that (24), under these conditions, expresses a necessarily false proposition; and the fact is it does not.

(22) and (23), therefore, do not express equivalent propositions. If 'George' is serving here as a proper name of George (i.e. the number 7) then the possibility of a world in which Harry shows us a blackboard eraser has no tendency at all to show that the proposition expressed by (22) thus understood is possibly true; what it shows is only that Harry could have been thinking of something distinct from George and that (22) could have expressed a proposition distinct from the one it *does* express.

Of course proper names do not always serve the function of proper-naming. Sometimes, for example, they function as general terms (or fragments thereof) as in "He is a veritable Daniel come to judgement". Indeed, the same name can function both ways in the same sentence; no doubt Daniel himself was a veritable Daniel come to judgement. And perhaps Camp takes it that in the situation he is thinking of, our referring to this object as 'George' is no more than a tacit agreement to use that name to abbreviate some such description as 'the thing Harry was talking about'.

Now surely we can, if we wish, use a proper name as an abbreviation for a definite description. (Indeed, we could use a preposition or a parenthesis for that purpose, if we chose.) And if we did, then sentences containing the name in question well express propositions distinct from the ones they otherwise would have. Suppose, for example, Harry tells us he is thinking of a number between 1 and 10; in fact he is thinking of 6. Now suppose we use 'George' to denote the number Harry is thinking of and ask whether the proposition expressed by

(25) George is prime

is possible. The answer will depend upon whether 'George' functions here as a proper name or as a surrogate for some such definite description as 'the number Harry is thinking of'. If the latter, then the possibility that Harry is thinking of 7 rather than 6 shows the proposition (25) expresses to be contingent. If the former, however, then that possibility shows at best that (25) could have expressed a true proposition. There is nothing here to suggest that the proposition it *does* express could have been true. Harry knows that (25) expresses a necessarily false proposition. We do not; we know only that the proposition it expresses is either necessarily true or necessarily false. That (25) is true, i.e. expresses a true proposition, is contingently false; this does not compromise the fact that the proposition it expresses is necessarily false.

The resolution of Camp's objection, then, is to be seen in the fact that what is usually a proper name does not always function as one. If, for example, we decide for some reason to use 'Socrates' as short for 'the snubnosed teacher of Plato', then

(26) Socrates never taught Plato

will express a necessarily false proposition. How does this bear on D_2 and D_3 (above, pp. 30–2)? As follows. 'Socrates' is indeed a proper name of Socrates (even if it is not functioning as one in (26)); hence K (Socrates, *snubnosedness*) will be necessarily false; hence by D_3 Socrates will be essentially snubnosed, which is absurd. Or more accurately, K (Socrates, *snubnosedness*) will not be well defined; there will be at least *two* inequivalent propositions about Socrates expressed by the sentence to which it directs us. The trouble, of course, is that while 'Socrates' is indeed a proper name of Socrates, in (26) it is not functioning as one. Strictly speaking, therefore, D_2 and D_3 are inadequate; in giving the kernel function we must add that the proper name in question is, in the sentence in question, to *function as* a proper name of x.

But what is this 'functioning as a proper name'? How can I explain *that*? Perhaps any revealing and adequate philosophical account of the function of proper names will involve essentialist notions. For example, an important part of their function, as we shall see in Chapter V, is to express *essences*; if so, perhaps any full and satisfactory philosophical analysis of the function of proper names will require reference to that notion, a notion that is essentialist *in excelcis*. But if I can explain the function of proper names only by adverting to essentialist notions, then is not my explanation of the *de re* by the *de dicto* ultimately circular, in some subtle or not so subtle fashion?[1]

This is a ticklish question. However, I think the answer is *no*. Of course D_2 and D_3 do presuppose certain truths (as I take them to be) about the function of proper names. For example, Frege and Russell held that a proper name, on a given occasion of its use, typically functions as an abbreviation for some definite description denoting the relevant bearer—a description incorporating a (possibly complex) property widely believed or believed by the user of the name to be unique to that bearer. So, for example, 'Socrates' might be synonymous with or an abbreviation for some such description as 'the snubnosed Greek Philosopher who was executed by the Athenians for corrupting the youth'. Presumably the more one knows about Socrates, the richer the description for which 'Socrates' is an abbreviation. My account presupposes that proper names do not work in this way. And the fact is they do not; a sentence containing a proper name does not in general express a proposition equivalent to the proposition expressed by the result of replacing that name by a coreferential definite description. It is closer to the truth to say that a sentence in which a proper name is used ordinarily expresses the same proposition as is expressed by the result of replacing it by a demonstrative ('this', 'that') when the latter is used to demonstrate or refer to the appropriate bearer of the name. That is to say,

(27) Jim Whittaker lives in Seattle

expresses the same proposition as

(28) This lives in Seattle

when the latter is uttered by someone who is referring to Jim Whittaker. This proposition is neither identical with nor even equivalent to any such item as

(29) The famous Northwest mountaineer who was the first American to reach the summit of Everest lives in Seattle.

So my account does indeed presuppose certain truths about

[1] Camp, op. cit., pp. 224–5.

proper names. Furthermore, a complete and philosophically revealing account of the function of proper names might indeed involve essentialist notions. But neither of these facts, I think, involves the present enterprise in objectionable circularity. For my aim in giving D_2 and D_3 is twofold. First of all, those of us who have the concept of *de re* modality and understand or think we understand *de re* locutions will find it interesting to note that every *de re* proposition is equivalent to some *de dicto* assertion. (The converse also holds: a proposition is necessarily true if and only if the property of *being true* is essential to it.) This fact is interesting and worth knowing in its own right. It is further interesting to see that for any sentence containing *de re* locutions there is an equivalent sentence containing only *de dicto* and non-modal locutions. And in this context it is hard to see how circularity can so much as rear its ugly head; there is no attempt to 'reduce' one kind of language to another or to replace the less clear by the more clear, or anything of the sort.

But secondly, there are philosophers who think to make tolerable sense of modality *de dicto* while finding modality *de re* utterly obscure. Such a person is perplexed by *de reist* talk of objects having properties essentially or necessarily; he feels he does not understand these alleged assertions and suspects a confusion somewhere. I have tried to remove the grounds for suspecting confusion and to help the sceptic understand what the *de re* modalist is asserting. The essentialist claims, let us say, that 9 is essentially composite or that Socrates is essentially a person, or that any given pain has the property of being a sensation essentially. The sceptic pleads inability to understand; he pleads utter bafflement in the face of such claims. My account is designed to help him. In the first place, it provides *truth conditions* for essentialist sentences—truth conditions that invoke only non-modal and *de dicto* notions. More, this account, if it is successful, enables him to find, for any essentialist assertion, a proposition that he understands and that is equivalent to that assertion. Still further, this account enables him to find, for any essentialist assertion, a proposition that he understands and that isn't even clearly distinct from the essentialist's claim. This *is* clearly something *further*, as the following consideration shows. Suppose

(30) Socrates is essentially a person

is true. If D_3 and D_4 are accurate, this is equivalent to

(31) Socrates is a person and *Socrates is not a person* is necessarily false.

But (given that a statement predicating necessity or impossibility of a statement is necessarily true if true at all) (31) is equivalent to

(32) Socrates is a person and *7+5 = 14* is necessarily false.

Hence (30) is equivalent to (32). Despite this equivalence, (32) leaves something to be desired as a *de dicto* explanation of the *de re* (30). But (30) is obviously more closely related to (31) than to (32); for the proposition expressed by (32), though equivalent to that expressed by (30), is none the less pretty clearly a different proposition. This is not so for (31).

So if my account is successful, it should eliminate or greatly reduce the sceptic's perplexity. Here, however, the possibility of circularity does indeed arise; presumably we would not have helped him much if the statement of the rule for finding the *de dicto* equivalent of an essentialist assertion itself contains a *de re* expression or some other expression he does not understand. But this is not the case here. The sceptic (or at any rate the sceptic I am addressing) *does* have the idea of a proper name; and he knows how proper names work. Granted, my account presupposes that proper names function in the way briefly outlined above, rather than in the Frege–Russell fashion; but this can be argued and recognized without recourse to essentialist notions. Granted further, a complete and philosophically adequate account of the function of proper names would involve essentialist notions; but the present enterprise does not require that the sceptic and I agree on such an analysis. It requires only that he and I agree (at least for the most part) as to what propositions are expressed by the sentences resulting from the indicated substitutions of proper names into '*x* has the complement of *P*'.

IV

WORLDS, BOOKS, AND
ESSENTIAL PROPERTIES

IN Chapter III we saw how to explain the *de re* by way of the *de dicto*; an object *x* has a property *P* essentially if and only if *x* has *P* and $K(x, P)$ is necessarily false. But there is another direction from which we can approach and articulate these ideas.

1. *Worlds*

In exploring and explaining the nature of necessity, Leibniz turns to the idea of *possible worlds*; we can do no better. So we must ask initially what sort of thing a possible world *is*. The first and rough answer is that it is a *way things could have been*; it is *a way the world could have been*; it is a *possible state of affairs* of some kind. There are such things as states of affairs; among them we find some that obtain, or are actual, and some that do not obtain. So, for example, *Kareem Abdul-Jabbar's being more than seven feet tall* is a state of affairs, as is *Spiro Agnew's being President of Yale University*. Although each of these is a state of affairs, the former but not the latter obtains, or is actual. And although the latter is not actual, it is a *possible* state of affairs; in this regard it differs from *David's having travelled faster than the speed of light* and *Paul's having squared the circle*. The former of these last two items is causally or naturally impossible; the latter is impossible in that broadly logical sense.

A possible world, then, is a possible state of affairs—one that is possible in the broadly logical sense. But not every possible state of affairs is a possible world. To claim that honour, a state of affairs must be *maximal* or *complete*. *Socrates' being snubnosed* is a possible state of affairs; it is not complete or inclusive enough to be a possible world. But what is this 'completeness'? Here we need a couple of definitions. Let us say that a state of affairs *S includes* a state of affairs S' if it is not possible (in the broadly logical sense) that S obtain and S' fail to obtain—if, that is, the conjunctive state of affairs S *but not* S' (a state of affairs that obtains if and only if S obtains and S' does not) is impossible. So, for example, *Jim Whittaker's being the first American to climb Mt. Everest* includes *Jim Whittaker's being an American*. It also includes *Mt. Everest's being climbed, something's being climbed*, and *no American's having climbed Everest before Whittaker did*. Similarly, a state of affairs S *precludes* a state of affairs S' if it is not possible that both obtain. Thus *Whittaker's being the first American to climb Mt. Everest* precludes *Luther Jerstad's being the first American to climb Everest* as well as *Whittaker's never having climbed anything*. But now it is easy to say what completeness is; a state of affairs S is *complete* or *maximal* if for every state of affairs S', S includes S' or S precludes S'. And a possible world is simply a possible state of affairs that is maximal. Of course *the actual world* is one of the possible worlds; it is the maximal possible state of affairs that is actual, that has the distinction of actually obtaining. Obviously *at least* one possible world obtains. Equally obviously, *at most* one obtains; for suppose two worlds W and W^* both obtained. Since W and W^* are distinct worlds, there will be some state of affairs S such that W includes S and W^* precludes S. But then if both W and W^* are actual, S both obtains and does not obtain; and this, as they say, is repugnant to the intellect.

2. *Books*

It is clear that a proposition like

(1) Socrates is snubnosed

is intimately related to a state of affairs like

(2) Socrates' being snubnosed.

Roderick Chisholm, indeed, thinks the relation so intimate as to constitute identity.[1] As he sees it, there are not *two* kinds of entities—propositions and states of affairs—but only one; propositions just *are* states of affairs. Perhaps he is right. Without entering that question, we may note that in any event there is an obvious respect in which (1) corresponds to (2); it is

[1] In "Events and Propositions", *Nous*, 4 (1970), 15–24 and "States of Affairs Again", *Nous*, 5 (1971), 179.

impossible, in that broadly logical sense, that (1) be true and (2) fail to obtain. We might extend the use of 'entails' and say that (1) *entails* (2).[1] But it is equally impossible that (2) obtain and (1) be false; (2) also entails (1). And obviously for any possible world W and proposition p, W entails p or entails the denial of p. Now for any possible world W, *the book on W* is the set S of propositions such that p is a member of S if W entails p. Like worlds, books too have a maximality property; if B is a book, then for any proposition p, either p is a member of B or else not-p is. And clearly for each possible world W there will be exactly one book. There is at least one, since for any world W and proposition p, W entails either p or its denial; so the set of propositions entailed by W will be maximal. There is also at most one; for suppose a world W had two (or more) distinct books B and B'. If B differs from B', there must be some proposition p such that B contains p but B' contains the denial of p. But then W would entail both p and its denial, in which case W would not be a possible state of affairs after all. So each world has its book. Similarly, each maximal possible set of propositions is the book on some world; and the book on the actual world is the set of true propositions. The book on a world W is the set of propositions *true in W*. To say that p is true in a world W is to say that if W had been actual, p would have been true. More exactly, if p is true in W, then W entails p; it is impossible that W be actual and p be false. The locution 'truth in W' (for specific W) denotes a property that a proposition has if it is not possible that W obtain and p fail to be true. *Truth-in-W* is to be explained in terms of truth *simpliciter*; not *vice versa*. A proposition is true in the actual world if it is true; it is true in W if it *would have been* true had W been actual.

3. *Existence and Properties in a World*

Objects or individuals *exist in* possible worlds, some like Socrates existing in only some but not all possible worlds, and others, like the number seven, existing in every world. To say that an object x exists in a world W, is to say that if W had been actual, x would have existed; more exactly, x exists in W if it is impossible that W obtain and x fail to exist. Again, it is the notion of existence

---

[1] Of course if propositions *are* states of affairs, this would not be an extension.

simpliciter that is basic; existence-in-*W* is to be explained in
terms of it. To say that Socrates exists in *W* is not, of course, to
say that Socrates exists, but only that he *would have*, had *W* been
actual. Still further, objects *have properties* in worlds. Socrates, for
example, has the property of being snubnosed. But no doubt
there is a possible state of affairs such that if it had been actual,
then Socrates would have had a nose of some other sort or
perhaps no nose at all.[1] Accordingly there are possible worlds
in which Socrates is not snubnosed. To say that Socrates has the
property of being snubnosed in a world *W*, is to say that
Socrates would have had the property of being snubnosed, had
W been actual; it is to say that the state of affairs *W's being actual
and Socrates' not being snubnosed* is impossible. It is equivalent to
the claims that *W* includes the state of affairs consisting in
Socrates' being snubnosed, and that the book on *W* contains the
proposition *Socrates is snubnosed*.

Each proposition, furthermore, as well as each book, exists in
each possible world. That is to say, for any proposition *p* and
world *W*, *p* would have existed had *W* been actual. So the set
of books (the library, as we might call it) remains the same from
world to world; what varies is the answer to the question which
book contains only true propositions. But in the same way, each
world exists in each world. This may sound excessively Plotinian.
What it means, however, is simple and obvious enough. The
actual world, for example (suppose we name it 'α' for ease of
reference), is a state of affairs that obtains. Had some other
world been actual, α would not have obtained; still, there *would
have been* such a thing as α; α would have been a merely possible
state of affairs. *Obtaining* or *actuality* for states of affairs is like
truth for propositions. The proposition

(3) G. Cantor is a mathematician

is true; had things been appropriately different, it would have
been false. *False*, but not *non-existent*; there would have *been* such
a proposition, but it would not have been true. In the same way,
α obtains. Had things been different, α would have been a merely
possible state of affairs; there would have *been* such a state of
affairs as α, although that state of affairs would not have been

---

[1] Here you may think that the "Problem of Transworld Identity" rears its ugly
head. I shall discuss this alleged problem in Chapter VI.

actual. There are any number of merely possible worlds; each of them exists—exists in the actual world—although none is actual.

4. *Actuality*

That is to say, none of these merely possible worlds is in *fact* actual. But of course each is actual at or in itself. Each world *W* has the property of actuality in *W* (and nowhere else). For take any world *W*: *W* (and *W* alone) would have been actual, had *W* been actual; and this is sufficient for *W*'s being actual in *W*.

It may be tempting to conclude that α's being actual does not significantly or importantly distinguish it from other possible worlds—that α is not fundamentally different from these others by virtue of being actual. The reasoning sometimes goes as follows. True enough, α and α alone is actual—that is, actual in the actual world, in α. α is actual in exactly one world: itself. But the same may be said for any other possible world; it too is actual in exactly one world: itself. Why then should α thus exalt itself at the expense of its fellows, claiming for itself alone the title 'the actual world'? Why should *we* make that claim on its behalf? True enough, α merits that title in the actual world —in α; but for each world *W* there is a world where *W* enjoys this same distinction. Therefore α's being actual does not significantly distinguish it from these others.[1]

This reasoning is confused. True enough, each world is actual at itself; at any other world *W* it is *W*, not α, that is actual. But how does this so much as suggest that α's being actual does not significantly distinguish it from other worlds? To say on this account that actuality does not significantly distinguish α from its fellows is like saying that Einstein's having discovered Relativity does not significantly distinguish him from other men; for, for each person *x* there are plenty of worlds where *x* discovers relativity—just as many as those where Einstein enjoys this distinction. No doubt you have wished that it was you who discovered the calculus, rather than Leibniz or Newton. Take

---

[1] David Lewis ("Anselm and Actuality", *Nous*, 4 (1970), 186–7) gives a different argument for this conclusion. I am not sure I understand his argument; in any case it seems to depend upon the view that each object exists in just one possible world. See below, Chapter VI, Sections 5–7.

heart: there are plenty of worlds where you do so; and Leibniz and Newton can claim no more.

But of course there is an important difference: Leibniz and Newton made these discoveries; the rest of us did not. α is actual; the other worlds are not. And the fact that each world is actual at itself does not compromise this difference. For what, after all, does this truth come to? We began by supposing we know what it is for a state of affairs to be actual; we then explained a possible world as a complete or fully determinate possible state of affairs. We added that a state of affairs S is *actual in a world W* if S would have been actual had W been actual, or if it is not possible that W obtain and S not obtain. To say, therefore, that every world is actual in itself is to say no more than that for every world W it is not possible that W be actual and W not be actual; it is to say that for every world W, if W had been actual, then W would have been actual. While this is indeed true, it is hard to see that it should lead us to minimize the difference between α, the actual world, and the other merely possible worlds.

We might make a similar point about propositions. We began by supposing that we know what it means for a proposition to be true. We then explained truth in a world as follows: p is true in a world W if p would have been true had W been actual; equivalently, if it is not possible that W be actual and p not be true. We could define *truth in a book* analogously; p is true in B if p is a member of B. Then every possible proposition is true in at least one world and in at least one book; for to say so is only to say, obviously, that for each possible proposition p there is at least one book of which it is a member and at least one state of affairs S such that if S had been actual, p would have been true. It would not be the method of true philosophy to infer, from this fact, that the difference between truth and possibility is of no ultimate significance.

5. *This World and the Actual World*

The predicate 'is actual' expresses the property of being actual; hence in each world W 'is actual' is true of W. As David Lewis puts it, "at any world W, the name 'the actual world' *denotes* or *names* W; the predicate 'is actual' *designates* or *is true of* W and

whatever exists in W; the operator 'actually' is *true of* propositions true at W, and so on for cognate terms of other categories".[1] This is certainly true for many uses of these locutions.
When in α I utter the sentence

(4) This is the actual world

what I say is true. In uttering (4) I use the name 'the actual
world' to refer to α; this name denotes α; and α is indeed the
actual world. There are other worlds in which I utter (4) (and
in which I speak English). Let W^* be any such world. If W^* had
been actual, I would have spoken truly in uttering (4); for 'this'
and 'the actual world' would have denoted W^*, which would
have been the actual world. Indeed, an occurrence of this sentence is true (in English) in any world W; for in any world W
and for any occurrence of this sentence, the occurrences of 'this'
and 'the actual world' denote W, which in W is the actual
world.

Some have concluded that the phrases 'this world' and 'the
actual world' are synonymous, or, less sweepingly, that the
sentence

(4) This is the actual world

expresses the same proposition as

(5) This world is this world.

But such a conclusion is mistaken; and in fact (4) and (5) do
not express the same proposition. For consider the proposition
expressed by (4). This proposition (or at any rate one logically
equivalent to it) is also expressed by

(6) α is the actual world.

But the proposition expressed by (6) is contingent, unlike the
proposition expressed by (5); so (4) and (5) do not express the
same proposition. Of course (4) (given its English meaning)
could not have been used to express a false proposition; that is,
for every world W, the proposition (4) expresses in W is true
in W. It does not follow that the proposition it *does* express—the
one it expresses in *this* world—is true in every world; and in fact
it is not.

    [1] "Anselm and Actuality", *Nous*, 4 (1970), 185.

Similarly, the sentence

(7) This world is not actual

is false (in English) in every world in which it is uttered. Nevertheless the proposition it expresses in a given world is not necessarily false. The proposition it expresses in α, for example, is true in every world *but* α. In this regard, (4) and (7) resemble

(8) I am speaking

and

(9) I am not speaking.

On any occasion of utterance, (8) is true and (9) is false. Nevertheless the propositions expressed by utterances of (8) and (9) are contingent.

In the same way, the property of being actual must be distinguished from the property of being this world. The words 'the property of being this world' do in fact denote a property: this is a property that a world has if and only if that world is α. This property is one that α alone has; further, it is one that α has in every world. There is no world in which α lacks the property of being this world—although of course there are worlds in which the English sentence

(10) This world is α

expresses a false proposition. The words 'the property of being actual' also denote a property and one that α alone has; but this property is one that α possibly lacks. There are worlds in which α lacks this property—indeed, α lacks it in every world distinct from α.

6. *Relative Possibility*

In semantical developments of modal logic, one meets the suggestion that a possible world may be possible *relative to* some but perhaps not all possible worlds.[1] To say that W is possible relative to W' is to say that W would have been possible if W' had been actual; alternatively, it is to say that every proposition true in W is possible in W', or that every state of affairs that

---

[1] See, for example, Saul Kripke's "Some Semantical Considerations on Modal Logic", *Acta Philosophica Fennica*, 16 (1963). Reprinted in *Reference and Modality*, ed. L. Linsky (Oxford: Oxford University Press, 1971), p. 64.

obtains in W is possible in W'. This relation of relative possibility is commonly taken, in such semantical treatments of modal logic, to be at least reflexive; every possible world is possible with respect to itself and every proposition true in a world is possible in that world. The usual semantical developments of modal logic yield as valid the formulas of Von Wright's system T if relative possibility is taken to be reflexive. If we add that it is also transitive, then we find that

(11) $\Box p \supset \Box \Box p$,

the characteristic formula of Lewis's S_4, is valid. If we go on to add that it is symmetric as well, we have the characteristic formula of S_5

(12) $\Diamond \Box p \supset \Box p$

as valid.[1]

This notion of relative possibility is useful in that '$\Box$' may be interpreted in a variety of ways. We might, for example, so construe it that the results of prefixing it to a sentence S is true if and only if the proposition expressed by S is *known* to be true. Then presumably neither (11) nor (12) would be true; a proposition could be known to George, let us say, although no one —not even George—knew that it was known to anyone. *A fortiori* (12) would not be true; there are many propositions p such that while it is not known that p is *not* known, it is also not known that p. So if we interpret '$\Box$' as 'it is known that' then a sound system will endorse neither (11) nor (12). We might also interpret '$\Box$' as 'it is provable (in mathematics, say) that'. Here perhaps we should want to endorse (11); if it is provable that p, then it is provable that it is provable that p. For presumably to produce a proof of p is to prove that p, but also that p is provable. But (12) would still be dubious at best: even if it cannot be proved that Fermat's Theorem cannot be proved, it hardly follows that it *can* be proved.

So the notion of relative possibility is in this way useful in semantical developments of modal logic; it permits a certain generality not otherwise easily attainable. But suppose we focus our attention on broadly logical necessity. Are there propositions that are *in fact* necessary, but would have been merely

[1] Loc. cit.

contingent if things had been different, if some other possible state of affairs had been actual?

(13) All bachelors are unmarried

and

(14) If all bachelors are unmarried and Dirk is a bachelor, then Dirk is unmarried

are necessary truths; could they have been merely contingent? If so, there must be some possible state of affairs S such that if S had been actual, then (13) and/or (14) would have been contingent. But *are* there states of affairs that with any show of plausibility could be said to meet this condition? One hears the following affirmative answer. That we use the word 'bachelor' in the way we do is surely a contingent fact; we could have used it to mean what we now mean by 'callow and beardless youth' for example. But if we *had* so used it, then (13) would have been contingent; so it is possible that (13) should be contingent.

But this argument betrays deplorable confusion. Had the envisaged state of affairs been actual, the *sentence* that expresses (13) would have expressed a contingent[1] proposition; it by no means follows that the proposition it *does* express would have been contingent. This confusion set aside, I think we can see that (13) and (14) are not merely necessary; they could not have been contingent. So when it is broadly logical necessity that is at stake, we shall want to accept (11). But surely the same goes for (12). Are there propositions that *in fact* are possible, but would have been impossible had things been different in some way?

(15) Socrates never married

and

(16) Socrates was a carpenter

are false but possible propositions; could they have been impossible? The answer, I think, is clear; while of course the *sentences* expressing (15) and (16) could have expressed impossible propositions, (15) and (16) themselves could not have been impossible. We may put the same question in a different way. Are there

---

[1] And probably false proposition; so what the argument would show, if successful, is that (13) is not necessary at all.

states of affairs that *in fact* could have obtained, but that would have lacked the property of possibly obtaining, had things been different in some possible way? That is, are there states of affairs that in *this* world have the property of obtaining in some possible world or other, but in *other* worlds lack that property? Again, I think we can see that there are no such states of affairs. I think we can see that

(17) If a state of affairs S is possible, then it is necessarily possible; that is, possible with respect to every possible world.

But then it immediately follows that

(18) Every possible world is possible with respect to every possible world.

It also follows that

(19) Any state of affairs possible with respect to at least one possible world, is possible with respect to every possible world.

For let S be a state of affairs possible with respect to some possible world W; and let W^* be any other possible world. There must be a possible world W' such that W' is possible with respect to W and such that S holds in W'. But W' is a possible world; hence by (18) it is possible with respect to *every* possible world; accordingly it is possible with respect to W^*. But then S is possible with respect to W^*;[1] (19), therefore, is true. And of course from (19) it follows that

(20) Every world possible with respect to at least one world is possible with respect to every world.

Since this is so, we may forgo further mention of the relation of relative possibility and speak simply of possibility as such.

---

[1] This argument depends upon my definition of a possible world as a maximal state of affairs that is *in fact* possible—possible with respect to the actual world. We might think to expand the membership of the class of possible worlds by adopting the following recursive definition of *possible world*:

A maximal state of affairs is a possible world if either it is possible with respect to the actual world or possible with respect to some possible world.

In view of (17), however, it is easily shown that every maximal state of affairs that is a possible world under *this* definition is also a possible world under the definition originally given.

7. *Truth and Truth-in-α*

Suppose we consider a proposition like

(21) Socrates is snubnosed.

(21) is in fact true. And since α is the actual world, (21) is true in α. Furthermore, the latter includes the state of affairs consisting in

(22) Socrates' being snubnosed.

Since α includes (22) and (22) entails (21), α entails (21). Accordingly, it is not merely true but necessarily true that (21) is true-in-α. That is to say, it is true in every world that (21) is true-in-α. (21) may be and doubtless is false in some world W; in that world W, none the less, the proposition that (21) is true-in-α, is true. Truth must thus be distinguished from truth-in-α. The former is a property that (21) (and any other contingent proposition) has in some worlds and lacks in others; the latter is one that a proposition has in every world if in at least one. Indeed, for any proposition p and world W, if there is a world in which p is true-in-W, then p is true-in-W in every world. Propositions of the form *p is true in α* and *p is true in W* are non-contingent, either necessarily true or necessarily false.

Every possible world, therefore, contains every other possible world in a dual sense. In the first place, as we have seen, each world W *exists in* each world W' in that if W' had been actual, W would have existed. But secondly, for any possible worlds W and W' and state of affairs S, if W includes S, then W' includes the state of affairs consisting in W's including S. In the same way, each book contains every other book in this sense: if B is the book on some world, then for any book B' and proposition p, if p is a member of B, then B' contains the information that p is a member of B. So in this way each book contains the entire library—or at the least a detailed and highly analytic card catalogue.

8. *Necessary Truth and Essential Properties*

A proposition, of course, is necessarily true if true in every possible world. But we have *several* fairly plausible options as to what it is for an object x to have a property P essentially: Socrates has P essentially if and only if

(23) Socrates has P in every world

or

(24) Socrates has P and has it in every world in which he exists,

or

(25) Socrates has P and there is no world in which Socrates has the complement $\overline{P}$ of P.

How are these related? The issue turns essentially on whether there are (or possibly are) objects that have properties but do not exist. We might suppose, for example, that Santa Claus, despite his failure to exist, does have such properties as being rotund and jolly and favourably disposed towards well-behaved children; he has these properties in α, the actual world. On the other hand, we might take it that a thing has properties in a world W only if it exists in W. I shall adopt the latter view, but defer argument for it until Chapters VII and VIII. Here I shall simply take it for granted.

But given this assumption, we see that (23) does not adequately characterize Socrates' having P essentially. For surely Socrates is a contingent being who does not exist in every world. Hence there is no property—not even self-identity—that he has in every world; (23) therefore implies that Socrates has no essential properties at all. More generally, (23) implies that only necessary beings have essential properties. So (23) is unacceptable. (24) and (25), on the other hand, equivalently and accurately characterize the idea of essential attribution. For if Socrates has P in every world in which he exists, then there is no world in which he has the complement of P. And if, conversely, there is no world in which Socrates has the complement of P, then (assuming that for every property P and world W in which Socrates exists, Socrates has P in W or else $\overline{P}$ in W) every world in which he exists is one in which he has P. Of course (24) and (25) diverge if we suppose that Socrates has properties in worlds in which he does not exist; for then he might have P in every world in which he exists, but have $\overline{P}$ in some world in which he does not.

9. *Some Putative Principles*

A. *Identity* de re *and* de dicto

Given the above remarks, it is easy to see that the burden of a *de dicto* assertion like

(26) Possibly something is red

is that the proposition *something is red* is true in at least one possible world. An assertion like

(27) Something is possibly prime

on the other hand, is a *de re* assertion conveying the information that there exists at least one object—the number 2 perhaps— that has the property of being prime in at least one possible world. A proposition like

(28) Necessarily, everything is self-identical

or

(28) $\Box(x)x = x$,

claims that the proposition *everything is self-identical* is true in every possible world;

(29) Everything is necessarily self-identical

or (letting '$\Box x = x$' represent the property of being essentially self-identical)

(29) $(x)\Box x = x$,

on the other hand, is the *de re* assertion that each object has the property expressed by '$\Box x = x$'—the property a thing has if and only if it has the property of self-identity in every world in which it exists. (29) has sometimes been viewed with suspicion[1] in that it is thought to entail such items as

(30) Necessarily, the tallest man in Boston = the tallest man in Boston,

a proposition arguably false since the proposition to which it attributes necessity arguably entails that there are some men in Boston. This, however, is unfair to (29) which says only that each object, including the tallest man in Boston, has the property

[1] See, for example, R. Chisholm, "Identity Through Possible Worlds: Some Questions", *Nous*, 1 (1967), 8.

of being self-identical in every world in which it exists. So taken, (29) entails no such *de dicto* items as (30).

B. *The Buridan Formula*

Jean Buridan once remarked that

    (31) Possibly everything is F

does not in general entail

    (32) Everything is possibly F.

That is, he rejected

    (33) Necessarily, if possibly everything is F, then everything is possibly F.

His counter-example is as follows. God need not have created anything; hence it is possible that

    (34) Everything is identical with God.

It does not follow from this, he says, that everything is possibly identical with God. You and I, for example, are not. A less dramatic counter-example can be constructed by turning to the contrapositive of (33):

    (35) Necessarily (if something is essentially F, then necessarily something is F)

or, as we might more perspicuously put it (letting '$\Box Fx$' express the property of being essentially F),

    (35) $\Box((Ex)\Box Fx \supset \Box(Ex)Fx)$.

Clearly enough Socrates has the property of being essentially identical with Socrates; hence something has the property. On the other hand, there are worlds in which Socrates does not exist, so that the proposition *Something is identical with Socrates* is not necessarily true.

We can also see that the converse of (33) and (35)

    (36) $\Box(\Box(Ex)Fx \supset (Ex)\Box Fx)$

is false. Obviously it is necessary that there be at least one contingently true proposition. There is no object that has essentially the property of being a contingently true proposition, however; for any such proposition would have the property of being true in every possible world (given that each proposition exists in every world) and would thus be necessarily rather than contingently true. Other examples abound.

c. *The Barcan Formula*

The proposition expressed by the Barcan Formula[1]

(37) $(x)\Box Fx \supset \Box(x)Fx$

is easily seen to be false or at any rate not necessarily true. No doubt there is a possible world W^* where no material objects exist—a world in which the only objects are such things as propositions, properties, sets, numbers, and God. Now such a thing as a set, of course, is an immaterial object. Furthermore, a set is essentially immaterial; for surely no set could have been a material object. It is therefore true that

(38) Every set is essentially immaterial.

This is not a merely accidental feature of our world; (38) is necessarily true, true in every world. Hence it is true in this world W^* of which we are speaking. And of course sets are not unique in this regard; the same goes for properties, propositions, numbers, and God. Hence

(38′) Everything is essentially immaterial

is also true in W^*. But

(39) Necessarily, everything is an immaterial object

is false in W^*, in view of the possibility of worlds like α in which there exists material objects.

Of the group of putative principles we are examining, only

(40) $\Box(x)Fx \supset (x)\Box Fx$,

has the distinction of being true. For suppose its antecedent is true and let x be any object—any actually existent object, that is—and W any world in which x exists. *Everything is F* is necessarily true and hence true in W. x, accordingly, has the property of being F in W. So x has that property in every world in which it exists—that is, x has it essentially.

---

[1] Named for Ruth Barcan, now Ruth Barcan Marcus, one of the pioneers of modern modal logic. What is at issue, of course, is not whether the *formula* (37) is *valid*; obviously in some semantical developments of modal logic it is and in others it is not. The question is whether a certain *proposition*—one naturally expressed by (37)—is *true*.

Of course this argument depends upon our characterization of essential attribution:

(41) *x* has *P* essentially if and only if *x* has *P* in every world in which it exists.

If instead we embraced

(42) *x* has *P* essentially if and only if *x* has *P* in every possible world,

then such a property as existence (conceding, *pace* Kant, that existence is a property) would constitute a counter example to (40).[1] For

(43) Everything exists

is of course true in every possible world; but many objects do not exist in every possible world. Hence

(44) Everything essentially exists

is false under (42). Such properties as *self-identity* and *being unmarried if a bachelor* would also constitute counter examples to (40), given (42), if we suppose, as I do, that an object has no properties in a world in which it does not exist; for while it is necessarily true that everything has self-identity, those of us who do not enjoy the status reserved for necessary beings will not have this property essentially under (42). This is best seen as a reason for rejecting (42). But (44) is true given the more plausible (41).

10. *What Properties are Essential to Socrates?*

An object *x* has a property *P* essentially, then, if and only if *x* has *P* in every world in which *x* exists—equivalently (given that objects have no properties in worlds in which they do not exist) if and only if there is no world in which *x* has the complement of *P*. But what sorts of properties do things have essentially? Which of Socrates' properties, for example, are essential to him? Consider first such properties as *self identity, being coloured if red, being something or other*, and *being either a prime number or else something else*. Clearly every object whatever has these properties and has them in every world in which it exists. Let us call such

---

[1] See S. Kripke, op. cit., p. 70.

properties *trivially essential*. Among them will be the property of existence—if, once more, we momentarily concede that existence is a property. Every object, clearly enough, exists in every world in which it exists; so everything has essentially the property of existing. This is not to be boggled at. Everything has existence essentially; but only some things—properties, propositions, numbers, God, perhaps—have *necessary existence*, the property an object has if it exists in every possible world.

So objects have trivially essential properties. But perhaps this truth is somewhat lacklustre; are there objects and properties that are not trivially essential, such that the former essentially have the latter? Certainly; the number 12 has the properties of *being an integer, being a number*, and *being an abundant number* essentially; Socrates has none of these properties and *a fortiori* has none essentially. Are there properties that some things have essentially and others have, but have accidentally? Indeed there are; *being non-green* is a property 7 has essentially and the Taj Mahal accidentally. *Being prime or prim* is essential to 7; it is accidental to Miss Prudence Allworthy, Headmistress of the Queen Victoria School for Girls.

But perhaps these fancy, cooked up properties—disjunctive or negative as they are—have a peculiar odour. What about Socrates and such properties as *being a philosopher, an Athenian, a teacher of Plato*? What about *having been born in 470 B.C., having lived for some seventy years*, and *having been executed by the Athenians on a charge of corrupting the youth*? Are any of these ordinary meat-and-potatoes properties of Socrates essential to him? I should think not. Surely Socrates could have been born ten years later. Surely he could have lived in Macedonia, say, instead of Athens. And surely he could have stuck to his stonecutting, eschewed philosophy, corrupted no youth, and thus escaped the wrath of the Athenians. None of these properties is essential to him. But what about their disjunction? No doubt Socrates could have lacked *any* of these properties; could he have lacked them all? I think he could have, as I have argued in elsewhere;[1] I shall not repeat these arguments here.

Socrates, therefore, has such trivially essential properties as *the property of having some properties* and *the property of being unmarried if a bachelor*. He also has essentially some properties not had by

[1] "World and Essence", *Philosophical Review*, 79 (1970), 466–73.

everything: *being a non-member* and *being possibly conscious* would be examples. These are properties he shares with other persons. Are there properties he has essentially and shares with some but not all other persons? Certainly. *Being Socrates* or *being identical with Socrates* is an essential to Socrates; there is no world in which Socrates exists but does not have the property of being Socrates, the property of being identical with Socrates. (Of course the property of being named 'Socrates' is not essential to Socrates; there are worlds in which he is named 'Plato' or 'Spiro Agnew' and worlds in which he has no name at all. The property *being Socrates* must not be confused with the property *being named 'Socrates'*.) *Being Socrates*, therefore, is essential to Socrates; *being Socrates or Plato* is a property essential to Socrates and one that he shares with Plato. This property is had essentially by anything that has it. *Being Socrates or Greek*, on the other hand, is one Socrates shares with many other persons and one he and he alone has essentially.

11. *World-Indexed Properties*

Consider once more the property of being snubnosed. This is a property Socrates has and has accidentally; there are possible worlds in which he has its complement. Let W^* be any such world. In W^* Socrates does not have the property of being snubnosed. However, he does have *the property of being snubnosed in α* in that world. But what kind of a property is *that*? *Being snubnised in α* is a property enjoyed by an object x in a world W if and only if (1) x exists in W and (2) if W had been actual, α would have included x's being snubnosed. Alternatively, x has the property *being snubnosed in α*, in a world W, if and only if x exists in W and in W α includes the state of affairs consisting in x's being snubnosed—if and only if, that is, x exists in W and W includes α's *including Socrates' being snubnosed*. More generally,

(45) where P is a property and W a world, x has the property *having P in W* in a world W^* if and only if x exists in W^* and W^* includes W's *including x's having P*.

Of course, W^* includes x's having P in W if and only if it is impossible in W^* that W obtain and x not have P. But, as we have already seen (above, p. 54), what is impossible does not vary from world to world; if a state of affairs is impossible in at least one world, then it is impossible in every world. So if *W* includes *x's having P* in at least one world, then *W* includes that state of affairs in every world. Accordingly, we can make a small but satisfying simplification in (45):

> (46) Where *P* is a property and *W* is a world, an object *x* has the property *having P in W* in a world *W** if and only if *x* exists in *W** and *W* includes *x's having P*.

Being snubnosed in α is a *world-indexed* property. We might characterize this notion as follows:

> (47) A property *P* is *world-indexed* if and only if either (1) there is a property *Q* and a world *W* such that for any object *x* and world *W**, *x* has *P* in *W** if and only if *x* exists in *W** and *W* includes *x's having Q*,

or

> (2) *P* is the complement of a world-indexed property.

We should note that the complement of a world-indexed property such as *being snubnosed in W* is not the property *being non-snubnosed in W*. The latter property is one that an object *x* has only if it exists in *W* and is non-snubnosed therein. The complement of *being snubnosed in W*, however, does not require that those who have it exist in *W*; it is enjoyed by any object that either does not exist in *W* or is non-snubnosed therein. So if *W** is a world in which Socrates does not exist, then Socrates lacks both *being snubnosed in W** and *being non-snubnosed in W**; he does, however, have the complements of both these properties.

It is easy to see that *being snubnosed in* α is essential to Socrates. For he has this property in a world *W** if and only if he exists in *W** and in that world α includes *Socrates' being snubnosed*. But α does include *Socrates' being snubnosed*; hence it includes it in every world; hence Socrates has *being snubnosed in* α in every world in which he exists—i.e. essentially. And of course the same goes for every other world-indexed property he has. But for any world *W* and property *P*, either Socrates has *P* in *W* or else he does not—in which case he has the complement of the world-indexed property *having P in W*. So for every world-indexed property *Q*, either Socrates has *Q* essentially or else he has its complement essentially. And of course the same will go for *existence*; Socrates has essentially the property of existing in α. Indeed, everything[1] has that property essentially. But no doubt there are worlds in which the proposition *everything exists in α* is false; this is so, at any rate, if there could have been more things than there are. So while everything has this property essentially, that everything has it is not a necessary truth.

Some, indeed, may think the very idea of a property like *being snubnosed in α* muddled, perverse, preposterous, or in some other way deserving of abuse. So Mrs. Marcus:

> A word of caution here. In specifying how we paraphrase, we hope to avoid a few muddles. Plantinga for example has staked several arguments on the claim that being snubnosed in *W* is a property Socrates has in all possible worlds which contain him and is therefore essential. Are we to suppose that 'Socrates is snubnosed in *W*' like 'Socrates was born in Athens' is one of those ordinary sentences we associate with sentence symbols of our interpreted QML, that in the domain of our interpretation there are places one of which is Athens and the other the world, which would put *W* in the domain of *W*.[2]

As a word of caution, this is to the point. We must not be misled by our terminology to suppose that a possible world is a place, like Wyoming, so that *being snubnosed in W* is like *being mugged in Chicago*. A possible world is a state of affairs, not a place; and far be it from me to claim otherwise. This stipulated, however, where exactly (or even approximately) is the muddle? Socrates has the property of being snubnosed in *W*, where *W* is a possible world, if and only if *W* includes *Socrates' being snubnosed*. If *W* is a world in which Socrates has the property of being snubnosed, then clearly enough Socrates has the property *being snubnosed in W*. It is not easy to see that this property merits much by way of scorn and contempt.

Professor Marcus goes on: "All that Plantinga's funny sentence (*P*) might come to is that . . . its truth assignment is *T* in *W* and so therefore must be the assignment to ◇*P*." I am unable to see which funny sentence of mine Professor Marcus is referring to as '*P*'. One possibility, perhaps, is this: *P* is 'Socrates is snubnosed'; and the assertion that Socrates is snubnosed in *W*

---

[1] Recall my assumption that there are no non-existent objects (although in other worlds there may be objects that do not exist in α); so the quantifier ranges over existent objects, that being the only kind there are.

[2] "Essential Attribution", *Journal of Philosophy*, 68 (1971), 195.

"comes to" the truth that since P is to be assigned truth in W, $\Diamond P$ is true in fact. This suggests that the propositions

(48) *Socrates is snubnosed* is true in W (for specific W)

and

(49) Possibly Socrates is snubnosed

come to the same thing, or are equivalent. But they are not. There are worlds W in which it is false that Socrates is snubnosed; let W be any such world. Then (48) will be false and (49) true. *Being true in W* (for specific W) entails[1] but is not entailed by *being possibly true*. In the same way, the property of being snubnosed in W is not to be confused with the property of being possibly snubnosed (a property that Socrates also has essentially); for if W is α, then while Raquel Welch has the latter, she lacks the former.

12. *Could Socrates have been an Alligator?*

That depends. We might think of an alligator as a composite typically consisting in a large, powerful body animated by an unimpressive mind with a nasty disposition. If we do, shall we say that any mind-alligator-body composite is an alligator, or must the mind be of a special, relatively dull sort? If the first alternative is correct, then I think Socrates could have been an alligator; for I think he could have had an alligator body. At least he could have had an alligator body during part of his career. We have no difficulty in understanding Kafka's story about the man who wakes up one morning to discover that he has the body of a beetle; and in fact the state of affairs depicted there is entirely possible. In the same way it is possible that I should awaken one morning and discover (to my considerable chagrin) that my body had been exchanged for an alligator body. Socrates, therefore, could have had an alligator body; if this is sufficient for his having been an alligator, then Socrates could have been an alligator. (Whether he could have had an alligator body *all along*—throughout the entire time during which he did have a human body—is of course a distinct question; but here too I am inclined to think he could have.)

[1] Where a property P entails a property Q if there is no world in which there exists an object that has P but lacks Q.

On the other hand, we might hold, with Descartes, that an alligator is a *material object* of some sort—perhaps an elaborate machine made of flesh and bone. Suppose that is what an alligator is; could Socrates have been one? Descartes has a famous argument for the conclusion that he is not a material object:

> I am therefore, precisely speaking, only a thinking thing, that is, a mind (*mens sive animus*), understanding, or reason—terms whose signification was before unknown to me. I am, however, a real thing, and really existent; but what thing? The answer was, a thinking thing. The question now arises, am I aught besides? I will stimulate my imagination with a view to discover whether I am not still something more than a thinking being. Now it is plain I am not the assemblage of members called the human body; I am not a thin and penetrating air diffused through all these members, or wind, or flame, or vapour, or breath, or any of all the things I can imagine; for I supposed that all these were not, and, without changing the supposition, I find that I still feel assured of my existence.[1]

How shall we construe this argument? I think Descartes means to reason as follows: it is at present possible both that I exist and that there are no material objects—that is,

(50) Possibly, I exist and there are no material objects.

But if so, then

(51) I am not a material object.

But is the premiss of this argument true? I think it *is* true, although here I shall not argue for that claim. The proposition that there are no material objects does not entail, it seems to me, that I do not exist. Furthermore, Descartes could have employed a weaker premiss here:

(50′) Possibly, I exist and no material object is my body.

But even if these premisses are true, the argument is at the best unduly inexplicit. We might as well argue from

(52) Possibly, I exist and no brothers-in-law exist

to

(53) I am not a brother-in-law.

What follows from (50) is not (51) but only its possibility:

(54) Possibly, I am not a material object.

---

[1] Descartes, *Meditations*, Meditation I.

At best, therefore, what the argument shows is that even if human beings are in fact physical objects, they are only contingently so. But something else of interest follows from (50) and (50′); it follows that there are worlds in which I exist and not only *am* not a body, but do not *have* a body. *Being embodied*, therefore, is not essential to human persons. Here we might be inclined to object that

(55) All human persons have bodies

is necessarily true. Perhaps so and perhaps not; in neither case does it follow that human persons are essentially embodied. What follows is only that, if they are not, then *being a human person* is not essential to human persons, just as *being a brother-in-law* is not essential to brothers-in-law. The property of being a human person (as opposed to that of being a divine person or an angelic person or a person *simpliciter*) may entail the possession of a body; it may be that whatever, in a given world, has the property of being a human person has a body in that world. It does not follow that Socrates, who is in fact a human person, has the property of having a body in every world he graces.

As it stands, therefore, Descartes's argument does not establish that he is not a body or a material object. But perhaps we can fill in some of the gaps. Suppose, first of all, that I am a material object—that I am identical with some material object. Which material object am I? With which such object am I identical? The answer seems clear: I am the object that I refer to as "my body". So if there is any material object at all with which I am identical, I am identical with my body (which for ease of reference I shall name 'B'). But

(56) It is possible that I exist at a time when B does not.

For it certainly seems possible that I should acquire a new body —either by exchanging bodies with someone else, or by having B replaced in one fell swoop or piece by piece by another body —perhaps one made of some synthetic and more durable material. But then clearly it is possible that I acquire a new body and continue to exist when B is destroyed. Accordingly there is a time *t* at which it is possible that I exist and B does not. That is to say, there is a possible world *W* such that in *W* I exist at *t* and B does not exist at *t*. Hence I have the property *exists at t in W*; B lacks that property. By the Indiscernibility of Identicals, therefore, it follows that I am not identical with B. But then surely there is no material object at all with which I am identical.

There is still another way of repairing Descartes' argument. G. H. von Wright suggests the following principle:

> If a property can be significantly predicated of the individuals of a certain universe of discourse then either the property is necessarily present in some or all of the individuals and necessarily absent in the rest or else the property is possibly but not necessarily (that is, contingently) present in some or all individuals and possibly but not necessarily (contingently) absent in the rest.[1]

We might restate and compress this principle as follows:

(57) Any property *P* had essentially by anything is had essentially by everything that has it.

Is (57) true? We have already seen that it is not; *being prime or prim, being Socrates or Greek* constitute counter examples. Still, the principle might hold for a large range of 'natural' properties; and it is plausible to suppose that it holds for the property of being a material object as well as for the complement of that property. It seems to me impossible that there should be an object that in some possible world is a material object and in others is not. That is to say, where '*M*' names the property of being a material object and '$\overline{M}$' names its complement,

(58) Anything that has *M* or $\overline{M}$, has *M* essentially or has $\overline{M}$ essentially.

And armed with this principle, we can refurbish Descartes' argument. For if I am not essentially a material object, then by (58) I am not one at all.

If these arguments are sound, therefore, then Descartes was right in holding that he (as well as the rest of us) is not a material object. But we can go further. If I do not have the property of being a material object, then by another application of (58) it follows that I have its complement essentially. Descartes, therefore, was correct; he is an immaterial object and, indeed, is such

---

[1] *An Essay in Modal Logic* (Amsterdam: North Holland Publishing Co., 1951), p. 27.

an object in every world in which he exists. Given (50) or (50′) or (56), what Descartes' argument establishes is that human persons are essentially immaterial. Socrates, therefore, could have been an alligator only if it is possible to be both an alligator and immaterial.

V

THE NECESSITY OF NATURES

1. *Essence Preliminarily Characterized*

So far we have seen that Socrates' essential properties include those that are trivially essential, but also such attributes as *being a non-number, being possibly snubnosed, being snubnosed in α,* and (perhaps a bit more tentatively) *being immaterial.* Can we go further? Does he also have an *essence* or *haecceity* or *individual nature*? And just what sort of thing would an essence be anyhow? The initial idea is this: an essence of Socrates is a property (or a group of properties) that Socrates has essentially and that is *unique* to him. We could say that an essence of Socrates *individuates* him; it must be a property nothing else has. But this is not sufficient; to be an essence of Socrates, a property must be such that nothing else *could have* had it. So we might say that

    (1) E is an essence of Socrates if and only if E is essential to Socrates and everything distinct from him has $\bar{E}$ (the complement of E) essentially.

But even this is not quite strong enough. If E is an essence of Socrates, then indeed nothing that *in fact* exists and is distinct from him could have had E; but we must say more: it must be impossible that there *should have been* an object distinct from Socrates that had E. So perhaps we shall want to say that

    (2) E is an essence of Socrates if and only if E is essential to Socrates and there is no possible world in which there exists an object distinct from Socrates that has E.

We might wish to go further still and require that

    (3) E is an essence of Socrates if and only if E is essential to Socrates and in every possible world everything distinct from him has $\bar{E}$ essentially.

But (3) really takes us no further; a property P is an essence of Socrates in the sense of (2) if and only if P is also an essence of

Socrates in the sense of (3). To see this, however, we must first argue for a principle that is important in its own right:

(4) Necessarily, for any objects x and y, if there is a possible world in which x and y are distinct, then there is no world in which x is identical with y.

Suppose for *reductio* that (4) is false; that is, that there is a possible world W in which there exist objects x and y that are distinct (in W) but identical in some world W^*. Now in W^*, of course, x has the property of being x-identical, the property of being identical with x. Furthermore, there is no world possible with respect to W^* where x has the property of being x-diverse—the property of being *distinct* from x. In W^*, therefore, x has the property *being nowhere x-diverse*. But then by the Indiscernibility of Identicals, the same can be said for y; that is, in W^* y also has the property of being nowhere x-diverse. In W^*, therefore, y's *being x-diverse* is an impossible state of affairs. But then by (19) of Chapter IV (above, p. 54) it follows that y's *being x-diverse* is impossible with respect to every possible world. In particular, y's being x-diverse is impossible with respect to W; in W, therefore (contrary to our supposition for *reductio*), it is *false* that y is distinct from x. (4), therefore, is true.

But now it is easy to see that if E is an essence of Socrates in the sense of (2), then E is also an essence of Socrates in the sense of (3). Suppose E is essential to Socrates and such that in every possible world everything distinct from Socrates has $\bar{E}$. We must show that in every possible world, everything distinct from Socrates has $\bar{E}$ essentially. Let W be any world and x any object in W that is distinct from Socrates; and let W^* be any world in which x exists. We must show that x has $\bar{E}$ in W^*. But in W^*, everything distinct from Socrates has $\bar{E}$. What must be shown, therefore, is that in W^*, x is distinct from Socrates. But this follows from (4) together with our supposition that x is distinct from Socrates in W.[1]

Our question, then, is whether Socrates has an essence in the sense of (2)—a property that is essential to him and such that in every possible world, everything distinct from him has its complement. But clearly he *does* have such a property; *Socrateity,*

---

[1] Obviously any property that meets the condition for essencehood laid down in (3) also satisfies that laid down in (1); hence if E is an essence in the sense of (2), it is also an essence in the sense of (1).

the property of being Socrates or being identical with Socrates is such a property. For surely Socrateity is essential to Socrates. There is no world in which Socrates exists and has the complement of Socrateity; there is no world in which Socrates exists and is distinct from Socrates. But, just as obviously, Socrateity is such that, for any world W, anything distinct from Socrates has its complement. Obviously there is no possible world in which there exists an object that is distinct from Socrates but has the property of being identical with Socrates.

2. The Nature of Essence

Accordingly, Socrateity is an essence of Socrates. But there are others. Each of Socrates' world-indexed properties, as we have seen, is essential to him. Now let P be any property he and he alone has—being married to Xantippe, for example, or being the shortest Greek philosopher, or being A. E. Taylor's favourite philosopher; and consider the world-indexed property having-P-in-α. I think we can see that this property is an essence of Socrates. We are given that it is essential to him; what remains to be shown, then, is that there is no world W in which there exists an object x that is distinct from Socrates but has the property of having-P-in-α. But suppose there is such a world W. In W, x is distinct from Socrates. By (4) (p. 71 above) it follows that x is nowhere identical with Socrates. But x has P-in-α; hence x exists in α and is distinct there from Socrates. In α, therefore, Socrates is distinct from x but both have P—contrary to our hypothesis that in α Socrates alone has P. Hence having-P-in-α is an essence of Socrates. Indeed, for any property P and world W, if in W Socrates alone has P, then having-P-in-W is one of his essences.

So an essence of Socrates is a property that he has essentially and such that there is no world in which there exists an object distinct from Socrates that has it. This suggests that an essence simpliciter (as opposed to an essence of Socrates) may be characterized as follows:

(5) E is an essence if and only if there is a world W in which there exists an object x that (1) has E essentially, and (2) is such that there is no world W^* in which there exists an object distinct from x that has E.

Given this conception of essencehood, it is easy to see that the essence of an object entails each property essential to that object. For let E be an essence of Socrates, let P be a property essential to him, and let W be any world in which E is instantiated by some object x. By clause (2) of (5), x is identical with Socrates in W. But then x has, in W, any property Socrates has in W. Since P is essential to Socrates, he has it in every world in which he exists; accordingly, he has it in W. So x has P in W. In no world W, therefore, is there an object that has E but lacks P; accordingly, E entails P.

We have noted that Socrates' world-indexed properties are essential to him. We might note further that for any world W, either Socrates exists in W or Socrates does not exist in W. That is, for any world W, either Socrates has the world-indexed property of existing-in-W or he has the complement of that property—the world-indexed property of not-existing-in-W. Hence, for any world W, either *existence-in-W* or *non-existence-in-W* is essential to Socrates and entailed by his essence. Notice also that for any property P and world W in which Socrates exists, either Socrates has P in W or Socrates has $\bar{P}$ in W. This, too, is a matter of his essence; so for any such world and property, any essence of Socrates either entails *having-P-in-W* or *having $\bar{P}$-in-W*. But what about those worlds in which Socrates does *not* exist? Does he have properties in *those* worlds? Take, for example, the property of being snubnosed, and let W be any world in which Socrates does not exist. Are we to suppose that if W had obtained, Socrates would have had the property of being snubnosed? Or that he would have had the complement of that property? Neither, I should think; had W obtained, Socrates would have had neither snubnosedness nor its complement. As I shall argue in Chapters VII and VIII, Socrates has no properties at all in those worlds in which he does not exist. We cannot say, therefore, that if E is an essence of Socrates, then for just any world W and property P, E entails either *having P in W* or *having $\bar{P}$ in W*; Socrates has neither P nor $\bar{P}$ in a world where he does not exist. We *can* say, however, that for any world-indexed property P, either Socrates has P or else he has its complement $\bar{P}$.[1] In general, then, among the properties essential to Socrates are to be found, for any

[1] Recall that the complement of *having Q-in-W* is *not-having-Q-in-W*: a property an object has if it does not exist in W. See above, p. 63.

world-indexed property P, either P or its complement $\bar{P}$. And hence if E is an essence of Socrates, then for any world W and property P, either E entails *has P in W* or E entails the complement of that property.

Suppose we say that a property P is *encaptic* if P is instantiated in some possible world and for every world-indexed property Q, P entails Q or P entails $\bar{Q}$. I have argued that every essence *of Socrates* is an encaptic property; but it is easy to see more generally that every essence whatever must be encaptic. For suppose E is an essence; that is, suppose there is a world W in which there exists an object x such that x had E essentially and such that for any world W^*, if there exists a y in W^* that has E, then y is identical with x. Now let P be any world-indexed property. Either x has P essentially or x has $\bar{P}$ essentially. Suppose the former. Then x has P in every world in which x exists. Let W^* be any world in which E is instantiated by some object y: clearly y is identical with x in W^*. But then y has P in W^*, since x does. So if x has P essentially, then E entails P. By the same reasoning, of course, if x has $\bar{P}$ essentially, then E entails $\bar{P}$. So either E entails P or E entails $\bar{P}$.

An essence, therefore, is an encaptic property that is *essentially instantiated* in some world or other; that is to say, such that there is a world W in which there exists an object that has E essentially. Conversely, every encaptic property that is essentially instantiated in some world or other is an essence. For suppose P is such an encaptic property. We must show that there is a world W in which there exists an object x that (1) has P essentially and (2) is such that in no world W^* is there an object distinct from x that has P. Let W be any world in which P is essentially instantiated by an object z; and let W^* be any world and y any object in W^* that is distinct from z. We must show that y does not have P in W^*. Suppose y does have P in W^*. P is encaptic; so either it entails *exists in W^** or it entails *does not exist in W^**. Since y has P and exists in W^*, P does not entail *does not exist in W^**. So it entails *exists in W^**. But then z exists in W^*, since z has P. And since z has P essentially, z has P in W^*. So both z and y have P in W^*. But for any property Q, P entails *has Q in W^** or *does not have Q in W^**. Hence for any property Q, z has Q in W^* if and only if y has Q in W^*, so that (contrary to our original hypothesis) z is identical with y in W^*.

Accordingly, we may characterize an essence as follows:

(6) E is an essence if and only if E is an encaptic property that is essentially instantiated in some world W.

(5) and (6) equivalently characterize the notion of essence.

But there are other interesting ways of delineating the idea of essence. A property P, we recall, is encaptic if for each world-indexed property Q, P entails Q or P entails its complement $\bar{Q}$. Now it is clear that some encaptic properties are not essentially instantiated in any possible world. *Being Socrates and snubnosed* for example, is encaptic; and (given that *being snubnosed* is not essential to Socrates) there is no world W in which there exists an object that has this property essentially. Indeed, *being Socrates and snubnosed* is (if I may put it so) *essentially accidental*: such that there is no world in which there exists an object that has it essentially. Now obviously an encaptic property may entail properties that are not world-indexed (just as *being Socrates and snubnosed* entails *being snubnosed*). Furthermore, two or more encaptic properties may *coincide on world-indexed properties*; P and Q coincide on world-indexed properties if and only if, for every world-indexed property P^*, P entails P^* if and only if Q entails P^*. Let us say that a property is a *smallest encaptic property* if it is encaptic and is entailed by every property that coincides with it on world-indexed properties. Like an encaptic property *simpliciter*, a smallest encaptic property may entail properties that are not world-indexed. *Socrateity*, for example, or *being Socrates* is a smallest encaptic property; and it entails such a property as *being Socrates or foolish*, which is not world-indexed. Unlike an encaptic property *simpliciter*, however, a smallest encaptic property P entails a non-world-indexed property Q only if Q is essential to anything that instantiates P—only if, that is, there is no world in which an object has P and has Q accidentally. Thus the property *being Socrates or foolish* is entailed by Socrateity, is not world-indexed, and is essential to what instantiates that property—that is, to Socrates himself.

Given the notion of a smallest encaptic property, we can characterize the idea of essence in still another way:

(7) P is an essence if and only if P is a smallest encaptic property.

I think we can see that (6) and (7) equivalently delineate the notion of essence. Let us note first that any smallest encaptic property meets the conditions for essencehood laid down in (6). Obviously, any such property is encaptic. But further, whatever instantiates a smallest encaptic property Q has Q essentially. For let W be any world in which there exists an object x that has Q, and let W^* be any world in which x exists. What must be shown is that x has Q in W^*. It suffices to show that in W^* x has every world-indexed property entailed by Q. But an interesting peculiarity of world-indexed properties, as we have seen, is that nothing in any world has any such property accidentally. Accordingly, since in W x has each world-indexed property entailed by Q, x has each such property in W^* as well; and hence x has Q in W^*.

On the other hand, any property P that meets the conditions for essencehood laid down in (6) is a smallest encaptic property. For let P be any property that meets these conditions. For any world-indexed property P^*, either P entails P^* or P entails $\bar{P}^*$. Accordingly, P entails some smallest encaptic property Q. Let W^* be any world in which there is an object that has Q. P is essentially instantiated; so there is a world W' in which there exists an object y that has P and has it in every world in which y exists. Now Q (and hence P) entails *existence in W^**; accordingly, y exists in W^*, has P in W^*, and has Q in W^*. Now clearly there is no world W in which two distinct objects share a smallest encaptic property; if for every property P^*, x has P^* in W if and only if y has P^* in W, then x is identical with y in W. In the present case, therefore, x and y are identical in W^*, for each has Q there. But y has E in W^*; hence so does x. Accordingly, there is no world in which there exists an object that has Q but lacks P; hence P both entails and is entailed by Q and is itself, therefore, a smallest encaptic property.

There is still another way to characterize an essence: instead of looking at it as itself a *property*, we could take it to be a *set* of properties. For suppose we consider complete sets of world-indexed properties—sets that contain, for every world-indexed property P, either P or its complement. Of course not every set of this sort is *consistent*—that is, such that there is a world in which some object x has each of its members. For such a set might include, for example, both *being-human-in-α* and *not-being-human-in-α*; or both *being-human-in-α* and *being-a-number-in-α*. But let us confine our attention to those complete sets of world-indexed properties that are possibly instantiated. We could then say that an essence is any complete and consistent set of world-indexed-properties. Obviously if E is an essence in the sense of (7) then anything that instantiates E has each property in some complete and consistent set of world-indexed properties; and anything having all the properties in such a set instantiates an essence in the sense of (7). So this gives us still another way to characterize the essence of essentiality:

(8) S is an essence if and only if S is a complete and consistent set of world-indexed properties.

Speaking of the essence of essentiality, by the way, we might note that essences themselves have both essential and accidental properties; indeed, essences have essences. Taking Socrateity, the essence of Socrates, to be a smallest encaptic property, we see that *being instantiated* is a property it has but has accidentally. *Being instantiated in some world or other*, on the other hand, is essential to Socrateity. The property *being an essence instantiated by Socrates*, furthermore, is a property that Socrateity alone has. Socrateity, however, has this property only in worlds in which *Socrates* exists—not in every world in which *Socrateity* exists. On the other hand, the property *being an essence instantiated by Socrates in* α is one that Socrateity has in every world in which it exists; and this property is one of its essences.

3. *Essences and Proper Names*

According to John Stuart Mill, proper names—such names as 'Socrates', 'George Washington', and 'Karl Marx'—have a denotation but no connotation.[1] Now it is not difficult to see what Mill had in mind when he said that such names have a denotation: a proper name denotes the object of which it is the name. Mill seems to take it for granted that each proper name denotes exactly one object; and of course here certain complications arise. It is plausible to suppose that some proper names— 'Pegasus', for example—have *no* denotation while others, like 'Socrates', appear to name several individuals. Names that denote exactly one object are apt to be pretty unlikely items like 'Paul John Zwier' or 'Willemina Lena Bossenbroek'.

[1] *A System of Logic* (New York: Harper and Brothers, 1846), p. 21.

But these matters are easily mended. It is not so easy, however, to see what Mill meant when he said that proper names have no connotation. How is this to be explained? "A non-connotative term", says Mill, "is one that signifies a subject only, or an attribute only. A connotative term is one which denotes a subject and implies an attribute." "Proper names", he says, "are not connotative; they denote the individuals who are called by them; but they do not indicate or imply any attribute as belonging to these individuals" (loc. cit.); and he adds that "Proper names are attached to the objects themselves, and are not dependent upon the continuance of any attribute of the object" (ibid., p. 22). Here Mill's meaning is not entirely evident. But perhaps the following is not wholly implausible as an explanation of this view. What Mill means is that proper names (as opposed to definite descriptions, which he calls 'connotative individual names') *do not express properties*.

But what does this come to? What does it mean to say of a proper name that it does (or does not) express a property? Perhaps we can get at this idea as follows. Consider a definite description such as 'the first American to climb Everest' and a sentence such as (9) that contains it:

(9) The first American to climb Mt. Everest never climbed a mountain.

(9) expresses a necessarily false proposition; part of the reason is that the description it contains "implies an attribute as belonging to" the individual that satisfies it: it implies the attribute of having climbed at least one mountain. We might put this as follows. A singular term t expresses a property P if and only if any result of replacing 'x' and 'P' in

(10) x has the complement of P

by t and a proper name[1] of P expresses a necessarily false proposition. 'The first American to climb Everest', therefore, expresses the properties *being an American, having climbed Everest, having climbed Everest before any other American,* and the like.

But clearly it also expresses any property entailed by any property it expresses. So in addition to the properties mentioned above, it also expresses such trifling truistic properties as *being*

---

[1] See above, p. 31.

something or other and *being either human or not human*. We might therefore desire a less indescriminate notion. We might say that *t exactly expresses* the strongest property it expresses; that is,

(11) *t* exactly expresses *P* if and only if *t* expresses *P* and expresses no property that entails but is not entailed by *P*.

It is then obvious that 'the first American to climb Everest' exactly expresses the property of being the first American to climb Everest.

Now Mill said proper names have no connotation; a possible interpretation is that proper names do not express properties. If this is what he meant, was he right? Clearly not. Clearly proper names express such trivial properties as *being either human or not*, *being unmarried if a bachelor*, and the like (and perhaps it was no part of Mill's programme to assert otherwise). But further, consider a sentence like

(12) Socrates is a number.

Does this express a necessarily false proposition? I think it does. No doubt it also expresses a proposition that is *not* necessarily false—indeed, one that is necessarily true—for no doubt on some occasion or other someone has named some number 'Socrates'. A sentence like (12) expresses many different propositions—one for each thing named 'Socrates'. Among these, however, is the one it expresses when 'Socrates' is used as a proper name of the teacher of Plato; and that proposition is necessarily false. (13), therefore, does express a necessarily false proposition; hence 'Socrates' does express a property.

Further,

(13) Socrates has the complement of the property of being Socrates

obviously expresses a necessarily false proposition. So it is evident that 'Socrates' expresses the property of being identical with Socrates. Still further, this name evidently expresses no property stronger than *being Socrates*. For take any such property *P*. Presumably *P* will be equivalent to a conjunctive property one conjunct of which is *being Socrates*, the other conjunct being some property *Q* logically independent of *being Socrates*. If so, however, it is possible for something to be Socrates without having *Q*.

Accordingly, the result of replacing 'x' and 'P' in 'x has the complement of P' by 'Socrates' and a proper name of Q will not express a necessarily false proposition. But then the same will hold for the result of the indicated replacements where it is P rather than Q that is at issue. So 'Socrates' *exactly expresses* the property of being identical with Socrates. But of course this property is an *essence* of Socrates. 'Socrates' expresses the essence of Socrates—more exactly and more pedantically, it expresses each of his essences. Of course it also expresses many other essences; for each thing x named 'Socrates', that name expresses the essence (or essences) of x. Proper names, therefore, do indeed express properties. They express properties of a very special sort: *essences*. Obviously it is because proper names express essences that one can explain the *de re* by the *de dicto* as I did in Chapter III.

It is sometimes said that proper names "denote the same object in every possible world". This suggests that there is no possible world in which the proper name 'Socrates' does not denote Socrates—that it would have denoted him no matter what. But this suggestion is misleading. It is misleading first because it is false; Socrates does not have essentially the property of being named 'Socrates'. His parents could have named him 'Xenophon' or 'Johan vander Hoeven'; had they done so (and had no one else named him 'Socrates') Socrates would not have been named 'Socrates'. It is misleading, second, because it is not true to the intentions of those who so speak of proper names and possible worlds. Their claim is to be understood as follows. To discourse of Socrates as he is in other possible worlds, we use the name 'Socrates'—even if, in these worlds, his name is 'Xenophon' or 'Johan' or he has no name at all. Thus Socrates could have been named 'Xenophon'; if Socrates had been named 'Xenophon', then his name would have begun with 'X'; if Socrates had not existed, then Socrates would not have been named 'Socrates'.

I therefore think it preferable to put the point as above: proper names express essences. The proper name 'Aristotle' expresses an essence of Aristotle. It therefore expresses a property P that is instantiated by the same object in every world— in every world in which P is instantiated, of course; for there are worlds in which Aristotle does not exist. What is characteristic of proper names, then, is that the properties they express are instantiated by the same objects in every world. In this regard they are to be contrasted with descriptions such as 'the first man to climb Rainier'. This latter, indeed, expresses a property—the property of being the first man to climb Rainier. But that property is not an essence: for different objects exemplify it in different worlds. In α it is E. van Trump that first climbed Rainier; but no doubt there are worlds in which W. C. Fields claims this distinction. This property, furthermore, is not encaptic; for it entails neither *being-snubnosed-in-α* nor *not-being-snubnosed-in-α*. It fails to entail the former, for there are worlds in which Jimmy Durante is the first to climb Rainier; but it also fails to entail the latter, for there are worlds in which it is Socrates who performs this feat.

So descriptions do not in general express essences. Of course *some* descriptions *do* express essences: 'the first man to climb Rainier in α', for example, expresses the property of being the first man to climb Rainier in α, and (as we have seen) such a property is an essence. Other descriptions that express essences are 'the number nine', 'the property of being composite', and 'the null set'. In Chapter III, therefore, we could have 'explained' the *de re* by the *de dicto* by stipulating that the kernel proposition with respect to *x* and *P* is to be the proposition expressed by the result to replacing '*x*' and '*P*' in '*x* lacks the complement of *P*' by any terms exactly expressing essences of *x* and *P*, adding that *x* has *P* essentially if and only if K(*x*, *P*) is necessarily false. This would have been a pretty low grade explanation—not because it yields the wrong results, but because the explanation crucially involves the notion of essence. Since this notion is essentialist *in excelsis*, no one who has doubts about the intelligibility of *de re* modal talk would have his doubts allayed by such an explanation.

4. *Hesperus and Phosphorus*

Hesperus, we know, is identical with Phosphorus. Indeed, if the foregoing is correct, there is no possible world in which, in the hauntingly beautiful words of an ancient ballad, "Hesperus and Phosphorus are entities distinct".[1] Stipulating for purposes of

---

[1] "Should Old Aquinas be Forgot?", a ballad whose origin has been obscured by the mists of antiquity.

argument that 'Hesperus' and 'Phosphorus' are both proper names of Venus, we note that each of these terms expresses an essence of Venus. But then

(14) Hesperus is distinct from Phosphorus

will express a proposition logically equivalent to that expressed by

(15) Phosphorus is distinct from Phosphorus;

accordingly, the proposition expressed by (14) is necessarily false. And do we not encounter a difficulty here? If (14) is necessarily false, then presumably

(16) Hesperus is identical with Phosphorus

is necessarily true. (16), however, was an astronomical *discovery*, and one of considerable magnitude. This proposition was discovered *a posteriori*; how then could it be necessarily true? Furthermore, astronomical science has been known to reverse itself; it is clearly possible that we should some time discover (14) to be true. If so, however, (14) *is* possibly true and (16) possibly false. We should therefore reject the view that proper names express essences.

This objection contains two connected strands. First, it is pointed out that (16) was discovered *a posteriori*; it is concluded that (16) is not necessarily true. And secondly, the objector proclaims the possibility of our discovering that Hesperus and Phosphorus are distinct; but if this is possible, then once more (16) is not necessarily true. Now suppose we waive the objection that (16), in view of the fact that it entails such contingencies as that there is such a thing as Phosphorus,[1] is at best contingently true. The objector takes it for granted that the discovery of necessary truth is not the proper concern of astronomy (or, presumably, any so-called empirical science). But this is dubious at best. As a historian I discover that Pico della Mirandola was born in 1463. I know that α is the actual world; so I also discover that

(17) α includes *Pico's being born in 1463*.

But (17), of course, is necessarily true. And, indeed, why could not a historian discover (17) *qua*, as they say, *historian*? Perhaps

[1] See Chapter VIII, Section 1.

the views of the historian, if properly come by, are *a posteriori*; it does not follow that they are also contingent. For presumably no human beings are capable of learning *a priori* such truths as that α includes, say, *the Greeks' winning the Battle of Marathon*, despite the necessity of

(18) α includes *the Greeks' winning the Battle of Marathon*.

And obviously there are as many propositions of this sort as you please—propositions that no one knows *a priori* but which are none the less necessarily true. For take any truth *T* of history or physics that has not been discovered *a priori*; the proposition that *T* is true in α will be a necessary truth that is known but not known *a priori*.[1]

But secondly, the claim was that

(16) Hesperus is identical with Phosphorus

could be discovered to be false, so that it must be contingent. But should this claim be allowed? Not if in fact (16) is true; and for familiar reasons. For clearly (16) is false, in any given world *W*, if and only if Hesperus exists in *W* and does not have *Phosphorus-identity* therein. So there is a world in which (16) is false only if Hesperus does not have *Phosphorus-identity* essentially —only if, that is, Hesperus does not have the property of being essentially identical with Phosphorus. Phosphorus, however, obviously has this property; so, therefore, must Hesperus. Of course there are possible worlds where

(19) the first heavenly body to appear in the evening is distinct from the last heavenly body to disappear in the morning

is true; and conceivably the objector is confusing this proposition with (16)—perhaps because he thinks of proper names as abbreviations for definite descriptions. It is also possible that the *sentence* (16) should have expressed a false proposition, as it would have, had two distinct heavenly bodies been named 'Hesperus' and 'Phosphorus'. Perhaps these two facts account for any initial inclination we may have had towards supposing it possible that (16) should have been false.

Still, doubts may persist. If my account is accurate, 'Hesperus' and 'Phosphorus' express essences. This conceded, it is plausible

---

[1] And this redeems a promissory note issued in Chapter I, p. 7.

to suppose that they express the very same essence. If so, however, does it not follow that the sentences

(20) Hesperus is identical with Phosphorus

(21) Hesperus was named 'Phosphorus'

and

(22) Hesperus has the property of being identical with Phosphorus

express the very same propositions as

(20') Phosphorus is identical with Phosphorus

(21') Phosphorus is named 'Phosphorus'

and

(22') Phosphorus has the property of being identical with Phosphorus?

I think it does. But what about the Babylonian *discovery* that Hesperus is identical with Phosphorus? Suppose for simplicity that the Ancient Babylonians spoke English rather than Ancient Babylonian. Prior to their discovery, the Babylonian astronomers would have accepted the primed items as trifling trivialities. But their attitude towards the unprimed items, one supposes, was quite different; here their attitude was one of suspension of belief if not outright denial. If 'Hesperus' and 'Phosphorus' are proper names of Venus, however, then (20) expresses the very same proposition as (20'). And if (20) expresses the very same proposition as (20'), then the Babylonians did believe the former, since they believed the latter. How, then, can we account for their sincere claim to reject (20)? Shall we suppose that they believed (20)—the proposition—but did not know or believe that they believed it? No; for no doubt they knew they believed (20'); and (20) is (20').

Perhaps we must say something like the following. The Babylonians believed that an utterance of the sentence 'this is identical with that' expresses a true proposition when the speaker accompanies 'this' with a demonstration (a pointing to) of Venus, and, an instant later, accompanies 'that' the same way. Had the circumstances surrounding the utterance of this sentence been different, however, the Babylonians would have been doubtful. Imagine it thus: pointing to the evening sky, to Venus, we say (very slowly) "*This* is not identical with (long pause) *that*" (pointing to the eastern sky, to Venus, some fine morning when Venus is the morning star). Now let us suppose that the sentence expresses the same proposition on these two occasions. Of course the Babylonians were not apprised of this fact. But why not? Not because they had an insufficient grasp of the semantic role of demonstratives such as 'this' and 'that', nor because of any other insufficiency in their command of the language. Their difficulty was rather their failure to realize that the second occurrence of 'that' was accompanied by a demonstration of the same heavenly body as was the second occurrence of 'this' and the first occurrences of 'this' and 'that'. And this defect in their knowledge issued in their failure to realize that the second occurrence of 'this is identical with that' expressed the same proposition as the first occurrence. The truth is they did not really know what proposition *was* expressed by that second occurrence.

In the same way, the Babylonian astronomers were ignorant of the fact that

(20) Hesperus is identical with Phosphorus

and

(20') Phosphorus is identical with Phosphorus

express the same proposition. They did not really know what proposition was expressed by (20). The latter did indeed express a proposition, and one with which they were acquainted. But they did not know that this proposition was the one (20) expressed. They knew that (20) expressed a proposition, and they knew that the proposition expressed by (20) was true if and only if the first heavenly body to appear in the evening had the property of lingering longer in the morning than any other heavenly body. Still, they did not know that (20) expresses the proposition that Phosphorous is identical with Phosphorous.

So the Babylonians did not know that (20) expresses the proposition that Phosphorous is identical with Phosphorus. They did not know what proposition (20) expresses. But why not? What stood in their way? Under what conditions does one fail to know what proposition is expressed by a given sentence? Of course such failure may be charged to a multitude of factors. For example, there is linguistic incompetence; no doubt there are those who do not know what proposition is expressed by

(23) David displays a defiantly apolaustic air

because they do not know the word 'apolaustic'. But the Babylonian failure was not of this sort.

Secondly, I might fail to know what proposition was expressed by a given sentence because of a *conceptual* inadequacy. Suppose I hear a couple of mathematicians discussing something they have named 'Fred'. As it turns out, Fred is a complicated topological function I have never heard of and could not grasp without two weeks of preliminary study. Then my failure to know what proposition is expressed by

(24) Fred is well behaved

is not due so much to linguistic inadequacy as to my inability to grasp this function. The proposition expressed by (24) (unlike that expressed by (23)) is simply beyond my powers of apprehension. I can refer to it in various ways—e.g. as the proposition expressed by (24) or as the proposition Paul mistakenly asserted—but I do not grasp or apprehend this proposition. The Babylonian failure, however, was also unlike this.

Take another kind of case. Suppose you have a couple of 150-foot, $\frac{1}{4}$-inch nylon rappel ropes. Each is braided red and white for half its length and blue and white the other half. These ropes are like trusted friends; indeed, you have named them 'Carol' and 'Alice'. You have detailed and intimate knowledge of their age, pedigree, load-bearing qualities, mode of construction, elongation-to-break factor, tensile strength, and all the rest. You have often inspected every inch for abrasions and bruises.

Now suppose you are about to descend the Grand Teton; you must make a 120-foot rappel. While you are inspecting the anchor point, an enthusiastic but clumsy novice in the party sets out to deploy Carol and Alice for the rappel. Unfortunately his well-intentioned efforts do not meet with success; Alice and Carol get wadded up into a large and enormously tangled ball of rope out of which disconsolately hang two ends—one red and white and the other blue and white. To cover his embarrassment, the novice idly picks up these two ends, names the ropes terminating therein 'Ted' and 'Bob', and asks the following question: is Bob identical with Ted?[1] Of course you do not know. Or rather, what you do not know is whether the sentence

(25) Bob is identical with Ted

expresses a true proposition. You do know that it expresses either

(26) Carol is identical with Carol

(27) Alice is identical with Alice

or

(28) Carol is identical with Alice;

but you do not know which. Here it is not that your acquaintance with the propositions involved is insufficient; your grasp of them is solid enough. It is your knowledge of (25) that is deficient; you do not know which of (26), (27), or (28) it expresses.

It is fairly clear, I suppose, that the Hesperus–Phosphorus case is like the case of Bob and Ted and Carol and Alice.[2] It was not that the Babylonian linguistic competence was insufficient, nor that they did not grasp or apprehend the proposition expressed by the sentence

(20) Hesperus is identical with Phosphorus—

that is, the proposition that Hesperus is identical with Hesperus. There may have been people who had no grasp of this proposition—people who had never studied astronomy or looked at the night sky, for example. But this was not the Babylonian trouble. Their problem was that they did not realize that (20) expresses the proposition that Hesperus is identical with Hesperus; and they were not apprised of this fact because they did not know that Hesperus bore the name 'Phosphorus' as well as the name 'Hesperus'.[3]

---

[1] I am indebted for this example to a conversation with Charles Daniels—who, however, drew a different conclusion from it.

[2] My apologies to David Kaplan for thus appropriating the title of his paper "Bob and Ted and Carol and Alice", forthcoming in *Approaches to Natural Language*, ed. J. Hintikka (D. Riedel, 1973).

[3] This corrects the account of the Babylonian intellectual economy given in "World and Essence", pp. 480–2.

VI

TRANSWORLD IDENTITY OR WORLDBOUND INDIVIDUALS?

1. *The Question*

SOCRATES, therefore, has both essential properties and an essence. The former are properties he has in every world in which he exists; the latter meets this condition and in addition is instantiated in any given world by Socrates or nothing. Of course not nearly all of Socrates' properties are essential to him and not nearly every property unique to him is one of his essences; but then it follows that Socrates exists in many possible worlds. Initially, this supposition seems harmless enough; it is natural enough to suppose that the same individual exists in various different states of affairs. There is, for example, the state of affairs consisting in *Socrates' being a carpenter*; this state of affairs is possible but does not in fact obtain. It is natural to suppose, however, that if it *had* obtained, then Socrates would have existed and would have been a carpenter; one plausibly supposes it *impossible* that this state of affairs obtain and Socrates fail to exist. If so, however, then Socrates *exists in* this state of affairs. But of course if he exists in this state of affairs, then he exists in every possible world including it. For clearly every possible world including *Socrates' being a carpenter* also includes *Socrates' existing*; each such world is such that if it had been actual, Socrates would have existed. So Socrates exists in many possible worlds.

At any rate, as I said, it is natural to make this supposition; but it is rejected by many philosophers otherwise kindly disposed towards possible worlds. Among them, there is, for example, Leibniz, whose credentials on this subject are certainly impeccable; Leibniz apparently held that each object exists in just one world.[1] The idealists, furthermore, in arguing

---

[1] As has been argued by Benson Mates in "Leibniz on Possible Worlds", *Logic, Methodology, and Philosophy of Science* III, ed. Van Rootselaar and Staal (Amsterdam: North Holland Publishing Co., 1968).

for their doctrine of internal relations, were arguing in essence that an object exists in exactly one possible world—indeed, some of them may have thought that there is only one such world. More recently, the view that individuals are thus confined to one world—let us call it 'The Theory of Worldbound Individuals'—has been at least entertained with considerable hospitality by David Kaplan.[1] Roderick Chisholm, furthermore, finds difficulty and perplexity in the claim that the same object exists in more than one possible world.[2] Still further, The Theory of Worldbound Individuals is an explicit postulate of David Lewis's Counterpart Theory.[3] In this chapter I shall explore this issue. Now perhaps the most important and widely heralded argument for the Theory of Worldbound Individuals (hereafter TWI) is the celebrated PROBLEM OF TRANSWORLD IDENTITY, said to bedevil the view that the same object exists in more than one world. Accordingly these two topics will occupy centre stage: TWI and the problem of Transworld Identity.

2. *Socrates in* α *and Socrates in* W

What then, can be said in favour of the idea that an individual is confined to just one world—that you and I, for example, exist in this world and this world only? According to G. E. Moore, the idealists, in arguing for their view that all relations are internal, were really arguing that all relational properties are essential to the things that have them. The argument they gave, however, if both sound and plausible, establishes that *all* properties—not just relational properties—are thus essential to their owners. And if this is correct then for no object *x* is there a possible state of affairs in which *x* lacks a property that in fact it has; so *x* exists only in the actual world.

Now an argument for a conclusion as sweeping as this must pack quite a punch. What did the idealists come up with? A confusion, says Moore. What the idealists asserted is

(1) 'If *P* be a relational property and *A* a term to which it does in fact belong, then, no matter what *P* and *A* may be, it may

---

[1] "Transworld Identification", read at an A.P.A. Symposium, Chicago, 1967.
[2] "Identity through Possible Worlds: Some Questions", *Nous*, 1 (1967), 1.
[3] "Counterpart Theory and Quantified Modal Logic", *Journal of Philosophy*, 65 (1968), 113.

always be truly asserted of them, that any term which had *not* possessed P would necessarily have been other than, numerically different from, A. . . .'[1]

Perhaps we may put this more perspicuously as

(1') For any object *x* and relational property P, if *x* has P, then for any object *y*, if there is a world in which *y* lacks P, then *y* is distinct from *x*

which clearly entails the desired conclusion that all relational properties are essential to their bearers. What they suggested as a reason for accepting (1), however, is

(2) "If A has P, and *x* does not, it *does* follow that *x* is other than A."[2]

If we restate (2) as the claim that

(2') For any objects *x* and *y*, if *x* has P and *y* does not, then *x* is distinct from *y*

holds in every world, we see that (2) is just the thesis that the Indiscernibility of Identicals is necessarily true. This thesis seems accurate enough, but no reason at all for (1) or (1'). But, as Moore says, (1) and (2) are easily conflated, particularly when put in the idealist's typically turbid and opaque prose; and the idealists seized this opportunity to conflate them.

Initially, then, this argument is unpromising. It has a near relative, however, that may conceivably be found in Leibniz and often surfaces in contemporary discussion. Leibniz writes to Arnauld as follows:

Besides, if, in the life of any person and even in the whole universe anything went differently from what it has, nothing could prevent us from saying that it was another person or another possible universe which God had chosen. It would then be indeed another individual.[3]

This is on its face a dark saying. What Leibniz says here and elsewhere, however, may suggest the following. Suppose Socrates exists in some world *W* distinct from α. Taking the term

[1] "External and Internal Relations", in *Philosophical Studies* (London: Routledge & Kegan Paul Ltd., 1922), p. 287.
[2] Ibid., p. 289.
[3] Letter from Leibniz to Arnauld, 14 July 1686. In *Discourse on Metaphysics* (La Salle, Illinois: Open Court, 1962), pp. 127–8. Leibniz makes very nearly the same statement in a letter to Count von Hessen-Rheinfels, May 1686 (p. 111).

'property' in a broad sense, we shall be obliged to concede that there must be some property that Socrates has in α but lacks in *W*. (If we let 'π' name the book on α, then taking the term 'property' in a *very* broad sense, one property Socrates has in α but lacks in *W* is that of being such that every member of π is true.) So let us suppose that there is some property—snubnosedness, let us say—that Socrates has in α but lacks in *W*. That is, the Socrates of α ('Socrates-in-α', as we might call him) has snubnosedness, while the Socrates of *W* does not. But surely this is inconsistent with the Indiscernibility of Identicals. For according to this principle, if Socrates-in-α has snubnosedness but Socrates-in-*W* does not, then Socrates-in-α is distinct from Socrates-in-*W*. We must conclude, therefore, that Socrates does not exist both in α and in *W*. There may be some person in *W* that much resembles our Socrates, Socrates-in-α; that person is none the less distinct from him. And of course a generalization of this argument, if successful, will show that nothing exists in more than one world.

Here, however, there is an unhappy hiatus between premiss and conclusion. We are asked to infer

(3) Socrates-in-α is snubnosed and Socrates-in-*W* is not

from

(4) Socrates is snubnosed in α but not in *W*.

But who is this 'Socrates-in-α'? More exactly, is the phrase 'Socrates-in-α', as it turns up in this argument, a denoting phrase? If so, what is it supposed to denote? Presumably the object that *in* α is Socrates—that is, 'Socrates-in-α' denotes Socrates. 'Socrates-in-*W*', furthermore, presumably denotes the thing that is Socrates *in W*—the thing that *would have been* Socrates, had *W* been actual. (Of course *Socrates* is the thing that would have been Socrates, had *W* been actual; but let us proceed slowly and beg no questions.) And what does it mean to say that

(3') Socrates-in-*W* is nonsnubnosed?

That Socrates-in-*W* is nonsnubnosed is inferred from the supposition that in *W*, *Socrates* has the property of being nonsnubnosed. Accordingly, (3'), if it is to follow from (4), cannot be taken to imply that the thing that in *W* is Socrates, is *in fact* nonsnubnosed; what it must mean is that this thing is nonsnub-nosed *in W*. Hence we must understand (3) as claiming that the thing that is Socrates in α is snubnosed in α, while the thing that is Socrates in *W*, is nonsnubnosed in *W*. So taken, (3) does indeed follow from (4).

But (3) (so taken) together with the Indiscernibility of Identicals by no means yield anything so startling as that Socrates-in-α is distinct from Socrates-in-*W*. For there is no property that (3) predicates of Socrates-in-α and withholds from Socrates-in-*W*. According to (3) Socrates-in-α (that is, Socrates) has the property of being snubnosed, all right, but *in* α. Socrates-in-*W*, however, lacks that property *in W*—that is, Socrates-in-*W* has the property of being such that, if *W* had obtained, he would not have been snubnosed. And of course this property is not the complement of snubnosedness, nor even incompatible with it; Socrates himself is snubnosed, but by hypothesis would not have been, had *W* been actual. So the Indiscernibility of Identicals does not apply here; there is no property that (3) predicates of Socrates-in-α but denies of Socrates-in-*W*. To suppose that Socrates has *P* in the actual world but lacks it in *W* is to suppose only that Socrates does in fact have *P* but would not have had it, had *W* been actual. The Indiscernibility of Identicals casts not even a hint of suspicion upon this supposition. This objection, therefore, is a snare and a delusion.

3. *The Problem of Transworld Identity*

A. *The Problem Stated*

A more popular and more promising argument for TWI is an appeal to the *Problem of Transworld Identity* said to confront one who rashly supposes the same object to exist in more than one world. Here the claim is that there are deep conceptual difficulties in *identifying* the same object from world to world—difficulties that threaten the very idea of Transworld Identity with incoherence. These difficulties, furthermore, presumably do not arise on TWI.[1]

But what, exactly, *is* the problem of Transworld Identity?

---

[1] So David Lewis: "P₂ the postulate according to which nothing exists in more than one world, serves only to rule out avoidable problems of individuation" (op. cit., p. 114).

What difficulties does it present for the notion that the same object exists in various possible worlds? Just how does this problem go? Although published statements of it are scarce,[1] the problem may perhaps be put as follows. Let us suppose again that Socrates exists in some world W distinct from this one—a world in which, let us say, he did not fight in the battle of Marathon. In W, of course, he may also lack other properties he has in this world—perhaps in W he eschewed philosophy, corrupted no youth, and thus escaped the wrath of the Athenians. Perhaps in W he lived in Corinth, let us say, was six feet tall, and remained a bachelor all his life. But then we must ask ourselves how we could possibly *identify* Socrates in that world. How could we *pick him out*? How could we *locate* him there? How could we possibly tell which of the many things contained in W is *Socrates*? If we try to employ the properties we use to identify him in *this* world, our efforts may well end in dismal failure—perhaps in that world it is Xenophon or maybe even Thrasymachus who is Plato's mentor and exhibits the splendidly singleminded passion for truth and justice that characterizes Socrates in this. But if we cannot identify him in W, so the argument continues, then we do not really understand the assertion that he exists there. If we cannot even identify him, we would not know whom we were talking about, in saying that Socrates exists in that world or has this or that property therein. In order to make sense of such talk, we must have a *criterion* or *principle* that enables us to identify Socrates from world to world. This criterion must consist in some property that Socrates has in each world in which he exists—and if it is to be sufficient to enable us to *pick him out* in a given world, distinguish him from other things, it must be a property that in no possible world is exemplified by something distinct from Socrates. Further, the property (or properties) in question, if it is to enable us thus to pick him out, must be, in some broad sense, 'empirically manifest': it must resemble such properties as having such-and-such a name, address, social security number, height, weight, and general appearance in that we can tell by broadly empirical means whether a given object has or lacks it. For how,

---

[1] But see R. Chisholm, "Identity through Possible Worlds: Some Questions", *Nous* 1 (1967), 1–8, and J. Hintikka, "The Semantics of Modal Notions", in *Semantics of Natural Language*, ed. D. Davidson and G. Harman (Dordrecht: D. Reidel, 1972), p. 402.

otherwise, could we use it to *pick out* or *identify* him? So if it is intelligible to suppose that Socrates exists in more than one world, there must be some empirically manifest property that he and he alone has in each of the worlds in which he exists. Now obviously we do not know of any such property, or even that there is such a property. Indeed, it is hard to see how there *could* be such a property. But then the very idea of Transworld Identity is not really intelligible—in which case we must suppose that no object exists in more than one world.

The first thing to note is that this objection seems to arise out of a certain *picture* or *image*. We imagine ourselves somehow peering—through a Jules Verne-o-scope,[1] perhaps—into another world; we ask ourselves whether Socrates exists in it. We observe the behaviour and characteristics of its denizens and then wonder which of these, if any, is Socrates. Of course we realize that his physical appearance might be quite different in *W*, if he exists there at all. He might also live at a different place, have different friends and different fingerprints, if, indeed, he has fingers. But how then can we tell which one he *is*? And does it so much as make sense to say that he exists in that world, if there is no way in principle of identifying him, of telling which thing there *is* Socrates?

B. *A Temporal Analogy*

Now perhaps this picture is useful in certain respects; in the present context, however, it breeds nothing but confusion. For this picture insinuates that the propositions *Socrates exists in other possible worlds* or *Socrates exists in a world in which he is not snubnosed* are intelligible to us only if we know of some empirically manifest property that he and he alone has in each world in which he exists. But why should we accept this idea? Suppose we consider an analogous temporal situation. In Herbert Spiegelberg's book *The Phenomenological Movement* there are pictures of Franz Brentano at the age of 20 and of 70 respectively. The youthful Brentano looks much like Apollo; the elderly Brentano resembles, instead, Jerome Hines in his portrayal of the dying Czar in Boris Godounov. Most of us believe that the same object exists at various distinct times; but do we know of some empirically manifest property *P* such that a thing is Brentano at a given time

[1] The word is David Kaplan's.

t if and only if it has P? Surely not; and this casts no shadow whatever on the intelligibility of the claim that Brentano existed at many different times.

But is the above argument not available here? No doubt there was a time at which G. Cantor was a precocious baby. But if I understand that assertion, must I not be able to *pick him out*, *locate* him at that time? If I cannot identify him, if I cannot tell which of the things that existed at that time was Cantor, then (so goes the argument) I cannot make sense of the claim that he existed at that time. But I could identify him, at t, only if I knew of some empirically manifest property that he and he alone had at t.

Here the argument is manifestly confused. To suppose that Cantor was a precocious baby at t it is not necessary that I be able to pick his picture out of a gallery of babies-at-t. Perhaps I must know *who he is* to understand this supposition; and perhaps to know that I must know of some property that he and he alone has. Indeed, we might go so far as to concede that this property must be 'empirically manifest' in some sense. But surely it is asking too much to require that I know of such a property that he and he only has *at every time at which he exists*. No doubt I must be able to answer the question 'which of the things that existed at t was Cantor?' but the answer is easy enough; it is Cantor himself. If this is correct, however, why suppose otherwise in the transworld case?

But perhaps the temporal analogy is not altogether convincing. "After all", it may be said, "times are linearly ordered; and at any times t and t' such that the interval between the two is small, there will indeed be some empirically manifest property that Cantor and Cantor alone has both at t and at t'. "Indeed", the objection continues, "this fact is a necessary condition of our being able to identify an object x at a time t' as the *same* object that existed at an earlier time t; and this ability to reidentify objects is a necessary condition of our intelligibly supposing that the same object exists at various distinct times. Nothing like this is available in the transworld case." Of course the objector is partly right; there is this difference between the transtemporal and transworld situations. I do not see, however, that this point invalidates the analogy. But let us focus our attention directly upon the transworld situation.

c. *The Problem Resolved*

I understand the proposition that there is a possible world in which Socrates did not teach Plato. Now let W be any such world. Why suppose that a condition of my understanding this is my knowing something about what Socrates would have looked like or where he would have lived, had W been actual? Perhaps I must know who Socrates is to understand this proposition; and conceivably this involves my knowing of some property that is empirically manifest (whatever exactly that comes to) and unique to Socrates. But what reason is there for supposing that I must know of some empirically manifest property he has *in that world W*?

The picture suggests that all of the possible worlds (W included) are somehow simultaneously "going on"—as if each world were actual, but at a different place or perhaps (as the best science fiction has it) in a "different dimension". It also suggests that I must be able to look into W and sift through its inhabitants until I run across one I recognize as Socrates—otherwise I cannot identify him, and hence do not know whom I am talking about. But here the picture misleads us. For taken literally, of course, this notion makes no sense. There is no such thing as "looking into" another possible world to see what is going on there. There is no such thing as inspecting the inhabitants of another possible world with a view to deciding which, if any, is Socrates. A possible world is a possible state of affairs. In saying that an individual x exists or has a property P in a state of affairs S, we are pointing to the impossibility that S obtain and x fail to exist or fail to have P. So, for example, consider the state of affairs consisting in Socrates' being a carpenter, and call this state of affairs 'S'. Does Socrates exist in S? Obviously: had this state of affairs been actual, he would have existed. But is there a problem of *identifying* him, *picking him out*, in S—that is, must we look into S to see which thing therein is Socrates? Must there be or must we know of some empirically manifest property he has in this and every other state of affairs in which he exists? Surely not.

We might define *existence in a proposition* analogously to existence in a state of affairs; that is, we might say that an object *x exists in a proposition p* if and only if it is not possible that p

be true and x fail to exist; and we might define 'x has property P in p' in appropriately similar fashion. Then clearly enough both Quine and Royal Robbins exist in the proposition

(5) Quine is America's foremost rock-climber and Royal Robbins is America's most distinguished philosopher.

But must we 'identify' Robbins and Quine in (5) in order to grasp or understand it? (Maybe it is really Quine who is the philosopher in (5)—after all, that role would certainly be more natural for him. And how will we recognize him when and if we come across him in (5)? What does he look like in this proposition? Royal Robbins? Or maybe Gaston Rebuffat?) Must we be apprised of some empirically manifest property Quine alone has in every proposition in which he exists in order to understand (5)? Of course not; there is no such property and the request for one is surely based upon nothing but confusion.

Similarly, then, for the possible worlds case. To understand the suggestion that there is a world W in which Socrates did not teach Plato, I need know nothing about which other persons exist in W or—except for his essential properties—which other properties Socrates has in that world. Indeed, how could I know more? All I have been told about W is that it is one of the many worlds in which Socrates exists but does not teach Plato; and for any property P Socrates has inessentially (except for those entailing the property of teaching Plato) there is a world that meets that description and in which Socrates has P. The claim that I must somehow be able to identify Socrates in W —pick him out—is either trivial or confused. Of course I must know which of the persons existing in W—the persons who would have existed had W been actual—I am talking about. But the answer, obviously and trivially, is Socrates. And to be able thus to answer I need know nothing further about what Socrates would have been like had W been actual.

D. *Essence and Transworld Identity*

Let us imagine the objector briefly regrouping. "If Socrates exists in several worlds", he says, "there must be properties that he has in each world in which he exists—properties essential to him, as we might put it. Furthermore, even if there need be no *empirically manifest* property that Socrates and Socrates alone has in each world in which he exists, there must at any rate be *some property or other* that he and he only has in each of these worlds. This property must meet two conditions: (1) Socrates has it in every world he graces, and (2) there is no possible world in which it is exemplified by something distinct from Socrates. Let us say that any such property is an *essence of Socrates*. Such a property, clearly, will entail each of his essential properties. But is not this idea—the idea that Socrates has an essence as thus characterized—at best extremely dubious? At best it is far from clear which (if any) of Socrates' properties are essential to him and even less clear that he has an essence. Nor does there seem to be any way of determining whether he has such a property, or, if he does, which properties are entailed by it; so is not the suggestion that he has an essence both gratuitous and problematic? We can and should avoid this entire mare's nest by accepting TWI." Thus far the objector.

What can be said by way of reply? First, that following this counsel has all the advantages of theft over honest toil, as Russell says in another connection. The question is whether Socrates has an essence and whether objects do or do not exist in more than one world—not whether we would be saved some work or perplexity if we said they did not. But second, the project of explaining and clarifying the notion of essence is not nearly so desperate as the objector assumes: I hope Chapter V has made that plain. More fundamentally, however, one cannot avoid the question which of Socrates' properties are essential to him by embracing TWI. For that theory gives an answer to this question, and an unsatisfactory one at that; it says that *all* of his properties are essential to him (since he exists in just one world) and that any property he alone has—that of being married to Xantippe, for example, or that of being the only famous Greek philosopher to fight in the Battle of Marathon—is one of his essences.

The objector, therefore, is right in claiming that if Socrates exists in several worlds then he must have an essence. His objection to the latter idea, however, is not impressive. So what are we to make of this so-called problem of Transworld Identity? Is there really something problematic, or obscure, or untoward in the idea that Socrates exists in several distinct worlds? Is there really any such thing as the problem of Transworld Identity? If there is, I am at a loss to see what it might be.

E. *Does Ramsification Destroy Information?*

Of course legitimate questions and problems lurk in the neighbourhood—for example the following. Take the book B_W of a
possible world W, conjoin its members, and take the existential
quantification with respect to all the individuals. The result
$(R(B_W))$ is a *Ramsey book*; and let $R(W)$ be the state of affairs
(the *Ramsey world*) corresponding to it. Now it may be plausible
to suppose that Ramsification results in no loss of information.
For consider the properties of Socrates: the Ramsey book on α
contains the information that there is exactly one individual that
has all these properties; and what do we add by saying that it
is *Socrates* who has them? So we may as well speak of Ramsey
worlds as of possible worlds as originally explained.

But now something like a problem of Transworld Identity
may arise. For it is plausible to suppose that no Ramsey book
entails that Socrates exists and no Ramsey world includes his
existence. If this *is* to be plausible, of course, we must refine the
notions of Ramsey book and world. For example, a book $B(W)$
may contain the proposition that Socrates has the property of
being the shortest Greek philosopher in α. But this property is
an essence of Socrates,[1] so that $R(B_W)$ *will* entail that Socrates
exists. So perhaps we must Ramsify with respect to worlds as
well as individuals. And something must be done about such
properties as *Socrateity*; perhaps we must say, vaguely, that only
'qualitative' or 'natural' or 'empirically manifest' properties are
to figure in Ramsey books and worlds.

But imagine these matters satisfactorily dealt with. Then (so
continues the objector) it seems that no Ramsey world includes
the existence of Socrates. $R(B_\alpha)$, for example, the Ramsey book
on α, does indeed entail the existence of some person with all the
'natural' or 'qualitative' properties of Socrates; but does it entail
the existence of *Socrates*? Perhaps someone else—Plato, maybe—
could have had all those properties; perhaps there is a possible
world in which he *does*. In that case $R(B_\alpha)$ does not entail that
Socrates exists; and $R(\alpha)$ does not include the existence of
Socrates—or, for that matter, his non-existence. So Socrates
does not exist in $R(\alpha)$. And if this is true for α, it will no doubt
be true for any other possible world W—that is, $R(W)$ will

---

[1] See above, p. 72.

include neither the existence nor the non-existence of Socrates. But a Ramsey book, we said, contains as much information as its unramsified compeer. Hence, we cannot say of Socrates that he exists in other possible worlds—or, for that matter, that he does not.

If this is not a problem of transworld identity, it is at the least a transworld anomaly. But does it occasion a difficulty for the idea that Socrates exists in various possible worlds? I think not. For it may be plausible to suppose that Ramsification does not destroy information and it may be plausible to suppose that no Ramsey world includes the existence of Socrates; it is not at all plausible, however, to follow the objector in making *both* suppositions. If Ramsey worlds do *not* include the existence of Socrates, then clearly information *is* lost in the process of Ramsification. Clearly enough the existence of Socrates is a possible state of affairs (since it obtains); and for any possible state of affairs, there is a maximal possible state of affairs that includes it. So if no Ramsey world includes the existence of Socrates, then information is indeed lost in Ramsification, and Ramsey worlds are not maximal states of affairs and hence are not possible worlds —in which case it does not matter whether Socrates exists in them. If, on the other hand, information is *not* lost in Ramsification, then $R(B_W)$ will entail each member of $B(W)$, including such items as that Socrates exists. Indeed if no information is lost, $R(W)$ will just be (or be equivalent to) W. But then $R(\alpha)$, for example, will include the existence of Socrates, since α does.

But *is* information lost in Ramsification? We may put this question in other ways: Ramsification is a function; is it one–one or many–one? Are Ramsey worlds equivalent to possible worlds? Is each essence equivalent to some intersection of 'qualitative' or 'natural' properties? Is it possible that you should have all of my qualitative properties and I all of yours? Are there worlds that differ solely by a permutation of individuals? These questions are equivalent and equivalently difficult; I do not know their answers, partly because of uncertainties about the alleged notion of a qualitative property. But perhaps they are best thought of as queries as to whether certain properties are essential to their bearers. For take Socrates and consider the intersection S_Q of his qualitative properties. The question is whether the complement of S_Q is essential to everything distinct

from Socrates—more exactly, whether that proposition is necessarily true. To put the question the other way around, consider
maximal possible intersections of qualitative properties—that
is, maximal intersections that are exemplified in some world.
Socrates exemplifies just one of these; he has the complements
of the rest. The question is whether he has these complements
essentially—whether, that is, the complement of the union of
these maximal intersections is essential to him.

If these are intelligible questions, I do not know their answers.
There are similar questions: is there a world W and an object x
existing in W such that x is identical with Socrates and x, let us
say, was born in 1500 B.C. or was an eighteenth-century Irish
washerwoman? Is there a world in which there exists something
identical with Socrates and the President of the United States?
These questions may advertise themselves as questions about
Transworld Identity; in fact they too are questions as to which
of Socrates' properties are essential to him. Could he have
had the property of being-disembodied-at-some-time-or-other?
Or the property of having-an-alligator-body-at-some-time-or-
other? (According to Socrates himself, everyone has the former
property, and some of his more snappish acquaintances may
have the latter.) These are real questions; we may be unable to
answer them. It would be overzealous, however, to conclude
that there is difficulty or confusion in the idea that Socrates
exists in many possible worlds. Our lack of confident answers
means only that Socrates has *some* properties such that we
cannot easily tell whether or not they are essential to him; it
does not so much as suggest that *all* his properties are thus
inscrutable. And, indeed, not all of them are. Obviously
Socrates could have been a bit shorter or a bit taller, a bit
wiser or a bit less upright. But then Socrates is not a worldbound individual; there are many possible worlds in which
he exists.

4. *Objections to TWI*

The arguments for the Theory of Worldbound Individuals,
then, are based upon error and confusion; but are there positive
reasons for rejecting this theory? It certainly seems so. The
theory's basic thrust is that no object exists in more than one

possible world; this implies the outrageous view that—taking 'property' in as wide a sense as you like—no object could have lacked any property that in fact it has. Had the world been different in even the tiniest, most Socrates-irrelevant fashion, Socrates would not have existed. On this theory, if God created both Socrates and *n* electrons, then it was absolutely impossible that he create both Socrates and n+1 electrons. TWI thereby fails to distinguish the relation in which Socrates stands to inconsistent attributes—being both married and unmarried, for example—from the relationship in which he stands to such an attribute as *fleeing to Thebes* or *being such that there are n+1 electrons.* It is as impossible, on this view, that Socrates should have had the latter as the former. *Every* attribute of Socrates is one that he has in every world in which he exists—there being only one such world; so no attribute he lacks is such that there is a possible state of affairs in which he has it. Accordingly, on this view each of Socrates' properties is essential to him.

Consider, furthermore, a proposition like

(6) Socrates is foolish,

a proposition which predicates of Socrates a property he lacks. Now presumably (6) is true, in a given possible world, only if Socrates exists in that world and has the property of being foolish therein. But on TWI there is no such world; accordingly, (6) is necessarily false. So on TWI any proposition predicating of Socrates a property he does not have will be necessarily false. Further, consider any proposition *p* that is false but contingent; since *Socrates exists* is true only in α, where *p* is false, there is no world in which *p* and *Socrates exists* are both true; the latter, therefore, entails the denial of the former. Accordingly, *Socrates exists* entails every true proposition. And surely all of this is clearly false. If we know anything at all about modality, we know that some of Socrates' properties are accidental to him, that *Socrates is foolish* is not necessarily false, and that *Socrates exists* does not entail every true proposition.

5. *Counterpart Theory*

But here we must consider an exciting new wrinkle to this old theory. Embracing the Theory of Worldbound Individuals,

David Lewis adds to it the suggestion that a worldbound individual typically has *counterparts* in other possible worlds:

The counterpart relation is our substitute for identity between things in different worlds. Where some would say that you are in several worlds, in which you have somewhat different properties and somewhat different things happen to you, I prefer to say that you are in the actual world and no other, but you have counterparts in several other worlds. Your counterparts resemble you closely in content and context in important respects. They resemble you more closely than do the other things in their worlds. But they are not really you. For each of them is in his own world, and only you are here in the actual world. Indeed we might say, speaking casually, that your counterparts are you in other worlds, that they and you are the same; but this sameness is no more a literal identity than the sameness between you today and you tomorrow. It would be better to say that your counterparts are men you would have been, had the world been otherwise.[1]

Fortified with Counterpart Theory, TWI seems no longer obliged to hold that each of Socrates' properties is essential to him; instead, a property is essential to him if and only if each of his counterparts (among whom is Socrates himself) has it: "In short, an essential attribute of something is an attribute it shares with all its counterparts. All your counterparts are probably human; if so, you are essentially human" (ibid., p. 122). So while indeed there is no world in which Socrates, *our* Socrates— the object that in our world is Socrates—lacks the property of being snubnosed, there are no doubt worlds containing *counterparts* of Socrates—counterparts that are not snubnosed. Hence the property of being snubnosed is not essential to him.

And now return to

(6) Socrates is foolish

TWI seems to imply, paradoxically enough, that (6) is necessarily false. Can Counterpart Theory be of help here? Perhaps. It is natural to suppose that (6) is true in a given world W if and only if the thing denoted by 'Socrates'—Socrates himself— is foolish in W. But this thing cannot enjoy the property of being foolish in W unless it *exists* in W. Hence it is natural to suppose that (6) is true in W only if Socrates—the Socrates of α—exists

---

[1] "Counterpart Theory and Quantified Modal Logic", *Journal of Philosophy*, 65 (1968), 114–15.

in W. This is a natural supposition; but it is not one the counterpart theorist accepts. He holds instead that the truth of (6) in W does not require the existence in that world of what is denoted by 'Socrates' in this. He could hold, for example, that a name such as 'Socrates' denotes different objects with respect to different worlds. With respect to α, it denotes a certain object—an object that exists in α alone. With respect to another world W, however, what it denotes (if anything) is not the thing that is Socrates in α, but the thing that is Socrates in W—one of the counterparts of our Socrates. On this view, then, 'Socrates', like 'the tallest man in Boston', denotes different objects with respect to different worlds.

We could put essentially this point another way: it is open to the counterpart theorist to hold that different things have the property of being Socrates in different worlds—just as, in different worlds, different objects have the property of being the tallest man in Boston; for he can hold that the property of being Socrates is the property unique to Socrates and his counterparts. Then, of course, the property of being Socrates— 'Socrateity' as we might call it—is not the property of being identical with the person who is Socrates in α, the actual world; it is not the property of being that person. *That* property, indeed, is exemplified in only one world: α; and it is not possible that it should have been exemplified by an individual distinct from the one that *does* exemplify it. *Socrateity*, on the other hand, is exemplified in many worlds; while in fact it is exemplified by the Socrates of α, it would have been exemplified (if at all) by something else had things been different in even the most minuscule fashion. (Indeed, on Counterpart Theory an object may have several counterparts in the same world; so no doubt there are worlds in which several distinct objects exemplify Socrateity.) This property is the one unique to Socrates and his counterparts. And the point is that (6) is true, in a given world W, just in case W contains an object that is both Socratic and foolish—that is, just in case Socrateity and foolishness are coexemplified in W. So (6) is equivalent to

(6') Something exemplifies both Socrateity and foolishness.

Of course this proposition will be true in some but not all worlds.

But what about

(7) Socrates exists?

If nothing exists in more than one world, then presumably Socrates does not, in which case on TWI (fortified with Counterpart Theory though it be), (7) still appears to be true in just one world and still appears to entail every true proposition. But perhaps appearances are deceiving; perhaps Counterpart Theory affords the means of denying that (7) is true in only one world. On counterpart theory as presently construed,

(6) Socrates is foolish

is true, we saw, in any world where Socrateity and foolishness are coexemplified—in any world, that is, where Socrates has a foolish counterpart. Perhaps then (7) can be held to be true in any world where Socrates has an existent counterpart—that is, in any world where he has a counterpart. This proposition is true in any world where Socrateity has an instance; since there are many such, there are many worlds in which it is true; hence (7) does not entail every true proposition.

But if (7) is true in many worlds, how does the central claim of TWI—that nothing exists in more than one—fit in? If Socrates (along with everything else) exists in only one world, that is if

(8) Socrates exists in more than one world

is false, how can (7) be true in more than one world? There is no difficulty here. Socrates exists in exactly one world; hence (8) is false. But the multiworld truth of (7) (construed as above) does not require that the object that has Socrateity in α exist in more than one world; it requires only that Socrateity be instantiated in several worlds. That it should be thus multiply instantiated is in no way inconsistent with the claim that what instantiates it here in α does not exist elsewhere.

Furthermore (perhaps by way of a genial effort to appear agreeable to his friends of transworldly orientation) the Counterpart Theorist can go so far as to deny that (8) is false. First, he could if he chose construe (8) as the entirely accurate *de dicto* claim that *Socrates exists* is true in more than one world. According to the central claim of TWI, nothing exists in more than one world. This claim, however, is not inconsistent with (8) construed as above. For let us suppose the predicate 'exists in more than one world' expresses a property that, according to TWI, no object has. Then (8), if true, must not be seen as predicating that property of Socrates: if it did, it would be false. What it does instead is predicate *truth in more than one world* of *Socrates exists*. There is an instructive parallel between (8) so construed and

(9) the number of planets is possibly greater than 9.

Read *de dicto*, (9) quite properly predicates possibility of

(10) the number of planets is greater than 9.

It is plausible to add, furthermore, that the words 'is possibly greater than 9' express a property[1]—the property a thing has just in case it is possibly greater than 9. Every number greater than nine enjoys this property; that is to say, each number greater than nine is *possibly* greater than nine. The number of planets, however, being nine, does not have the property in question. (9) therefore, can be read as a true *de dicto* assertion; but, thus read, it does not predicate of the object named by 'the number of planets' the property expressed by 'is possibly greater than 9'.

Similarly, then, for (8). Although the words 'exists in more than one world' express a property that (if TWI is true) nothing has, (8) does not predicate that property of anything and hence need not (at any rate on that account) be false. And hence the argument from

(11) Nothing exists in more than one world

to the falsehood of (8) is unacceptable, as we can see if we compare it with another:

(12) Every number greater than 7 is necessarily greater than 7

(13) the number of planets is greater than 7

hence

(14) the number of planets is necessarily greater than 7.

If we construe (14) as the *de dicto* claim that

(15) the number of planets is greater than 7

---

[1] See below, Appendix, Section 2.

is necessarily true, then it obviously fails to follow from (12) and (13). (12) quite accurately says that every number meeting a certain condition has a certain property—that of being necessarily greater than 7. (13) properly points out that the number of planets meets that condition. (14), however, is not the consequent *de re* assertion that the number of planets has that property, but the false (and inconsequent) *de dicto* assertion that (15) is necessarily true. And the same can be said for (8). Under the present proposal this is not the *de re* assertion that some specific object has the property that (11) says nothing has; it is instead the *de dicto* allegation that *Socrates exists* is true in more than one world—an allegation quite consistent with (11).

But there is a second way in which the Counterpart Theorist can join his transworldly colleagues in upholding the truth of (8). Return to

(6) Socrates is foolish.

We said that (6), on Counterpart Theory, is contingently false despite the fact that there is no world in which Socrates (the Socrates of α) has the property of being foolish. But perhaps it is open to the Counterpart Theorist to hold that there is a sense —perhaps somewhat attenuated and Pickwickian—in which Socrates *does* have this property in other worlds. For perhaps he can say that Socrates has the property of being foolish in a world W (in this new and broader sense of 'has') if he has a counterpart in W that has foolishness there (in the old and strict sense of 'has').[1] But of course then he can hold that there are worlds in which Socrates—our Socrates, the Socrates of α—has the property of being foolish. Similarly for (8). I pointed out that (8) could be thought of as true *de dicto* but false *de re*. But the Counterpart Theorist can hold alternatively that it is both true and *de re*. For he can hold that Socrates exists in a world W, in this new and broader sense, if he has a counterpart in W; and in this broader sense of 'exists' it will be accurate to say that Socrates exists in more than one world. In the original and

---

[1] Alternatively he could hold that in a new and broader sense, Socrates satisfies the open sentence 'x is foolish' with respect to a world W if Socrates has a counterpart in W who satisfies 'x is foolish' in the old and narrower sense. This suggestion is made by David Lewis in his unpublished "Counterfactuals and Comparative Possibility", 1971. In correspondence, Lewis has suggested that Socrates *vicariously* satisfies 'x is foolish' in worlds in which he has foolish counterparts.

narrower sense of 'exists', Socrates and the rest of us exist in just one world; in the new and broader sense, Socrates and everyone else exists in several worlds.

So in this way the partisan of TWI can preserve at any rate an appearance of harmony with those who hold that Socrates exists in several worlds. He can go so far as to join the upholder of Transworld Identity in affirming the truth of (8). You may think this course on his part is less ingenuous than ingenious; and so, perhaps, it is. But so far the addition of Counterpart Theory seems to provide TWI with a remedy for ills it could not otherwise cope with.

6. *Semantic Inadequacies of Counterpart Theory*

Counterpart Theory promises relief from the varied ills of TWI. This promise, however, in my view remains unfulfilled. For TWI, fortified with Counterpart Theory though it be, is still open to decisive objection. These objections are of two sorts, corresponding to two ways we might approach Counterpart Theory. On the one hand, this theory makes a number of metaphysical allegations. For example, it affirms the existence of possible worlds; it adds that everything exists in some world or other and that just one world is actual. More importantly, it holds that each object exists in exactly one world. But Counterpart Theory does something else. It makes assertions about such items as

(16) Socrates could have been incorporeal.

According to Counterpart Theory, (16) is true if and only if some of Socrates' counterparts are incorporeal, or if and only if some of his counterparts satisfy the formula 'x is incorporeal'. This semantic aspect of Counterpart Theory can be regarded in several ways. Consider (16), for example: does Counterpart Theory discourse of the *sentence* (16) specifying truth conditions for it, thereby aiming to give us insight into the meaning of this sentence and the modal words it contains? Or is its subject instead the *proposition* (16)—the proposition that is in fact expressed by the sentence (16)—its claim being that this proposition is equivalent, in some strong sense, to the proposition that Socrates has at least one incorporeal counterpart? Perhaps it is more natural to take the theory the first way. Let us so take it, bearing in mind the other possibility. Thus understood, Counter-part Theory provides a semantics for a modal fragment of our language, or for a regimented version of such a fragment. And, so taken, the theory will be successful only if it does not assign to a clearly true sentence a truth condition that according to the theory itself is unfulfilled. Here, it seems to me, the theory is not entirely successful; we might say that it suffers from certain semantic inadequacies. I shall outline two kinds.

A. *Socrates and Xenophon*

Obviously, Socrates could have been importantly different. He could have had many properties he lacks and lacked many he has; and this with respect to just those properties to which we look in deciding whether someone *resembles* Socrates. Consider these properties; among them we find such items as courage, intelligence, wisdom, rectitude, being the teacher of Plato, being born in Athens in 470 B.C., fighting in the Battle of Marathon, being executed by the Athenians on a charge of corrupting the youth, and the like. Now clearly things could have gone differ-ently with Socrates. He could have had a different appearance. Indeed, if Chapter IV is right, he could have had an alligator body; but here we need not go as far as all that. He could have been less upright than he was. He could have been a scoundrel, and one that was not very bright at that. If he *had* been like this, then he would have been less like he was *in fact* than, say, Xenophon was. After all, Xenophon too was an intelligent, courageous, upright Athenian citizen who has left his mark on the history of the Western world. So if Socrates had been a tall, skinny, dimwitted scoundrel who looked like Ichabod Crane— if he had lived in Thebes, never met Plato, and never been heard of after his death—then he would have been less like he *actually* was than Xenophon was. We might put this by saying that he would have resembled the Socrates of α less than does the Xenophon of α.

It is therefore possible that Socrates should have been less like he was in α than Xenophon was. But if this is possible, then surely it is possible that Socrates should have been very different from what he was in fact, while Xenophon should have been very much like *he* was in fact. It therefore follows that Socrates and Xenophon could have been such that the former was less like Socrates as he was in fact (in α) than the latter. If we suppose that Socrates and Xenophon exist in more than one world, we could put this by saying that there is a world W distinct from α such that Socrates and Xenophon both exist in W, and in which Xenophon resembles Socrates as he is in α more than Socrates does. Accordingly,

> (17) Socrates and Xenophon could have been such that the latter should have resembled Socrates as he was in the actual world more than the former

is true. That is, this sentence expresses a true proposition.

The truth conditions assigned to (17) by Counterpart Theory, however, are, according to that theory, unfulfilled. For on this theory (17) is true only if there is a world W in which Socrates and Xenophon have counterparts S_w and X_w such that X_w resembles Socrates (the Socrates of α) more than S_w does. But the theory also holds that a counterpart of Socrates in a world W resembles Socrates more closely than does anything else that exists in W: "Your counterparts resemble you closely in content and context in important respects. They resemble you more closely than do the other things in their worlds."[1] We might say therefore that the denial of (17) is *valid* on Counterpart Theory in that the theory entails that the truth conditions it assigns to that sentence are unfulfilled. But clearly enough (17) is in fact true.

B. *Socrates and Socrates-identity*

A second semantic difficulty: consider

> (18) Everyone is at least as tall as he is.

It is plausible to see this proposition as predicating a certain property of each person—a property that is universally shared. It predicates of Kareem Abdul-Jabbar, for example, the property *being-at-least-as-tall-as-he-is*, a property that in no way distinguishes him from anyone else. But now consider an instance of (18) such as

> (19) Kareem Abdul-Jabbar is at least as tall as Kareem Abdul-Jabbar.

---

[1] D. Lewis, op. cit., p. 114.

(19), of course, predicates of Jabbar the property (18) says everything has. But it also predicates of him a property he does not share with others; for what it also says of him is that he has the property of being at least as tall as Kareem Abdul-Jabbar— a property nearly unique to him.

The same thing holds for

(20) Everything is identical with itself.

This proposition predicates of each object the property of being self-identical—a common property indeed. And an instance of (20)—

(21) Socrates is identical with Socrates

for example, predicates self-identity of Socrates. But (21) also says of him that he has identity-with-Socrates—that is, the property *being-identical-with-the-thing-that-actually-is-Socrates*, or *identity-with-the-thing-that-is-Socrates-in-α*; this property is unique to him. Since these properties do not characterize the same objects they are clearly distinct; we might say, however, that they *coincide on* Socrates, in that it is impossible that he have either one without the other. The same duality, furthermore, characterizes such a proposition as

(22) Everything is essentially identical with itself.

Such an instance of (22) as

(23) Socrates is essentially identical with Socrates

says of Socrates that he has the property of being essentially self-identical; but it also says of him that he has essentially the property of being identical with *Socrates*—quite another matter.

And here TWI fortified with Counterpart Theory runs into difficulty. For on this theory self-identity and identity-with-Socrates (i.e. *identity-with-the-thing-that-actually-is-Socrates*) do not coincide on Socrates. While it is impossible, according to Counterpart Theory, that Socrates lack *self-identity*, it is not impossible that he lack *identity-with-Socrates*. (This latter property is of course distinct from Socrateity; it is not the property common to Socrates and his counterparts, but rather the property of being identical with the object that in fact exemplifies Socrateity.) According to Counterpart Theory, this property is essential to Socrates only if each of his counterparts has it.

But of course only Socrates of all his counterparts has identity-with-Socrates. So the properties of self-identity and identity-with-Socrates do not, according to Counterpart Theory, coincide on Socrates: he could not have lacked self-identity but he could have lacked identity-with-Socrates. He has self-identity essentially, but identity-with-Socrates accidentally. That is to say, on Counterpart Theory the sentences

(24) Socrates could have been distinct from Socrates (taken *de re* with respect to both occurrences of Socrates)

or

(24') Socrates could have been distinct from the person who actually is Socrates

or

(24*) Socrates could have been distinct from the person who is Socrates in α, the actual world

are true. For on Counterpart Theory an object could have had a property P if it has a counterpart with P. And (unless he himself is his only counterpart) Socrates does indeed have counterparts that have the property of being distinct from the person who actually is Socrates—the person who is Socrates in α, the actual world. Indeed, all but one of his counterparts have this property. Hence Counterpart Theory assigns to (24), (24'), and (24*) a truth condition that according to Counterpart Theory is fulfilled; and this despite the fact that these sentences obviously express a false proposition.

Of course, what is paradoxical here is the claim that these *sentences* are true, express a true proposition. It is not paradoxical to claim that the *truth conditions* Counterpart Theory assigns to them hold. For a counterpart of Socrates is an object very much like but distinct from him. And no doubt he does have counterparts in other possible worlds—whether or not he himself exists in other worlds! According to Counterpart Theory, the proposition expressed by these three sentences is equivalent to

(25) There exists a world in which there exists an object very similar to but distinct from Socrates;

and no doubt (25) is true.

But the fact is the proposition ordinarily expressed by (24),

(24′), and (24*) is not true. For that proposition is true only if Socrates—the thing that exemplifies Socrateity—could have existed and been distinct from the thing that exemplifies Socrateity. It would be true only if Socrates could have been distinct from Socrates. And he could not have.

And of course there will be related difficulties. Consider

(26) Socrates could have been wiser than he is.

The Counterpart Theorist will not hold, of course, that (26) is true only if there is a world W in which Socrates has a counterpart S_W who is wiser than S_W is; rather, what (26) requires is that there be a world W in which Socrates has a counterpart S_W who is wiser than our Socrates. So (26) in all probability is true. But then similarly

(27) Socrates could have been a different person from the one he is

will be true just in case there is a world W in which Socrates has a counterpart S_W such that S_W is a different person from the one our Socrates is. And of course every counterpart of Socrates (except for Socrates himself) is a different person from our Socrates. Since the Counterpart Theorist will certainly hold that Socrates has personal counterparts in other worlds, he will be obliged to hold that (27) is true. But it is not. That is, (27) does not in fact express a true proposition.

Further, consider

(28) If Socrates had been taller than he is, he would have been wiser than he is.

According to Counterpart Theory, this sentence is true if (but not necessarily only if) each counterpart of Socrates who is taller than our Socrates is also wiser than our Socrates. In all likelihood, this is false. But then look at

(29) If Socrates had been taller than he is, he would have been a different person from the one he is.

The Counterpart Theorist will have to hold that (29) is true, for clearly every counterpart of Socrates who is taller than our Socrates is a different person (or, if he has non-personal counterparts, a different thing) from the one our Socrates is; each such counterpart is distinct from our Socrates. But again, (29) is not in fact true. Indeed, the Counterpart Theorist must accept

(30) For any property P that Socrates has, Socrates has essentially the property of either having P or being a different person from the one he is.

For Socrates has a property essentially if all his counterparts have it; but Socrates has P, and each of his other counterparts —the counterparts of Socrates that are distinct from him—has the property of being a different person (or thing) from the one our Socrates is.

7. *Metaphysical Inadequacies of Counterpart Theory*

Counterpart Theory, therefore, is subject to certain semantical inadequacies. But perhaps there are remedies for these troubles. Indeed, perhaps they can be handled simply by judiciously restricting the portion of our language for which we take the theory to provide a semantics. Perhaps other remedies are available. Furthermore, if we think of this theory as a semantics, it is natural to think of it less as an effort to tell the sober metaphysical truth than as a sort of image or aid to the imagination —useful as a source of insight into the working of our language, but not to be taken seriously as metaphysics. We might treat Counterpart Theory in something like the way we treat pictures and diagrams in mathematics; we might take it as a heuristic device whose value is to be found in the insight it affords into the workings of our language. So taken, the theory is to be judged by the amount of insight it does in fact provide.

But we may also take Counterpart Theory as an effort to spell out the sober metaphysical truth about modality; and it is the theory thus taken that is crucial to our present concerns. So let us turn our attention away from the semantical question and instead consider Counterpart Theory as a set of metaphysical assertions. Among these assertions, then, are the claims that there are possible worlds, that exactly one possible world is actual, that objects exist in possible worlds, and the like. And of course the central item here is the claim that nothing exists in more than one world. Or perhaps less sweepingly, the claim is that concrete objects—ships and shoes and filing clerks and cabbages and kings—exist in only one world; the Counterpart Theorist need make no claims about the transworld existence of such abstract objects as sets, numbers, properties, propositions, and possible worlds themselves. Concrete objects such as persons, however, exist in just one world.

This in itself is not at all easy to believe. Asked to think of possible states of affairs that do not obtain, we come up with such items as *Socrates' being a carpenter* or *Royal Robbins' being America's foremost philosopher*. We suppose that if the first of these had obtained, then Socrates—the very person we know and love so well—would have existed and would have had some property that he lacks. We suppose that this state of affairs includes the existence of a person who does in fact exist—of the person we call 'Socrates'; we do not suppose that it includes instead the existence of someone very similar to but none the less distinct from him. If this state of affairs had been actual, then this very person—the Socrates of α—would have existed and would have had some property that in fact he lacks. But of course Counterpart Theory, taken as metaphysics, entails that if Socrates was not in fact a carpenter, then there is no possible state of affairs such that if it had been actual, then Socrates himself would have existed and would have been a carpenter. And this is a hard saying indeed.

But we must go further. Earlier we noted three problems with TWI unfortified with Counterpart Theory: first it appears to entail that Socrates has all of his properties essentially; secondly it entails that if Socrates is wise, then

(6) Socrates is foolish

is necessarily false; and thirdly it yields the consequence that

(7) Socrates exists

if true, entails every true proposition. Counterpart Theory promised to assuage these difficulties. But in fact it does not help. For if the central contention of this theory is true—if nothing exists in more than one world—then these unsavoury consequences do indeed follow.

Consider the first; and take any property Socrates has accidentally—wisdom, perhaps. According to Counterpart Theory, Socrates—the person who actually is Socrates, the Socrates of α, if you wish—exists in just one world: the actual world. In that world he is wise. Accordingly, there is no world in which he is unwise. There is no possible state of affairs such that if it had been actual, then this very person would have been unwise. There is no possible state of affairs including this person's being unwise. Accordingly, it is impossible that he should have been unwise; he could not have been unwise. But then he has the property of being wise essentially. And the same will go for any other property he enjoys.

Of course the Counterpart Theorist will reply that Socrates —the Socrates of α—no doubt has unwise counterparts, which is sufficient for the truth that he could have been unwise. But how are we to take this reply? In either of two ways, perhaps. On the one hand he may mean to hold that the proposition

(30) There are worlds in which there exist unwise counterparts of Socrates

is sufficient for the truth of

(31) Socrates could have been unwise.

But how is (30) so much as relevant to (31)? According to (30) there is a world W (distinct from α) that includes the existence of an unwise counterpart of Socrates. If this world had been actual, then there would have existed an unwise person much like but distinct from Socrates. And how is that even relevant to the claim that Socrates himself—the Socrates of α—could have been unwise? There could have been a foolish person a lot like Socrates; how does this fact show that *Socrates* could have been unwise? How is the former a reason for the latter? We might as well claim that there is a property P such that Socrates could have had both P and its complement P̄—on the grounds that there are worlds where Socrates has a *pair* of counterparts, one with P and the other with P̄. No doubt there is a possible state of affairs including the existence of an unwise person who is similar to Socrates; but this fact is totally irrelevant to the truth that Socrates—Socrates himself—could have been unwise.

But the Counterpart Theorist might respond to quite another fashion. We noted earlier that he can appeal to a new and looser sense of 'has' and 'exists' such that Socrates can be said in this sense to exist and have properties in other possible worlds. Socrates has P in a world W, in this sense, if he has a counterpart that has P in W in the old and strict sense. We may therefore imagine him replying as follows. "When I say that Socrates could have been unwise I do not mean that there is a possible world in which Socrates—our Socrates—in the strict and literal sense is unwise; I mean only that there is a world in which in the new and looser sense he has that property. I so use the sentence 'Socrates could have been unwise' that what it expresses is entailed by the truth that Socrates has foolish counterparts." Thus perhaps he speaks with the vulgar but thinks with the learned. He genially agrees that there is a world in which Socrates is unwise and concludes that Socrates could have been unwise. By adopting this course he preserves verbal agreement with the rest of us who do not look upon Socrates as a worldbound individual.

But of course the agreement is only verbal. For it is only in this loose and Pickwickian sense that he concedes the existence of a world in which Socrates is unwise; and his use of 'Socrates could have been unwise' is therefore similarly loose and Pickwickian. If in his use the sentence 'Socrates could have been unwise' expresses a proposition entailed by the fact that Socrates has unwise counterparts, then the Counterpart Theorist is using that sentence to express a proposition different from the one the rest of us express by it. While he assents to our sentence, he denies the proposition we take it to express. Furthermore, he does not really disagree with us when we say that Counterpart Theory entails that Socrates could not have been unwise. For his counter claim was only that his theory does not entail that Socrates had no foolish counterparts. The justice of this claim is incontestable; but it is quite consistent with our claim that Counterpart Theory entails that if Socrates is wise, then he could not have been unwise. For our claim, of course, is that Counterpart Theory entails the proposition *we* take to be expressed by these words.

Suppose I were to claim that no resident of California has ever been outside the boundaries of that state. "That is ridiculous," comes your indignant reply, "why not long ago Ronald Reagan was in Washington, D.C." To which my reply goes as follows: "Actually, Reagan—California's Reagan, that is—never got beyond the Nevada border. For at the border he was replaced by someone else who had the good fortune to be extremely similar to him. The resemblance was absolutely uncanny. Furthermore," I add, "the sentence

(32) Reagan was in Washington

as I use it, is true; for what I mean thereby is that someone very similar to Reagan—more like him than anyone else in Washington—was in Washington. So my theory does not have the absurd implication that if Reagan is a Californian, then he has never been in Washington." Here I am maintaining a verbal agreement with others by conceding that (32) is true. But in fact I do not concur with those who accept (32); for in their mouths it expresses a proposition I hold to be false. And the Counterpart Theorist does something similar. He holds that nothing exists in more than one world; we point out the consequence that Socrates could not have been unwise; he repudiates this unwholesome result on the grounds that

(31) Socrates could have been unwise

as he uses it, expresses a proposition true if Socrates has an unwise counterpart. But his apparent agreement with us is illusory; for while indeed he holds, with us, that (31) expresses a true proposition, the one we use it to express is, on his theory, flatly false.

A cardinal difficulty with TWI in its original Leibnizian form was its implication that each object has each of its properties essentially; and the original attractiveness of Counterpart Theory was its promise to overcome that difficulty. I think we now see that this promise is unfulfilled. Of course we can define locutions of the form 'x has P essentially' in the way suggested by Counterpart Theory; and then we shall be in verbal agreement with the truth that objects have some of their properties accidentally. But the agreement, I suggest, is *only* verbal. For on TWI, if I have a property P, then there is no world in which I —the person I use 'I' to denote—lack that property. So it is not possible that I should have lacked it. No doubt, as the Counterpart Theorist may retort, there are possible states of affairs including the existence of persons *similar* to me that lack P; but this is irrelevant to the question whether I could have lacked P —whether it is possible that I should not have had P. It is no more to the point than the possibility that there be something or someone with my *name* that lacks *P*. Hence I do not think Counterpart Theory succeeds in overcoming this objection to TWI; that difficulty persists.

And the same holds for the two remaining difficulties I ascribed to TWI in its original form. Return again to the proposition

(6) Socrates is foolish.

TWI entails that (6) is necessarily false; and the addition of Counterpart Theory does not relieve it of this embarrassing implication. Again, of course, we shall be told that (6) is true in any world where Socrates has a foolish counterpart. We shall be told that (6) is equivalent to

(33) Socrateity and foolishness are coexemplified,

where *Socrateity* is the property unique to Socrates and his counterparts. This property is one that could have been exemplified by someone distinct from the person who does exemplify it, the Socrates of α. Indeed, in any other world in which it is exemplified, it *is* exemplified by someone else.

But in fact (6) is not equivalent to (33). That is to say, the proposition ordinarily expressed by the sentence 'Socrates is foolish' is not equivalent to (33). For the former would have been true only if Socrates himself—the person who exists in α— had existed and had been foolish. This proposition is true in a world *W* only if that person exists and is foolish in *W*. Hence it is not entailed by (33), which is true in a given world if someone distinct from but sufficiently similar to Socrates is foolish there. Indeed, what (6) declares is not that foolishness and *Socrateity* are coexemplified, but that foolishness and *Socraticness* are, where Socraticness is the property an object has only if it is identical with the person who is in fact Socrates. This is a property Socrates shares neither with his counterparts nor with anything else. From the point of view of Counterpart Theory, Socraticness is the property unique to the object that exemplifies Socrateity in α. And it is *this* property that (6) holds to be coexemplified with foolishness. Of course the Counterpart Theorist can choose to use the sentence (6) to express (33), thus preserving verbal agreement with those of us who hold that (6) is contingent. But all the while he holds that the proposition *we* take (6) to express, is necessarily false.

The third and final difficulty afflicting TWI was that on this view

(7) Socrates exists

is true only in the actual world and thus entails every true proposition. This difficulty remains when TWI is fortified by Counterpart Theory. Again we shall be told that (7) is equivalent to

(34) Socrateity is instantiated,

a proposition that is no doubt true in many worlds. But the fact is the proposition expressed by the sentence (7) is not equivalent to (34). For the former is true in a world W only if Socrates himself—the person who actually is Socrates—exists in W. It is not sufficient that someone very similar to him exist there. The fact is, (7) is equivalent not to (37) but to

(35) Socraticness is exemplified.

And while once more the Counterpart Theorist can choose to use the sentence (7) to express (34), this course does not blunt the objector's point. For that point concerns the proposition *we* use (7) to express—that is, (35) or one equivalent to it; and the point is that *this* proposition, according to TWI, is true only in the actual world. That point remains; TWI, with or without the fortification of Counterpart Theory, implies that this proposition is true in the actual world alone and thus paradoxically entails every true proposition.

We must therefore conclude, I believe, that Counterpart Theory (taken as sober metaphysics) affords no real remedy for the ills besetting the Theory of Worldbound Individuals; this latter theory, then, is false.

VII

POSSIBLE BUT UNACTUAL OBJECTS:
THE CLASSICAL ARGUMENT

1. *The Question*

I HAVE argued that there are possible worlds, that objects have both essential and accidental properties as well as essences, and that the same object typically exists in different possible worlds. Socrates, for example, exists in this world and in many others. Of course there are worlds in which he does not exist; Socrates is not a necessary being. Let W* be any such world and suppose W* had been actual. Then Socrates would not have existed; but would there none the less have *been* such a thing as Socrates—would there have been a thing that was Socrates and was a possible but unactual or nonexistent object? To put the question differently: suppose it is possible that there exist a person distinct from every person (past, present, and future) that does exist. Does it follow that there is at least one unactualized but possible person? Are there, or could there be, possible but nonexistent objects? Of course there are related questions: can we *talk about* nonexistent objects? Is it possible to *refer to* nonexistents? If so, does it follow that there are some to be talked about and referred to? If there are nonexistent objects, do they have properties? If there are possible but un-actualized objects, are there also some that are impossible and unactualizable? In asserting a negative existential proposition do we refer to or specify some object and then predicate nonexistence of it? Are creatures of myth and fiction— Mr. Pickwick, Captain Marvel, Pegasus, King Lear, and their like—possible but non-existent objects? These perplex-ing and difficult questions are the subject of this and the next chapter.

So are there any nonexistent objects? But how are we to take this assertion? What might it mean to say there are some individuals that do not exist? It may be difficult indeed to see just what is meant; but perhaps we can say something about what is *not* meant. It is not suggested, of course, that there exist some things that do not exist, 'exist' being taken the same way in each occurrence. Secondly, this is not just a picturesque way of stating the fact that in the company of true sentences there are to be found such items as 'Pegasus does not exist' or 'there is no such thing as Santa Claus'. We may perhaps *argue from* the fact in question to the claim in question; but surely the latter is not just a misleading way of putting the former. Thirdly, the suggestion is not just that there are some things—numbers or classes, for example—that do not exist in space in time; nor, for that matter is it that there are some things—persons and material objects, let us say—that do not exist in timeless and spaceless splendour. Fourthly, the use of 'there is' here is not *idiosyncratic*, as when, upbraiding someone for playing fast and loose with the truth, you say "After all, there is such a thing as honesty, Archibald"; here your aim is less to make pronouncements upon what there is than to establish Archibald in truthfulness. Fifth, its use here is not *elliptical*, as when in a lecture of the merits of *Henry IV* one hears 'then, of course, there is this fantastic fellow Falstaff, who . . .'. Presumably this amounts to something like '*in the play* there is this fantastic character Falstaff . . .'; and this does not much resemble the use of 'there is' in the serious philosophical assertion that there are some things that do not exist.

What *do* these words mean, then? Perhaps we cannot sensibly expect much of an answer; perhaps what is meant by 'there is' and 'exists' cannot be helpfully explained in other terms. In any event, we seem to have a certain initial grasp of this assertion, hesitant and infirm though it be. And here we are not alone; the question has a long and distinguished history. It is part of current folklore that Meinong claimed there were possible but nonexistent objects; but of course the question goes much further back. It was prominent, for example, in medieval discussions of the doctrine of creation. God has created you and me and the rest of us. Does this consist in his having actualized some possible persons? Are there other possible persons he could have actualized in our places? How did he decide which possible persons to actualize? Is there some sort of injustice in his passing over those he does not actualize, supposing that there are some? More recently, the idea that there are possible but nonexistent objects has been endorsed or taken seriously by Leibniz, Brentano, Meinong, Russell, G. E. Moore, and many others.

2. Modal Logic and Possible Objects

This question, therefore, has had a distinguished career. But it receives renewed impetus from important recent developments in the philosophy of logic, especially the semantics of quantified modal logic and allied semantical studies. Of course more than one semantical system has been offered for quantified modal logic, and these systems differ significantly among themselves. For the sake of definiteness, therefore, I shall focus attention upon Saul Kripke's 1963 *Acta Philosophica Fennica* systems;[1] most other recent systems do not differ from this one in respects relevant to what I wish to say.

To spare the reader a trip to the library, I shall give a brief account of Kripke semantics. Suppose we have a propositional modal logic. For the semantics we invoke the idea of *possible worlds* in which propositions are true or false. A *model structure* is a triple (G, K, R) where G is a member of K and R a reflexive relation on it; we may think of G, says Kripke, as the real world and K as a class of possible worlds. R is to represent the relation of 'relative possibility'; a world W^* is possible *relative to* a world W if and only if every proposition true in W^* is possible in W. (By varying the properties of R we get different classes of valid formulae: for example, if R is transitive as well as reflexive we have as valid the theorems of Lewis's S_4; if it is also symmetrical we get S_5.) A *model* on a model structure is just a function of two variables $\phi(A, W)$ that assigns T or F to each propositional variable in each world. Truth values for the complex formulae are inductively defined in the natural way: $V((A\&B), W) = T$ if and only if $V(A, W) = T$ and $V(B, W) = T$; $V(\sim A, W) = T$ if and only if $V(A, W) = F$; and $V(\Box A, W) = T$ if and only if $V(A, W') = T$ for every W'

---

[1] "Semantical Considerations on Modal Logic", reprinted in *Reference and Modality*, ed. L. Linsky (Oxford: Oxford University Press, 1972), p. 63.

such that W R W'. Here we exploit Leibniz's idea of necessary truth as truth in every possible world.

For quantified modal logic we add, for each positive integer n, a list of n-adic predicate letters (propositional variables taken as 0-adic), together with individual variables and quantifiers. A *quantificational model structure* is then a model structure together with a function $\psi(W)$ that assigns to each W in K a domain of individuals—intuitively, says Kripke, these are the individuals that exist in that world. A quantificational model $\phi(P^n, W)$ on a quantificational model structure is then a function of two variables that assigns a set of n-tuples of members of $\mathscr{U}$ ($\mathscr{U} = \mathrm{U}(\psi(W))$, $W \in K$) to P^n if n < 0; otherwise $\phi(P^n, W)$ will be T or F. In this way a truth value is induced for each well-formed formula A with respect to each world (relative to an assignment of members of $\mathscr{U}$ to the free variables of A). The steps for negation, conjunction, and necessity have already been given. If A is a propositional variable, $\mathrm{V}(A, W) = \phi(A, W)$ (and $\phi(A, W)$, as we remember, is T or F); if A is an atomic formula $P^n(x_1, ..., x_n)$, $\mathrm{V}(A, W) = \mathrm{T}$, relative to the assignment of $a_1, ..., a_n$, to the x_i, if and only if the n-tuple $(a_1, ..., a_n)$ is a member of $\phi(P^n, W)$; if A is $(x)A(x, y_1, ..., y_n)$, $\mathrm{V}(A, W) = \mathrm{T}$, relative to the assignment of $b_1, ..., b_n$ to the y_i if and only if $\mathrm{V}(A(x, y_1, ..., y_n), W) = \mathrm{T}$ for every assignment of a member a of $\psi(W)$ to x.

It is clear, then, that quantification is over existing members of U; that is, a universally quantified formula of the form $(x)F^1x$ is true with respect to a given world W if and only if every object *in the domain of individuals of W* is assigned to F^1 in W; the fact, if it is a fact, that there are other objects from $\mathscr{U}$ —objects not in the domain of W—that are not assigned to F^1 in W in no way compromises its truth. By way of illustration:

(1) (x) if x is a horse, then x has no wings

is true with respect to G, the actual world, even if (what, for the sake of illustration, we may momentarily concede)[1] Pegasus is a horse and has wings. Since Pegasus does not in fact exist, he is not in the domain of the actual world; hence he offers no obstacle to the truth of (1) in G. And a formula A is valid then, if $\mathrm{V}(A, W) = \mathrm{T}$ for every quantificational model on a quantificational model structure.

[1] But see below, Chapter VIII, Sections 1 and 2.

3. *How Shall we Take the Semantics?*

Now how, exactly, does the question of possible but unactual objects rear its ugly head with respect to this semantical system? To answer this question, we must ask another: how, exactly, are we to take such a semantics for modal logic? What is the point of offering such a system? Why do we need one and what is it designed to do for us? For a variety of reasons and to serve a number of different goals, no doubt, all of which somehow come under the heading of deepening our insight into our modal notions and the modal portion of our language. In Chapter VI (Section 7) I pointed out that Counterpart Theory can be thought of in two quite different ways. We can take it as a heuristic device, an aid to the imagination whose metaphysical imagery makes for vividness but is not to be taken seriously; but we can also take it as an attempt to spell out the sober metaphysical truth about modality. A semantical system such as Kripke's can be looked at in these same two ways. We may regard its talk of possible worlds and sets of individuals as convenient but dispensable imagery whose cash value is to be found in the insights provided into the workings of our language. And if we do look at these semantical systems in this light, then we need not be troubled by embarrassing metaphysical questions about the nature of possible worlds and the status of objects that, as we picturesquely put it, exist only in other possible worlds. Here these questions do not arise.

This attitude towards the semantics, however, is an extremely sophisticated one that does not always stop short of sophistry. Furthermore, the insights to be gained in this way are limited and somewhat elusive. For example, the semantics may be invoked to elucidate the idea that an object has some but not all of its properties essentially; an object has a property essentially, we may say, if it has it in every world, or every world in which it exists. We may then propose to explain 'Johan is essentially a person but contingently a philosopher' as the assertion that Johan has both these properties and has the former but not the latter in every world he graces. If we take the possible worlds scheme seriously, this is straightforward and to be understood after the manner of Chapter IV. But suppose we refuse to say that there really are any possible worlds or disclaim any views as to what they might be like, or reject any responsibility for the assertion that Johan has properties in some that he lacks in others: then it requires a well-trained eye to see just what our explanation accomplishes.

Take another case. As we saw in Chapter I, Aquinas solves a paradox about divine omniscience and human freedom by remarking that

(2) Whatever is seen to be sitting is necessarily sitting

is true taken *de dicto* but false taken *de re*. Fortified with the semantics we may understand St. Thomas as endorsing the claim *de dicto* that

(3) Whatever is seen to be sitting is sitting

is true in every possible world, while disputing the claim *de re* that

(4) Whatever is seen (in this world) to be sitting is sitting in every possible world.

Again we may try to follow St. Thomas but repudiate the apparent implications of our explanation—that there are possible worlds, that propositions are true or false therein and that people and things have properties in them—as metaphysical imagery useful here to apprise us of a distinction that stands on its own legs. And again it is not entirely easy, from this point of view, to see just what the semantical explanation, so taken, contributes.

In any event, there is another way to take the semantics. We may look to it, not for heuristic aids to the imagination, but for literal explanation and articulation of our modal notions. We may take seriously its talk of possible worlds and the vicissitudes of persons and propositions therein. And here these questions about the nature and status of possible worlds and their inhabitants do indeed arise.

4. *Pure and Applied Semantics*

But now for a crucial distinction. What is offered in the Kripke system, strictly speaking, is a formal or *pure* semantics. A model structure, for example, is a purely set theoretical construction that as such has no obvious connection with modal notions at all; it is just any ordered triple (G, K, R) where K is a set of which G is a member and on which R is a reflexive relation. K could be, for example, a set of chessmen with G the king and R the relation *is at least as large as*. A quantified model structure, again, is just an ordered pair whose first member is a model structure, the second being a function $\psi(W)$ assigning to each member W of K a set of individuals—a set of marbles, for example. Then $\mathcal{U}$ is just the set-theoretical union of the sets assigned to the members of K by $\psi(W)$. If K is the set of prime numbers, for example, and $\psi(W)$ assigns to W the set of integers W exceeds, then $\mathcal{U}$ is the set of integers. To accept the pure semantics, therefore, is not, as such, to acquiesce in any philosophical doctrine at all. The pure semantics commits itself to little more than a fragment of set theory.

But by the same token it is not to the pure semantics as such that we must look for the promised insight into our modal notions—not, at least, if we take the semantics seriously rather than as a heuristic device. The pure semantics does not give us a meaning for '$\Box$', or tell us under what condition a proposition is necessarily true, or what it is for an object to have a property essentially. Instead, it simply defines 'is a valid formula' for each of the systems treated. It tells us that a formula A—

(5) $(\exists x)\Box Fx \supset (\exists x)\Box(Fx \vee Gx)$,

for example—is valid in a given system S_i if and only if $V(A, W) = T$ in every S_i quantificational model on a quantificational model structure. So the pure semantics as such provides a meaning for 'is a valid formula of (e.g.) S_5'; it does not, as such, assign a meaning to '$\Box$'. Nor does the pure semantics tell us what a sentence like

(6) $(Ex)\Box x$ is a person

might mean.

Logicians commonly distinguish between pure and *depraved* or (less censoriously) *applied* semantics; to get a meaning for such sentences as (6) (as well as for '$\Box$' itself) we must turn to an appropriate applied semantics. An important difference between a pure and an applied semantics is that the latter places more conditions upon the notion of modelhood.

Intuitively [says Kripke] we look at matters thus: K is the set of all 'possible worlds'; G is the 'real world'. If H_1 and H_2 are two worlds, $H_1 R H_2$ means intuitively that H_2 is 'possible relative to' H_1; i.e., that every proposition *true* in H_2 is possible in H_1 . . .'

Intuitively $\psi(H)$ is the set of all individuals existing in H. Notice, of course, that $\psi(H)$ need not be the same set for different arguments H, just as, intuitively, in worlds other than the real one, some actually existing individuals may be absent, while new individuals, like Pegasus, may appear.[1]

These remarks are really hints as to the intended or associated applied semantics. In the intended applied semantics, therefore, a model structure will not be just *any* triple (G, K, R) where G is a member of K, and R is reflexive; K will be a set of possible worlds (not chessmen)—possible states of affairs of a certain kind —of which G is a member. And $\psi(W)$ will not assign just any domain of objects to a member W of K; it will assign to it the set of objects existing in W; the set of objects, that is, that would have existed had W be actual. We are to suppose, still further, that the members of $\mathcal{U}$ (i.e. the union of the domains of the possible worlds) *have properties* in these various worlds or, alternatively, are such that various predicates are *true of* them with respect to these worlds, it being entirely proper for the same individual to have different properties in different worlds. Then to endorse (5) is to say, perhaps among other things, that any substitution instance of it is true in every possible world—i.e., would have been true no matter what possible world had obtained. And we also get a meaning for

(6) $(\mathrm{E}x) \square x$ is a person;

what this now tells us is that in the actual world there exists an object that in every world has the property of being a person. And of course if we look at a semantics of this kind as a sober and literal account of modality—one whose talk of possible works and all the rest is to be taken seriously—then what is crucial is the applied, not the pure, semantics.

5. *Applied Semantics and Possible Objects*

Now how do possible but unactual objects enter the picture? As follows. In the pure semantics we have for each member H

---

[1] Op. cit., pp. 64–5.

of K the set $\psi(H)$; "intuitively", says Kripke, "$\psi(H)$ is the set of all individuals existing in H". In the associated applied semantics, then, $\psi(H)$, for a given world H, will be the set of objects existing in H. (And for the moment let us put to one side questions about the cardinality of $\psi(H)$—$\psi(\alpha)$, for example —as well as scruples about the sense of such locutions as 'the set of all individuals existing in a possible world H'.) In the pure semantics, furthermore, we have associated with each model structure the set $\mathcal{U}$—the union of $\psi(H)$ for each H in K. So presumably in the intended applied semantics we shall have the set of all those objects that exist in any possible world (or perhaps any world possible with respect to the actual world). And it is natural to think that among the members of $\mathcal{U}$ there will be some things that do not in fact exist. In "Semantical Considerations on Modal Logic" Kripke does not shrink from this conclusion:

Intuitively $\psi(H)$ is the set of all individuals existing in H. Notice, of course, that $\psi(H)$ need not be the same set for different arguments H, just as, intuitively, in worlds other than the real one, some actually existing individuals may be absent, while new individuals, like Pegasus, may appear.

And:

. . . are we to assign a truth value to the substitution instance 'Sherlock Holmes is bald'? Holmes does not exist, but in other states of affairs he would have existed.[1]

So it is natural to suppose that $\mathcal{U}$ contains objects that do not exist. But can we say something stronger? Is the applied semantics really committed to the idea that there are some things that do not exist? Perhaps not. As applied semanticists we need not initially insist, of course, that there is no possible

---

[1] p. 65. These quotations do not accurately represent Kripke's present views: "I thus could no longer write, as I once did, that 'Holmes does not exist, but in other states of affairs he would have existed.' . . . The quoted assertion gives the erroneous impression that a fictional name such as 'Holmes' names a particular possible-but-not-actual individual." "Addenda to Saul A. Kripke's paper 'Naming and Necessity'", in *Semantics of Natural Language*, ed. Davidson and Harman (Dordrecht: D. Reidel, 1972), p. 764. He does, however, reaffirm the point of the quoted passage: "The substantive point I was trying to make . . . remains and is independent of any linguistic theory of the status of names in fiction. The point was, that in other possible worlds 'some actually existing individuals may be absent while new individuals . . . may appear'."

world in which every member of $\mathcal{U}$ exists; no corresponding stipulation is made in the pure semantics. Perhaps there are many possible worlds W such that $\psi(W) = \mathcal{U}$. Perhaps α is one of them. On the other hand, there may be good reason to believe that there is no world W such that $\psi(W) = \mathcal{U}$, or at any rate good reason to think that $\psi(\alpha) \neq \mathcal{U}$. Is there an argument from the applied semantics and obvious truths for the conclusion that there are objects that do not exist? Consider the following: it is presumably possible that there be purple cows, though in fact there are none. Now on the semantical scheme

(7) Possibly there are purple cows

is true only if

(8) There is at least one purple cow

is true in some possible world. (8), however, is true in some world only if $\mathcal{U}$ contains an object that in some world W falls within the extension of 'purple cow'—only if, that is, there is a member of $\mathcal{U}$ that in some world W has the property of being a purple cow.

But of course this does now show that $\mathcal{U}$ has a member that does not in fact exist; since, for all we know, any actually existing cow (complete with its dirty black and white Holstein hide) is a purple cow in some other possible world. Indeed, perhaps Bucephalos, Alexander the Great's horse, is a purple cow in some other possible world. So this argument is inconclusive.

Perhaps we can approach the matter as follows. Consider all those things that exist in α and are or could have been persons —all those things, that is, that are possibly persons. (If every nonperson is a nonperson *essentially*, then these things are just all the persons there are.) It is plausible to suppose that there could have been a person distinct from each of these things. But then there is a world W in which there exists a person x that is distinct from each object that exists in α and is possibly a person. Accordingly, x is distinct from each object that exists in α—that is, from each object that exists. So $\mathcal{U}$ contains a member that is distinct from each object that exists; $\mathcal{U}$, therefore, contains possible but nonexistent objects.

To put the matter in terms of the ideas of Chapter V, it is

plausible to suppose that there is at least one uninstantiated essence. But clearly no object that exists in α exemplifies this essence in some other world; for of course every object displays the same essence in each world in which it exists, and no object exemplifies more than one (nonequivalent) essence in any world. This essence is exemplified in *some* world, however, and hence by an object distinct from any object that exists. $\mathcal{U}$ therefore contains a member that exemplifies this essence in some world or other, but does not in fact exist. So $\mathcal{U}$ contains possible but nonexistent objects.

I say it is plausible to suppose that there are uninstantiated essences; it is not easy, however, to show that this plausible supposition is *true*. Hence it is not easy to show that the applied semantics is committed to the idea that there are possible things that do not exist—although, of course, anyone who accepts it and also accepts the view that there could have been an object distinct from each object that does exist, will be so committed. It is obvious, however, that the semantical scheme is at any rate committed to the *possibility* that there are such objects (and no doubt it is fantastically unlikely that α is one of these world W where $\psi(W) = \mathcal{U}$, even if there are any such worlds). For surely any one of us could have failed to exist. So there are possible worlds in which you and I do not exist: these worlds are impoverished, no doubt, but not on that account impossible. There is a possible world W where we do not exist; but then $\psi(W) \neq \mathcal{U}$. So if W had been actual, then $\mathcal{U}$, the set of possible objects, would have had members that did not exist.

6. Are There Nonexistent Objects?

You might think that such objects are no more to be boggled at than possible but unactual worlds or states of affairs. There is an important difference, however. For it is not that possible but unactual worlds do not exist; they exist all right, but they just are not actual. There is such a state of affairs as *Socrates' being a carpenter*; this state of affairs is possible, but does not obtain. This is not to say, however, that it does not *exist* (but could have); what is meant is that it does indeed exist, but happens not to be actual. Here states of affairs resemble propositions. There are possible but false propositions entailing that Socrates was a carpenter. This is not to say that there *could have* existed such propositions although *in fact* no such proposition exists; for the truth is such propositions do exist but are false. So a possible but unactual state of affairs is not a *nonexistent* state of affairs; it exists just as serenely as your most solidly actual state of affairs. But a possible object that does not exist is a horse of a different colour. This is a thing such that there exists no such thing, to paraphrase Meinong—a monumentally perplexing idea. What could such a thing be like? Of course if there are overwhelming or even good reasons for supposing that there are such things, we can do no more than swallow our puzzlement and make the best of it. But *are* there any such reasons? Why should we believe that there are or could have been nonexistent objects?

First an argument—more like an intuitive impression, perhaps—that may be suggested by reflection on the idea of possible worlds. There are properties that are possibly but not actually exemplified. Among them, no doubt, there are some whose complement is essential to every object that exists in α—uninstantiated essences would be examples, as would the property *is distinct from everything that exists in* α. So in other possible worlds there must be objects that exemplify these properties—objects that are distinct from anything that exists in α. And in saying that there are possible but nonexistent objects, we do no more than call attention to these objects.

Suppose we concede the argument's premisses: in some possible world there exist objects distinct from any that exist in α. The studied vagueness of its conclusion may leave us perplexed. Is the claim only that there could have been objects distinct from any that exist in α? This is no doubt so; but it seems excessively dramatic to put this point by saying that there are some possible but nonexistent objects. Is the claim instead to be taken literally as the suggestion that there really are some things that do not exist? Then the concluding step seems totally unwarranted. Indeed there is a possible world *W* where there exists an object that does not exist in this. If *W* had been actual, then there *would have been* an object that does not in fact exist. But why conclude that there *is* an object that does not exist but would have, had *W* been actual? The conclusion seems entirely gratuitous.

7. *The Classical Argument*

Historically the most important argument for possible but non-existent objects goes in a different direction. G. E. Moore puts it as follows:

... the strongest excuse for making a sharp distinction such as Mr. Bradley makes, still seems to me to lie in the fact from which I started—the fact that it seems as if purely imaginary things, even though they be absolutely self contradictory like a round square, must still have some kind of *being*—must still be in a sense—simply because we can think and talk about them. .... And now in saying that there is no such thing as a round square, I seem to imply that there *is* such a thing. It seems as if there must be such a thing, merely in order that it may have the property of not-being. It seems, therefore, that to say of anything whatever that we can mention that it absolutely *is not*, were to contradict ourselves: as if everything we can mention must be, must have some kind of being.[1]

In *Some Main Problems* Moore ultimately rejects this argument; but he takes it with the utmost seriousness: "I am as sure as you can be that there is no such thing as a centaur: that is the side I want to take: I wish to maintain that, in the proper sense of the words, there really *is* no such thing and never has been. But I am not at all sure how to get over the opposing argument" (213).

We have learned at our mother's knee that Meinong offered a similar argument:

Any particular thing that isn't real must at least be capable of serving as the object for those judgments which grasp its unreality. In order to know that there is no round square, I must make a judgment about the round square. .... Those who like paradoxical modes of expression could very well say: 'There are objects of which it is true to say that there are no such objects'.

If I should be able to judge that a certain object is not, then I appear to have had to grasp the object in some way beforehand, in order to say anything about its non-being, or more precisely, in order to affirm or deny the ascription of non-being to the object.[2]

---

[1] *Some Main Problems of Philosophy* (London: George Allen & Unwin, 1953), p. 289.

[2] "The Theory of Objects", in *Realism and the Background of Phenomenology*, ed. R. Chisholm (Glencoe, Illinois: The Free Press, 1960), pp. 82, 84.

But so did Russell: in "On Denoting" he asks "How can a nonentity be the subject of a proposition?" And in *Principles of Mathematics*:

Being is that which belongs to every conceivable term, to every possible object of thought—in short to everything that can possibly occur in any proposition, true or false, and to all such propositions themselves. Being belongs to whatever can be counted. If *A* be any term that can be counted as one, it is plain that *A* is something, and therefore that *A* is. "*A* is not" must always be either false or meaningless. For if *A* were nothing, it could not be said not to be; "*A* is not" implies that there is a term *A* whose being is denied, and hence that *A* is. Thus unless "*A* is not" be an empty sound, it must be false— whatever *A* may be, it certainly is. Numbers, the Homeric gods, relations, chimeras and four-dimensional spaces all have being, for if they were not entities of a kind, we could make no propositions about them. Thus being is a general attribute of everything, and to mention anything is to show that it is.[1]

Arguments such as these have a distinguished company of adherents and a long history going back at least as far as Plato. What is central to them is the belief or intuition that it is impossible to talk or think about what does not in any sense have being or existence. If chimeras and Homeric Gods had no being or reality of any kind whatever, it would be impossible to speak of or refer to them; but we do speak of nonexistents, most poignantly in saying that they do not exist. Such things as chimeras, therefore, must have being of *some* kind, therefore, even if they do not have the good fortune to exist.

Of course these arguments, if successful, seem to show that there are *impossible* nonexistents as well as the more domesticated possible variety. This may give us pause. But suppose we waive that consideration for the moment and look more closely at the argument. It has essentially two premisses:

(9) In asserting negative existential propositions, we talk and think about what does not exist,

and

(10) Anything we can talk and think about must have being of some sort or other.

Now the notion of aboutness is a notoriously frail reed; yet we

[1] p. 449.

do use and understand it, at least to some extent. Let us therefore proceed, keeping its frailty in mind and placing upon it no
more weight than it can easily bear. A popular response to (9)
is to deny that negative existentials are about what does not
exist; it is often held that such a proposition as

(11) Carnivorous cows do not exist[1]

is not really about carnivorous cows at all; instead it is about
the property *carnivorous bovinity* or perhaps the predicate 'carnivorous cow', asserting of the former that nothing has it or of
the latter that it is true of nothing. On this view (11) is less
misleading if put as

(12) There are no carnivorous cows

which perhaps does not offer as much encouragement to suppose that it is about carnivorous cows. And perhaps indeed this
is a plausible response to the argument. Perhaps it is more
natural to look upon (11) in this way than as a proposition
valiantly trying to predicate nonexistence of each carnivorous
cow.

The classical argument gains strength, however, when we
turn to singular propositions, and in particular singular propositions expressed by sentences containing proper names (or
descriptions used referentially) in subject place. Consider
Socrates, for example; he exists in the actual world but not in
every world. That is, there are possible worlds in which Socrates
does not exist. Let W be such a world: had W obtained, then

(13) Socrates does not exist

and

(14) Possibly Socrates exists

would have been true. Had W obtained, therefore,

(15) There is at least one nonexistent possible object

would have been true.

Now this argument will invite suspicion at more than one

---

[1] The example is Richard Cartwright's; see his "Negative Existentials", *The Journal of Philosophy*, LVII, 31 (1960), 629.

point. But at the least it is improperly inexplicit. For if we accept the inference of (15) from (13) and (14), we implicitly endorse

> (16) Any world in which *Socrates exists* is false but possible, is one in which there are possible beings that do not exist.

And when we take a careful look at (16) we may wonder why or whether we should accept it. It is indeed true that if Socrates did not exist, then *Socrates exists* would be false but possible; how can we conclude that if Socrates did not exist, there would have been at least one possible but nonactual object? Well, perhaps as follows. No doubt existence is not an ordinary property; perhaps it does not much resemble such properties as *being red* or *being six feet tall*. Still, it *is* a property of *some* sort. And if it is, then it must have a complement—there must be a property P such that x has P if and only if x does not exist. Now (13) is the false proposition that Socrates has that property; it is a singular proposition that predicates of Socrates the property of nonexistence. (13) is in fact false; but if W had obtained, it would have been true. If W had obtained, Socrates would not have existed; still, there would have been a true proposition that was both about him and predicated a property of him. But how could there be a true proposition about Socrates—in particular one predicating a property of him—in W if, in W, he had no kind of being or ontological status at all? If there is no sense of 'is' such that in that sense it is correct to say of Socrates that in W he *is*, then surely no proposition predicating a property of Socrates could be true in W.

It is easier to patronize this argument than to give a good reason for rejecting it. What is central is the claim that any world in which there is a true proposition about Socrates, a proposition predicating some property of him, is a world in which he must *be* in some fashion or other; there cannot be propositions about what in no sense has being. Call this *The Ontological Principle*. Although this claim is perplexing, it also has a certain attraction that is hard to resist. Let us see if we can state this principle and with it the classical argument a bit more precisely. Let us say, provisionally, that a *singular* proposition is one that is about some specific object—its subject—and either predicates or denies some property of that object. No doubt this characterization is in the long run deficient in several respects; it may still serve our present purposes. Thus

(17) Royal Robbins is America's most distinguished rockclimber

and

(18) Royal Robbins is not America's most distinguished rock-climber

are singular propositions. Royal Robbins is the subject of both, and the first predicates of him a certain property—*being America's most distinguished rockclimber*—that the second denies of him. Now the classical argument has three essential premisses:

(19) Such negative existentials as *Socrates does not exist* are singular propositions,

(20) Many singular negative existentials are possibly true

and

(21) Any world in which a singular proposition is true, is one in which *there is* such a thing as its subject, or one in which its subject has either existence or being.

(21), of course, is the Ontological Principle; and from (19) and (21) it obviously follows that

(22) Any world in which a singular negative existential is true, is one in which there is an object that does not exist

which together with (20) entails that there are or could have been some individuals that do not exist.

8. *Proper Names and Negative Existentials: Russell*

Now the classical argument presumes that both existence and nonexistence are properties. Of course many arguments have been deployed for the conclusion that neither of these is in fact a property; most of these arguments, however, are at best inconclusive.[1] At best what they show is that existence, if a property, is in many ways atypical, a conclusion in which the advocate of our argument can rest with equanimity. Of course the argument also presumes that assertions like *Socrates exists* and

---

[1] See my *God and Other Minds* (Cornell University Press, 1967), Chapter II.

Socrates does not exist are singular propositions predicating a property of Socrates. Many have denied that a sentence like

(23) Socrates exists

expresses a singular proposition—one that is about Socrates and predicates existence of him. According to Russell, for example, what are ordinarily called proper names serve as abbreviations for definite descriptions.[1] So, for example, 'Socrates' is short for something like 'the Greek philosopher who drank hemlock' or 'the teacher of Plato' or some more complicated description. On this view (23) is more explicitly put as something like

(24) The Greek philosopher who drank hemlock exists

which under Russell's analysis of definite descriptions expresses not a singular but a general proposition: something like

(25) There exists just one Greek philosopher who drank hemlock.

(25) is no more about Socrates than (12) is about carnivorous cows; and of course

(13) Socrates does not exist

is similarly not about Socrates.

This view of proper names, however, suffers from at least one annoying defect: it is clearly false. There is no description of the appropriate sort that is synonymous with 'Socrates'. Certainly such items as 'the teacher of Plato' and 'the Philosopher who drank hemlock' are not; for neither

(26) Socrates never drank hemlock

nor

(27) Socrates never taught Plato

express necessarily false propositions, as they would if 'Socrates' were synonymous with one of these descriptions. (Perhaps *some* descriptions are synonymous with proper names—perhaps, for example, 'the person identical with Socrates' is synonymous with 'Socrates'; but of course this is of no use to Russell's view.) Russell's view of proper names, therefore, gives us no good reason for supposing that 'Socrates does not exist' does not express a singular proposition.

---

[1] "The Philosophy of Logical Atomism", in *Logic and Knowledge*, ed. Robert Marsh (London: George Allen & Unwin Ltd., 1956), p. 175. According to Russell, of course, what are ordinarily called proper names are not proper names at all.

9. *Proper Names and Negative Existentials: Searle*

John Searle offers a subtler argument for the same conclusion. He begins by pointing out that there are 'criteria of identification' associated with the use of a proper name such as 'Aristotle':

> Though proper names do not normally assert or specify any characteristics, their referring uses nonetheless presuppose that the object to which they purport to refer has certain characteristics. But which ones? Suppose we ask the users of the name "Aristotle" to state what they regard as certain essential and established facts about him. Their answers would be a set of uniquely referring descriptive statements. Now what I am arguing is that the descriptive force of "This is Aristotle" is to assert that a sufficient but so far unspecified number of these statements are true of this object. Therefore, referring uses of "Aristotle" presuppose the existence of an object of whom a sufficient but so far unspecified number of these statements are true. To use a proper name referringly is to presuppose the truth of certain uniquely referring descriptive statements, but it is not ordinarily to assert these statements or even to indicate which exactly are presupposed.[1]

So there are what we might call 'identity criteria' associated with a name such as 'Aristotle' or 'Socrates'; these are what the users of the name regard as essential and established facts about him. Suppose we take these criteria to be properties of Socrates rather than facts about him. Then among them we should certainly find such properties as *having been born about 470 B.C., having married Xantippe, being a Greek Philosopher, being the teacher of Plato, having been executed by the Athenians on a charge of corrupting the youth,* and the like.

Searle goes on to make an interesting claim about these properties:

> Suppose most or even all of our present factual knowledge of Aristotle proved to be true of no one at all, or of several people living in scattered countries and in different centuries. Would we not say for this reason that Aristotle did not exist after all, and that the name, though it has a conventional sense, refers to no one at all? (p. 168)

A bit further on:

> We are now in a position to explain how it is that 'Aristotle' has

[1] "Proper Names", *Mind*, 67 (1958), 171. See also Searle's *Speech Acts* (Cambridge: Cambridge University Press, 1969), p. 169.

a reference but does not describe, and that the statement 'Aristotle never existed' says more than that 'Aristotle' was never used to refer to any object. The statement asserts that a sufficient number of the conventional presuppositions of referring uses of 'Aristotle' are false.

And in *Speech Acts*:

How is it possible that a proper name can occur in an existential statement? A statement such as 'Aristotle never existed' states that a sufficient, but so far unspecified, number of the descriptive backing of 'Aristotle' are false. (p. 169)

We may put Searle's point as follows: If S_1, S_2, ..., S_n are the criteria of identification for 'Socrates' then the statement

(13) Socrates did not exist

with its variants is the assertion that no one person had a sufficient number of the S_i.

There are problems here: can the same use of the name have different criterial sets associated with it, for example, by different people? Suppose all I know about Melchizedek is that he was the mysterious "priest of the most high God" whose meeting with Abraham is described in Genesis 14. Then on Searle's account, the sentence

(28) Melchizedek was not a high priest and neither met Abraham nor was mentioned in Genesis,

as *I* use it, would express a necessarily false proposition. But no doubt Melchizedek's wife associated quite a different set of identifying descriptions with his name; and no doubt (28) (or its Hebrew equivalent) expressed a contingent proposition as she used it. Does this matter? And even on my use of 'Melchizedek' it scarcely seems that (28) expresses a *necessarily* false proposition. Surely there is at most falsehood, not necessary falsehood, in the idea that Melchizedek only pretended to be a high priest, met Isaac rather than Abraham, and was never mentioned in Genesis. What is presently interesting, however, is this: if Searle is right, then (13) is not a singular statement that predicates a property of Socrates, but a general statement to the effect that no person has enough of S_1–S_n. And, similarly, of course,

(23) Socrates exists

and its variants do not predicate of Socrates the dubious property of existing; instead they assert that some object does (or did) have enough of the S_i.

Now the negative aspect of Searle's thesis seems at least partly right. When a person seriously asks whether King Arthur, say, or Melchizedek really existed, he does not seem to be referring to a specific person and asking whether that person existed. Suppose a pair of classicists have a dispute as to whether or not Homer existed; it would be incorrect, I think, to represent them as referring to the same person—namely Homer—and disagreeing as to whether that person had the property of existing. The one who takes the affirmative, I think, is not singling out or specifying a person by his use of the name 'Homer' and then predicating existence of him; his opponent is not using that name to specify a person of whom he then goes on to predicate nonexistence. Take another example. You and I might disagree as to whether Leigh Ortenburger (author of *The Climber's Guide to the Tetons*) ever did a 5·9 route in Yosemite; here we should no doubt be specifically referring to a person—Leigh Ortenburger—and disagreeing about his possession of a certain property. We are then talking about this person and predicating or denying a propery of him. Suppose, however, that you come to doubt the existence of Ortenburger. How, you say, could any one man know as much about the Tetons as the *Climber's Guide* contains? You come to believe that the Stanford mathematics department collaborated on the *Guide*—and that, inspired by the example of Bourbaki, they invented Ortenburger out of whole cloth, playfully ascribing the *Climber's Guide* to him. When you then say 'Leigh Ortenburger does not exist' you neither refer nor purport to refer to Ortenburger; and you do not predicate nonexistence of him or of anything else. You are doing something altogether different.

But what, exactly? Suppose I came to believe that Socrates never existed; just what would I be believing? Not that the man Socrates—the man who was born in *c*. 470 B.C., who taught Plato, was executed by the Athenians, etc.—had the property of nonexistence. But what then? According to Searle, I would believe that no single person had enough of the S_i. This is plausible, but perhaps not quite right. For first of all

(29) Socrates existed but had none (or nearly none) of the S_i

is a consistent proposition. The S_i, we recall, are the properties we use to identify Socrates. They are the properties we mention in answer to the question 'Who was Socrates?' But a historian could coherently claim to discover that Socrates existed, all right, but lacked most of the S_i. He could coherently hold that Socrates was born a year earlier than we thought, that he died a year later, that he was not executed but actually committed suicide by drinking not hemlock but some other poison, that his friends (for reasons best known to themselves) conspired to make it appear that the Athenians had executed him, that he actually had little aptitude for philosophy but was vastly idealized by Plato, who as a young man had borrowed sizeable sums from him.[1] Of course there are limits here; our historian could not coherently claim to discover *just anything* along these lines. For example, he could not coherently hold that Socrates was really a horse belonging to Alcibiades, or an illiterate eighteenth-century Irish washerwoman, or a bellboy at a large New York hotel. And this is so even if there is a world in which Socrates *is* a New York bellboy—even if, that is, the property of *not* being such a bellboy is not essential to Socrates.

We should note, by the way, that the isue here is *not* whether the disjunction of the S_i is essential to Socrates. Even if Searle were right in holding (29) to be inconsistent, this latter would not follow. For (29) is equivalent, on Searle's view, to something like

(30) The person that had most of the S_i had nearly none of the S_i;

and the inconsistency of this does not entail that the man who had the S_i had their disjunction essentially. To suppose otherwise is to confuse the *de dicto*

(31) It is necessarily false that the man who had most of the S_i, lacked most of them

with the *de re*

(32) The man who had most of the S_i could not have lacked most of them.

(31) is obviously true; but (32) does not follow.

---

[1] See "World and Essence", pp. 472–3.

To return to the argument: it looks as if (29) is consistent. Indeed,

(33) Socrates unfortunately met with a fatal accident at the age of six months, thus lacking nearly all of the S_i

is clearly consistent and entails (29). So the latter is consistent. If so, however, then the same goes for its conjunction with

(34) No one other than Socrates had enough of the S_i.

This conjunction entails

(35) Socrates existed but no one had enough of the S_i

which accordingly is also consistent. But then 'Socrates did not exist', contrary to Searle, does not express the same proposition as 'no one had enough of the S_i'.

10. *Proper Names and Negative Existentials: the Historical Chain View*

How then are we to understand such negative existentials as

(13) Socrates does not exist?

Kripke and Donnellan suggest that the reference of a proper name is determined not by some description or descriptive backing the user is prepared to offer in its stead, but by a sort of historical chain extending from the use in question to the person so named. As Kripke puts it:

A rough statement of a theory might be the following: an initial baptism takes place. Here the object may be named by ostension, or the reference may be fixed by description. When the name is 'passed from link to link' the receiver of the name must, I think, intend when he learns it to use it with the same reference as the man from whom he heard it.[1]

And according to Donnellan:

The main idea is that when a speaker uses a name intending to refer to an individual and predicate something of it, successful reference will occur when there is an individual that enters into the historically correct explanation of who it is that the speaker intended to predicate something of. That individual will then be the referent

[1] "Naming and Necessity", in *Semantics of Natural Language,* ed. Davidson and Harman (Dordrecht: D. Reidel, 1972), p. 302.

and the statement made will be true or false depending upon whether it has the property designated by the predicate.[1]

There are differences here between Kripke's and Donnellan's version; and neither is worked out in great detail. Still, this idea has the ring of plausibility. Certainly its negative aspect seems right; proper names are not in general related to descriptions in the Russell–Frege–Searle fashion. And our present question is this: if we take this view, how shall we understand a negative existential such as (13)?

No doubt we could go in various directions. One possibility (suggested but not endorsed by Donnellan's paper) is to take (13) as equivalent to some statement about the historical vicissitudes of the appropriate use or uses of the appropriate name. In seriously asserting (13), on this view, perhaps I assert a proposition to the effect that my use of 'Socrates' (or one of my uses of it, since I may use this name to name several persons) does not trace back to any person. Or perhaps I say that there is no historical chain of the appropriate sort terminating in this use; the details of the view do not matter at present. In any event, on this Donnellan-like approach, as on Searle's and Russell's, a serious utterance of such an item as (13) does not normally express a singular proposition predicating non-existence of Socrates. And here these views, I believe, are correct.

11. *Some Varieties of Singular Existentials*

But now we encounter a point of first importance. For although such sentences do not *normally* express singular propositions when taken *alone*, they *are* used to do so in other contexts. Perhaps we can see this as follows. On the Donnellan-like view, a sentence such as

(13) Socrates does not exist

normally expresses a proposition detailing some facet of the historical career of the name 'Socrates', or the provenance of someone's use of that name. If so, then its denial

(23) Socrates exists

[1] "Reference and Nonexistence", unpublished.

also expresses some proposition about that name. But clearly enough it is also true that Socrates could have existed, no matter what the history of anyone's use of 'Socrates' was; for he could have had another name or no name at all. There is a possible world W in which Socrates exists and in which our use of 'Socrates' has just the history that on the Donnellan-like view makes (23) false and (13) true. (Similarly there is a possible world W* in which Socrates does not exist and where our use of 'Socrates' has the sort of history that on this view makes (23) true and (13) false.) When we say, therefore, that *Socrates exists* is true in W but false in $W*$ we are not using 'Socrates exists' to express a proposition whose truth or falsity depends upon historical facts about the name 'Socrates'. Here the proposition in question is a *singular* proposition whose subject is Socrates— a proposition about Socrates that predicates existence of him.

Again, this singular existential proposition is probably not the one we would be most likely to assert in uttering (23). It is probably not the proposition a historian would assert to express his view that there really was such a person as Socrates, that he was not a fictional character created by Plato. It is none the less a perfectly good proposition. And, as we have seen, it figures in other propositions that *are* seriously asserted. So, for example, we may plausibly hold that

(36) Every world in which Socrates teaches Plato, is one in which Socrates exists.

(36), clearly enough, is not equivalent to

(37) Every world in which Socrates teaches Plato is one in which 'Socrates' has the right kind of history.

In (36), 'Socrates exists' serves to express that singular existential proposition whose subject is Socrates, as it does in

(38) *Socrates teaches Plato* entails *Socrates exists*.

Further: Even if there is something peculiar or Pickwickian about asserting these singular existentials, they *can* be asserted. Bemused by Cartesian meditations, Peter might say 'Peter really exists'. If he did, he would be making a comment neither about the history of his use of his name nor about the identity criteria he or someone else associates with it. He would be asserting a singular proposition whose subject was himself; he would be talking about himself and predicating existence of himself. A man might point to the Taj Mahal and say: "The Taj Mahal exists", thereby asserting a singular proposition. If he did, he would be right, although his assertion might be pointless or foolish. He might add, furthermore, "The Taj Mahal might not have existed".[1] In so doing he would not be making a comment about the possible vicissitudes of the name 'The Taj Mahal' nor pointing out that a set of identity criteria need not have been satisfied. He would instead be talking about the Taj Mahal itself—not its name or identity criteria—and quite properly claiming that there are worlds in which that thing does not have the property of existing.

So

(23) Socrates exists

can be used to express two quite different kinds of propositions. One of these—the one a historian would seriously assert—is perhaps properly accounted for by some combination of the Searle- and Donnellan-like views.[2] The other, however, is a singular proposition predicating of Socrates the property of existence. Suppose we call this latter (23*). The contrast between (23) and (23*) is mirrored by that between

(13) Socrates does not exist

(taken non-singularly) and (13*), which we could put as

(13*) Socrates does not have the property of existing.

This latter is the contradictory of (23*) and is a singular proposition. Once more, a historian who uttered the sentence (13) would doubtless not be asserting (13*); he would not be referring to Socrates and holding that the latter did not have the property of existence. Indeed, neither a historian nor anyone else could coherently claim to *discover* (13*). The reason is that if it were true, no one—no human being, anyway—could be

---

[1] See G. E. Moore, "Is Existence a Predicate?", in *Proceedings of the Aristotelian Society*, Supplementary Volume XV, 1936, pp. 175–88.

[2] The non-singular proposition expressed by (23) can also turn up in conditionals. You and I are discussing Pegasus. Agreeing that no such creature exists, you say "But I know that if he *did* exist, he would have wings". Here the antecedent does not express a singular proposition whose subject is Pegasus; it is instead to be understood in something like the Searle- or Donnellan-like way. It is interesting to note, by the way, that it is not the singular propositions expressed by (13) and (23) that are elusive and problematic—it is the *other* ones!

sufficiently acquainted or *en rapport* with this proposition to consider, entertain, believe, doubt, or deny it. Suppose Socrates had not existed: no doubt the rest of us would have been impoverished. This impoverishment, however, is one of which we would have been totally unaware; for we would have been unable so much as to consider or entertain the singular proposition *Socrates does not exist*. Such a proposition has a peculiar epistemological status: if it had been true we could not have discovered or believed it; its falsehood is a necessary condition of our being able to consider, entertain, be aware of, believe, or doubt it.

But if it is impossible that it be discovered, does it not follow that it is necessarily false? No. There are many contingent propositions that share this status with (13*). It is possible that you and I do not exist; still we should scarcely hope to be able to discover such a thing. There are worlds in which no discoveries are made; in none of them is that fact discovered. The falsehood of *I have never entertained a proposition* is a necessary condition of my entertaining it; yet this proposition is not necessarily false. Still another example: according to the Augustinian version of the *Cogito*, a necessary condition of my doubting my own existence is the truth of what I doubt. So we might say that

(39) I do not exist

is *pragmatically inconsistent* for me: although it is *contingently* false, its falsity is a necessary condition of my affirming, denying, or considering it. But the same really goes for (13*). This too I could believe or entertain only if it were false.

So if Socrates had not existed, we should have been unable to believe or assert that fact. Of course we do sometimes assert negative existentials and sometimes we are right. What we assert, therefore (at least on those occasions) are not singular negative existentials. Perhaps this together with the peculiarity mentioned in the last paragraph is what has led philosophers— Russell, for example—to overlook singular negative existentials, or to deny their existence, or to suppose that there is a confusion involved in recognizing and accepting them. But this is a great mistake. It is indeed a fact that *if* (13*) had been true, we should have been unable to assert or even consider it. But of course it is *false*; Socrates *does* exist; and so we have no trouble whatever in entertaining or considering (13*). We can also consider possible worlds in which it is true and assert conditionals in which it functions as antecedent or consequent. For example, if no persons had existed, then Socrates would not have existed. And if Socrates had not existed, then at least one essence which *is* instantiated would not have been. Furthermore, any world in which Socrates does not exist is one in which he did not teach Plato. If Socrates had not existed, Plato would not have been his student, the Athenians would not have executed him, Plato would not have recounted his views in the *Dialogues*, and histories of philosophy would contain no references to him. And in all of these propositions what is involved is (13*), not (13). So there is such a thing as a singular negative existential proposition; and so far the Classical Argument has emerged unscathed.

VIII

POSSIBLE BUT UNACTUAL OBJECTS: ON WHAT THERE ISN'T

1. *Predicative and Impredicative Singular Propositions*

OUR subject has been the venerable contention that there are or could be possible objects that do not exist—more specifically, the Classical Argument for that claim. This argument, you recall, had three essential premises:

(1) There are some singular negative existential propositions,

(2) Some singular negative existentials are possibly true,

and

(3) Any world in which a singular proposition is true, is one in which *there is* such a thing as its subject, or in which its subject has being if not existence.

In Chapter VII we examined objections to (1); we have found them wanting. Among the things there are we do indeed find such singular existential propositions as

(23*) Socrates exists

i.e. Socrates has the property of existing; and such singular negative existentials as

(13*) Socrates does not have the property of existing.

Furthermore, some of these singular negative existentials are indeed possible. So if we accept the Ontological Principle (above, Chapter VII, Section 7) we seem to find the original argument intact. We seem committed to the supposition that there are or could have been possible but nonexistent objects.

But now suppose we take a closer look at singular propositions and the Ontological Principle. The former, we recall, come in two varieties: those that *predicate* a property of their subject, and those that *deny* a property of it. We may call them respectively *predicative* and *impredicative* singular propositions.

(4) Socrates was snubnosed,

for example, is a predicative singular proposition. What would be an example of an impredicative singular proposition?

(5) Socrates was not snubnosed,

we say, pleased with our alacrity. But the sentence (5) is ambiguous; it may express either

(5′) Socrates was nonsnubnosed

which is really a predicative singular proposition, or

(5″) It is false that Socrates was snubnosed

which is properly impredicative. There is a *de re–de dicto* difference here; (5′) predicates of Socrates the property of being nonsnubnosed, while (5″) predicates of (4) the property of being false.

Now the Ontological Principle does have a certain attractiveness and plausibility. But (as presently stated, anyway) it exploits our tendency to overlook the difference between (5′) and (5″). Its plausibility, I suggest, has to do with *predicative* rather than impredicative singular propositions; with propositions like (5′) rather than ones like (5″). It *is* plausible to say that

(6) Any world in which a *predicative* singular proposition is true, is one in which the subject of that proposition has being or existence.

Call this *The Restricted Ontological Principle*. Not only is this plausible; I think it is true. For any world in which there is a true predicative singular proposition whose subject is Socrates, let us say, is a world in which Socrates has some property or other. If such a world had been actual, Socrates would have had some property. And how could he have had a property if there simply were no such thing as Socrates at all? So (6) is true. But if we fail to note the distinction between

(5′) Socrates was nonsnubnosed

and

(5″) It is false that Socrates was snubnosed

we may inadvertently credit the Ontological Principle with a plausibility that properly belongs to the Restricted Ontological Principle alone. For if we fail to note that a proposition *denying* a property P of Socrates need not predicate its complement of him, we easily fall into the error of supposing that the contradictories of predicative propositions are themselves predicative. And in the presence of this error the Restricted and unrestricted Ontological Principles are equivalent. Feeling the legitimate tug of the former, we seem obliged to assert the latter, which together with the truths (1) and (2) entails that there are or could have been things that do not exist.

But once we recognize the distinction between predicative and impredicative singular propositions, we can give the Restricted Ontological Principle its due without endorsing the Classical Argument. For this distinction applies of course to singular existentials as well as to other singular propositions. We must distinguish the impredicative

(13*) Socrates does not have the property of existing

better put, perhaps, as

(13*) It is false that Socrates has the property of existing

from the predicative

(13**) Socrates has the property of nonexistence.

(13*) is the contradictory of (23*) and is true in just those worlds where the latter is false. We need not conclude, however, that (13**) is true in those or any other worlds; and in fact, I suggest, this proposition is true in no possible worlds whatever. If there *were* a world in which (13**) *is* true, then certainly in that world Socrates would be but not exist. But the fact is there are no such worlds. (13**) is necessarily false; and Socrates is essentially existent.

2. *The Classical Argument Fails*

The sentence 'Socrates does not exist', therefore, can be used to express three quite different propositions: (13), the proposition, whatever exactly it is, that a historian might claim to discover; (13*), the impredicative singular proposition; and (13**), a necessarily false proposition predicating of Socrates the property of nonexistence. Accordingly, the proper response to the Classical Argument is this. Indeed some singular negative existentials are possibly true: those that are impredicative. But once we have the distinction between predicative and impredicative singular propositions clear, we see that it is the Restricted Ontological Principle, not its unrestricted colleague, that is intuitively plausible. Given this principle and the possible truth of impredicative singular negative existentials, however, it does not follow that there are or could have been things that do not exist.

A firm grasp on the distinction between predicative and impredicative singular propositions enables us to clear up a residual anomaly attaching to (6). That principle affirms that a world in which a singular predicative proposition is true, is one in which its subject either exists or *has being*; but now we see that this second disjunct is as pointless as it is puzzling. The truth of the matter is

(7) Any world in which a singular predicative proposition is true, is one in which its subject *exists*.

Failing to note the distinction between predicative and impredicative singular propositions (and consequently assuming them all predicative) we may reason that (7) must be false as follows: clearly there are worlds where singular negative existentials are true; but by hypothesis their subjects do not *exist* in those worlds; so (7) must be false. But now we see the error of our ways: although some singular negative existentials are possibly true, none of these are predicative. So this implausible notion of being or thereisness is uncalled for; and there remains no obstacle to accepting (7)—which, after all, is both the source of the attractiveness of the Ontological Principle and the truth in it.

Accordingly, singular propositions like

(8) Socrates is wise

and

(9) Socrates is unwise

are true only in worlds where their subject exists. (8) and (9) are not true where Socrates does not exist, where Socrateity is not exemplified. If W is a world where Socrates does not exist, both (8) and (9) are false in W and their impredicative denials are both true. In worlds where he does not exist, Socrates has no properties at all, not even that of nonexistence.[1]

---

[1] And this redeems a promissory note issued in Chapter IV, Section 8.

3. *Creatures of Fiction*

But now we must recognize a consideration that has been clamouring for attention all along. Statements like

(10) Hamlet was unmarried

and

(11) Lear had three daughters

are obviously, we shall be told, true singular statements about Hamlet and Lear. Hence Hamlet and Lear must be objects of some kind or other and must have being of some kind or other. Now Hamlet and Lear do not in fact exist; but clearly they could have. So there must be possible worlds in which Lear and Hamlet exist; hence they are possible but unactual objects; hence there are some.

Essential to this argument is the idea that when we say 'Hamlet was unmarried' we are talking about an object named 'Hamlet' and describing it by predicating of it a property it actually has—the idea that such statements as (10) and (11) are indeed singular statements about objects named 'Hamlet' and 'Lear'. Call this 'the Descriptivist Premiss'; and suppose we examine it. Stories (taken broadly) are to be thought of as descriptions of something or other; they consist in true assertions about objects of a certain sort. Ophelia was indeed Hamlet's girl friend, just as the play has it; and when we make this assertion we are predicating that property of an object that does not exist but could have.

There are initially at least three objections to this account— three peculiar and interesting facts about fiction that the view in question does not easily accommodate. First of all, both 'Lear exists' and 'Lear does not exist' express true propositions. Although Lear does not *really* exist, he does exist *in the play*—just as certainly as he has three daughters in the play. In this regard, his status differs from that of the Grand Inquisitor in the *Brothers Karamazov*; the latter is only a character in Ivan's parable and exists neither in reality nor in the novel. On the Descriptivist Account it is easy to see that Lear does not exist; after all he is a nonexistent possible object. But how then shall we contrast his status with that of the Grand Inquisitor? Shall we say that the latter is a merely possible possible object?

Secondly, sentences such as

(12) Santa Claus wears a size ten shoe

seem to have a peculiar status. The myths and legends say nothing about the size of Santa's feet. It seems wrong, however, to say that we just do not happen to *know* whether (12) is true or false; there seems nothing *to* know here. But on the descriptivist view presumably Santa Claus (who clearly has feet) does have either a size ten foot or else a foot of some other size.

Thirdly, such statements as (10) and (11) are presumably *contingent* on the Descriptivist View. In fact Lear had just three daughters, but no doubt in other possible worlds he has maybe one son and three daughters. Now how did Shakespeare know just how many children to give him? If it is only a contingent truth that he has just three daughters, then is it not quite possible that Shakespeare made a mistake? Perhaps he had only two daughters, Goneril being the fruit of an illicit liaison between Lear's wife and Gloucester. Perhaps Shakespeare, in ignorance of this, made a simple factual mistake. Or perhaps Shakespeare was unaware of the fact that Lear once took a trip through the Low Countries, was enamoured of a Frisian milk-maid, and became the progenitor of a long line of Calvinist clergymen.

But of course these suppositions are absurd. *You and I* can get Lear's properties wrong; not having read the play recently I may perhaps think that he had just one daughter; but Shakespeare could not have made that sort of mistake in creating the play. Still, does the Descriptivist View not imply that he could? If Shakespeare, in writing his play, is *describing* something, it would certainly seem plausible to suppose that he could *misdescribe* it, get its properties wrong. And how can the descriptivist view accommodate this fact?

Another difficulty has been emphasized by David Kaplan. According to Descriptivism, (10) and (11) express singular predicative propositions about Hamlet and Lear. If so, then 'Lear' in (11) must be functioning as a proper name—a name of a possible but unactual object. But how could it be? On the Searlean view of proper names, one who thus uses 'Lear' must be able to produce an *identifying description* of what he uses it to name. And how could he do that? He starts as follows: Lear is the possible individual who has the properties $P_1, P_2, ... P_n$. But why does he suppose that there is just *one* possible individual with the P_i? If there are *any* possible objects that have the P_i there will be as many as you please. For take any property $P_n + 1$ such that $P_n + 1$ and its complement are both consistent with the P_i; there will be a possible object that has the P_i and also $P_n + 1$, and another with the P_i and the complement of $P_n + 1$. So how can he single out any one possible but unactual object? A similar fate awaits this view on the historical chain account of names. For the latter requires that a name originate in some kind of dubbing or baptism, broadly conceived. But this means that some person or persons were able to specify or identify the dubbee—perhaps ostensively, perhaps by description. And how could this be done? Clearly no possible but non-existent individual was dubbed 'Lear' by someone who had it in full view and solemnly (or frivolously) intoned "I dub thee 'Lear'". So it must have been by description. But then we are back to the previous problem: what was the description and what reason is there for thinking there is just *one* possible individual meeting it? As Kaplan says,

I fear that those who would so speak have adopted a form of dubbing which corresponds to the logician's existential instantiation: There is at least one cow in yonder barn. Let's call one of them 'Bossie'. Now, how much do you think she weighs? I am skeptical of such dubbings. The logician is very careful in *his* use of such names.[1]

Still the Descriptivist is perhaps not entirely without reply. Suppose we try to develop his reply, as much, perhaps, in the spirit of playful exercise as in that of sober inquiry. No doubt we cannot name just *one* possible object, just as it is not possible (without further ado) to name just one of the cows in Kaplan's barn. But perhaps we need not name things one at a time. Perhaps we can name *all* the cows in the barn at one fell swoop —we could name them all 'Bossie'. If we felt so inclined, we could name every lion in Africa 'Frazier'. No doubt this would be a pointless procedure; still, it could be done. Now why cannot the friend of possibles do the same? He thinks there are many possible objects with the properties Shakespeare attributes to

[1] "Bob and Carol and Ted and Alice", forthcoming in *Approaches to Natural Language*, ed. J. Hintikka (Dordrecht: D. Reidel).

Lear. Why not suppose that when Shakespeare writes his play, he engages in a peculiar kind of dubbing? Perhaps in telling this story Shakespeare is naming every possible object that fits the specifications of the play; he is naming them all 'Lear'.

But here we meet a couple of complications. First, consider these possible objects he is naming 'Lear'. *Where* do they have the relevant properties? According to Descriptivism, the answer is in α, the actual world. But there are reasons for doubt; a wiser answer would be that these are the things that have those properties *in some world or other*. For first, a story may imply that one of its characters is unique. Suppose Frederick Manfred (formerly Feike Feikema) writes a story about someone described as the meanest man in North Dakota. Presumably the friend of possibles will not wish to commit himself to the claim that there is a possible man in North Dakota that has the property of being meaner than any other man—actual or possible—in North Dakota. He may prefer to hold that for any degree of meanness you pick, there is a possible North Dakotan meaner than that. And even if there is a maximal degree of North Dakotan mean-ness—one such that it is not possible to be both meaner and in North Dakota—it is at best extremely unlikely that Manfred's hero displays it. On the other hand, there are (on this view) any number of possible objects and worlds such that the former have in the latter the property of being the meanest man in North Dakota. Secondly, a story may detail certain relationships between its characters and actual objects. In H. G. Wells's *War of the Worlds* the Martians destroy New York City sometime during the first half of the twentieth century. But the fact is New York was not destroyed during that period. Not in α, that is; but in plenty of other possible worlds. So Wells's story must be about creatures that destroy New York City in some world distinct from α. Thirdly, we have already seen that some fictional characters are presented as really existing—Ivan, for example, as opposed to the Grand Inquisitor. But Ivan does not exist in α; so the story describes him as he is in some other possible world.

A second complication: Hamlet is not the only character in *Hamlet*; there are also Ophelia, Rosencrantz, Polonius, and all the rest. So in writing the play Shakespeare is not confined to naming things 'Hamlet'. He also dubs things 'Rosencrantz',

'Guildenstern', 'Polonius', and the like. (Indeed, perhaps he is naming some object both 'Rosencrantz' and 'Guildenstern'; for perhaps there is a possible object x and worlds W and W^* such that x has the properties the play ascribes to Rosencrantz in W and those of Guildenstern in W^*.) The play determines a complex n-place relation (n fixed by the number of its characters); and where R is this relation, the playwright gives the name 'Hamlet' to each possible object x_1 for which there are $n-1$ possible objects $x_2, ..., x_n$ such that there is a possible world in which $x_1, x_2, ..., x_n$ stand in R.

So on this neo-Descriptivist view sentences like

(10) Hamlet was unmarried

and

(11) Lear had three daughters

express singular propositions. Indeed, each expresses an enormous multitude of such propositions: (10), for example, expresses a different singular proposition for each possible object named 'Hamlet'—one for each object that is the first member of some appropriate n-tuple. Now none of these propositions is true in α; but where, then, *are* they true? Consider the possible worlds in which R is exemplified by an n-tuple of objects that do not exist in α: call these *Hamlet Worlds*. For each possible object x dubbed 'Hamlet' by the play, there is a class of Hamlet Worlds in which x exists and has the appropriate properties. Furthermore, there will be some state of affairs S such that S but no state of affairs including but distinct from S, obtains in each Hamlet World; these are *Hamlet Situations*. For each object named 'Hamlet' there is a distinct Hamlet Situation. And a sentence like (10) expresses a multitude of propositions, each true in[1] at least one Hamlet situation. So propositions from fiction are not in *fact* true; when we say of such propositions as (10) that they *are* true, we are to be understood as pointing out that they are true in some Hamlet Situation.

Thus (10) expresses indefinitely many singular propositions; this embarrassment of riches is no real embarrassment, however, since each is true—that is, each is true in a Hamlet Situation.

[1] Recall that a proposition P is true in a state of affairs S if and only if it is impossible that S obtain and P be false; similarly P is false in S if and only if it is impossible that S obtain and P be true.

Hence for most purposes we can ignore their plurality and pretend that (10) expresses but one proposition. And now note how neatly we thus elude the three difficulties that initially beset descriptivism. First, there was the objection that both 'Hamlet exists' and 'Hamlet never really existed' seem to express true propositions. Now we see that the second expresses a bevy of propositions each true in fact, in the actual world, while the first expresses a host of propositions true in the fashion appropriate to fiction—that is, each is true in a Hamlet Situation. Secondly, there was the fact that a sentence like

(13) Hamlet wore size ten shoes

seems to have a peculiarly indeterminate status: we feel uncomfortable ascribing either truth or falsity to it. Now we see that our hesitation is justified; for while this sentence expresses a vast company of propositions, none is true or false in any Hamlet Situation. Thirdly, we asked how the Descriptivist can handle Shakespeare's apparent immunity from error in asserting what appear to be contingent propositions. But now we see that in writing the play he concurrently names objects 'Hamlet' and selects states of affairs—the very states of affairs in which the named objects have the properties with which he credits them. So it is no wonder that he cannot easily go wrong here.

Thus does neo-Descriptivism retain the descriptivist posture. But perhaps we must concede that it has about it an air of the arcane and epicyclic. And anyway a descriptivism without the claim that stories give us the sober literal truth—truth in the actual world—about possible objects is like a Platonism without the forms: emasculated, at best. More important, however, is the following point. The Descriptivist position as initially presented contained an *argument* for the claim that there are nonexistent possibles. This argument loses whatever force it may have had once the descriptivist concedes that stories do not apprise us of properties their subjects have in the actual world. For if descriptivist intuitions are satisfied by the suggestion that a story describes its characters as they are *in other possible worlds*, why not hold instead that a piece of fiction is about n-tuples of *actual* objects, ascribing to them properties *they* have in other worlds? If we think stories must be *about* something, why not think of them as about existent objects? No doubt there are possible worlds in which Ronald Reagan, for example, is named 'Rip van Winkle' and has the properties depicted in Irving's story. If we are bent upon a descriptivist account we may suppose that Irving is describing Reagan as he is in these worlds (and the rest of us as we are in our Rip van Winkle worlds). For any fictional character there will be real objects and worlds such that the former have in the latter the properties credited to the fictional character. And hence we have no reason for supposing that stories about Pegasus, Lear, and the rest are about possible but unactualized objects—even if we accept the dubious supposition that they must be about objects of some kind or other.

4. *Names: Their Function in Fiction*

The fact, however (or so it seems to me), is that names such as 'Lear', 'Hamlet', 'Superman', and the like do not (as they normally function in fiction) serve to denote any objects at all. How then *do* they function? Perhaps as follows. Someone writes a story entitled "George's Adventures": "Once upon a time", he begins, "there was a boy named George who lived in Jamestown, North Dakota. George had many splendid adventures. For example, once he was attacked by an aroused prairie dog when he inadvertently stepped on its burrow. . . ." No doubt "George's Adventures" will not win many prizes; but what, fundamentally, is the author doing in telling this story? Fundamentally, I suggest, he presents and calls our attention to a certain proposition or state of affairs. He brings it to mind for us, helps us focus our attention upon it, enables us to entertain, explore, and contemplate it, a procedure we find amusing and titillating or edifying and instructive as the case may be.

But what sort of proposition does the author present? In the simplest typical case—where, let us say, the story has only one character—a general proposition, one that could be expressed by an existentially quantified sentence whose conjuncts correspond roughly to the results of replacing 'George' in the story's sentences by the quantifier's variable. Let us call the proposition thus related to a story the story's *Story Line* and such an existentially quantified sentence expressing it a *Stylized Sentence*. The initial segment of a Stylized Sentence expressing the Story Line of "George's Adventures" will look like this:

(14) (E*x*) *x* was named 'George' and *x* had many splendid adventures and. . . .

where the succeeding conjuncts result from the story's succeeding sentences by replacing occurrences of 'George' therein by the variable '*x*'. Of course the correspondence is *rough*. For example "George's Adventures" could have begun thus: "George lived in Jamestown, North Dakota. Many interesting things happened to him there; for example, one day. . . ." Here the Story Line is the same as in the previous case even though the author does not explicitly say that someone was named George. But for each fictional name in a story, I suggest, a stylized sentence expressing its Story Line will contain a quantifier and a conjunct introducing that name.

Now of course only an author wooden *in excelsis* could present the Story Line by means of a Stylized Sentence such as (13). A more accomplished storyteller employs an artful mode of presentation complete with all the cunning and pleasing embellishments of stylistic technique. So naturally he replaces subsequent occurrences of the variable by the name introduced in the first conjunct; and he will probably omit that conjunct altogether. Then (unless he is writing in German) he breaks up the result into a lot of shorter sentences and adds his other embellishments.

The essential feature of this account (tentative and incomplete as it is) is that names such as 'George' in "George's Adventures" do not serve to denote anything at all; they function substantially as stylistic variants of variables appearing in a Stylized Sentence. To ask "Who or what does 'George' denote in 'George's Adventures'?"—is to misunderstand. This name denotes nothing at all in that story. To illustrate a point or give a counterexample I might speak of a pair of philosophers, McX and Wyman,[1] who hold peculiar views on some topic or other. Here it would be the sheerest confusion to ask for the denotation of 'McX' and 'Wyman'. It is the same in the case of serious fiction.

---

[1] See W. V. Quine, "On What There Is", in *From a Logical Point of View* (New York: Harper & Row, 1963), p. 2.

Of course this account requires much by way of supplementation and qualification before it can be so much as called an account; many questions remain. For example, real persons and places often turn up in fiction, as do Jamestown in "George's Adventures" and Denmark in *Hamlet*; then the Story Line entails the existence of these persons or objects. Sometimes real people and places are given fictitious names, as is Grand Rapids, Michigan, in Frederick Manfred's *The Primitive*. Sometimes the author pauses to express his own views on some appropriate subject, as Tolstoy does in *War and Peace*; he then briefly deserts fiction for sober assertion. Sometimes it is difficult to discern the Story Line; we may be unable to tell whether it includes the existence of a real person—Henry Kissinger, let us say—detailing his adventures in a state of affairs quite different from the actual world, or whether it only includes the existence of someone similar to Kissinger. Sometimes a story appears to be inconsistent or incoherent as in some time-travel fiction and fairy stories about people who turn into teacups or pumpkins. But then what goes into the Story Line of such a story?

There are plenty of other questions about what to include in the Story Line. Whatever is entailed by what the author explicitly says? Shall we therefore suppose that all of mathematics and necessary truth generally is included in every Story Line, and that *everything* is included in the Story Line of an inconsistent story? Does the Story Line include causal laws if the author seems to be taking them for granted but explicitly mentions none? Does it include trivial and obvious truths known to the author and his intended audience—e.g. that most people are under nine feet tall? Does it include items of misinformation—e.g. that a bilious person suffers from an excess of bile—the author shares with his audience or thinks shared by his audience? These questions all await resolution; I shall say nothing about them here.

So the peculiar talent and virtue of author of fiction is his wide-ranging and fertile imagination; he helps us explore states of affairs we should never have thought of, left to our own devices. Of course he does not *assert* the propositions that form his stock in trade; as Sir Philip Sydney puts it,

Now for the poet, he nothing affirms, and therefore never lieth. For, as I take it, to lie is to affirm that to be true which is false . . .

But the poet (as I said before) never affirmeth . . . And therefore, though he recount things not true, yet because he telleth them not for true, he lieth not—without we will say that Nathan lied in his speech before-alleged to David; which as a wicked man durst scarce say, so think I none so simple would say that Aesop lied in the tales of his beasts; for who thinks that Aesop writ it for actually true were well worthy to have his name chronicled among the beasts he writeth of.[1]

The author does not assert these propositions; he exhibits them, calls them to our attention, invites us to consider and explore them. And hence his immunity from error noted earlier on.

Of course *we* are not thus immune. A critic who insists that Othello was an Eskimo has fallen into egregious error, whether through excess of carelessness or sophistication. For

(15) Othello was a Moor

is true and

(16) Othello was an Eskimo

is false. The first is true (again, roughly and subject to qualification and amendment) because the appropriate Story Line entails the existence of a Moor named Othello. (16), however, is false, because the Story Line entails the existence of someone named Othello who was not an Eskimo and it does not entail the existence of anyone else named Othello. (Here I venture no necessary and sufficient conditions for truth and falsehood in fiction; I mean only to indicate a promising line of approach.) But surely there will be sentences such as

(17) Hamlet wore size 13 shoes

that are neither true nor false. The appropriate Story Line does not entail the existence of someone named 'Hamlet' who wore size 13 shoes; but neither does it entail the existence of someone named 'Hamlet' who did not wear size 13 shoes. So (17) is neither true nor false. Of course a careless critic writing a book on literary characters with large feet might write "Hamlet, furthermore, wore size 13 shoes, as did . . .". Such a critic would probably be saying what is false; for very likely he would be asserting something that entails that (17) is true; and *that* is false.

[1] *Apology for Poetry*. Quoted in N. Wolterstorff, "A Theory of Fiction", unpublished.

As I said, this account requires much by way of development and supplementation and qualification. Here I am less interested in filling out the account than in simply sketching its basic features, thus pointing to an understanding of fiction according to which stories are about nothing at all and the names they contain denote neither actual nor possible objects.

IX

GOD, EVIL, AND THE METAPHYSICS OF FREEDOM

1. *The Problem*

IN this and the following chapter I wish to apply some of the foregoing ideas to two traditional topics in the philosophy of religion: the Problem of Evil (which will occupy this chapter) and the Ontological Argument. Perhaps the former constitutes the most formidable objection to theistic belief—or so, at any rate, it has seemed to many. A multitude of philosophers have held that the existence of evil is at the least an embarrassment for those who accept belief in God.[1] And most contemporary philosophers who hold that evil constitutes a difficulty for theistic belief claim to detect *logical inconsistency* in beliefs a theist typically accepts. So, for example, according to H. J. McCloskey:

> Evil is a problem for the theist in that a *contradiction* is involved in the fact of evil, on the one hand, and the belief in the omnipotence and perfection of God on the other.[2]

J. L. Mackie urges the same charge:

> I think, however, that a more telling criticism can be made by way of the traditional problem of evil. Here it can be shown, not that religious beliefs lack rational support, but that they are positively irrational, that the several parts of the essential theological doctrine are *inconsistent* with one another.[3]

And Henry David Aiken substantially repeats this allegation.[4]

Now the alleged contradiction arises, of course, when we consider the fact that evil exists together with the belief that God

---

[1] Epicurus, for example, as well as David Hume, some of the French Encyclopedists, F. H. Bradley, J. McTaggart, J. S. Mill, and many others.

[2] "God and Evil", *Philosophical Quarterly*, 10 (1960), 97.

[3] "Evil and Omnipotence", *Mind*, 64 (1955), 200.

[4] "God and Evil", *Ethics*, 68 (1957–8), 79.

exists and is omniscient, omnipotent, and wholly good or morally perfect. Obviously these propositions are not *formally* inconsistent; the resources of logic alone do not enable us to deduce an explicit contradiction from their conjunction. But then presumably the atheologian—he who offers arguments against the existence of God—never meant to hold that there was a formal contradiction here; he meant instead that the conjunction of these two propositions is necessarily false, false in every possible world. To show that he is right, therefore, he must produce a proposition that is at least plausibly thought to be necessary and whose conjunction with our original two formally yields a contradiction.

I have argued elsewhere[1] that it is extremely difficult to find any such proposition. I have also argued[2] that the *Free Will Defence* can be used to show that in fact these propositions are not inconsistent. In what follows I wish to look again at the issues involved in the *Free Will Defence*—this time from the vantage point of the foregoing ideas about *possible worlds*.

2. *The Free Will Defence*

The Free Will Defence is an effort to show that

(1) God is omnipotent, omniscient, and wholly good

(which I shall take to entail that God exists) is not inconsistent with

(2) There is evil in the world.

That is, the Free Will Defender aims to show that there is a possible world in which (1) and (2) are both true. Now one way to show that a proposition p is consistent with a proposition q is to produce a third proposition r whose conjunction with p is consistent and entails q. r, of course, need not be true or known to be true; it need not be so much as plausible. All that is required of it is that it be consistent with p, and in conjunction with the latter entail q. What the Free Will Defender must do, therefore, is find such a proposition.

But first, some preliminary definitions and distinctions. What does the Free Will Defender mean when he says that people are or may be *free*? If a person S is free with respect to a given

---

[1] *God and Other Minds*, Chapter 5.   [2] Ibid., **Chapter 6.**

action, then he is free to perform that action and free to refrain; no causal laws and antecedent conditions determine either that he will perform the action, or that he will not. It is within his power, at the time in question, to perform the action, and within his power to refrain. Consider the state U of the universe up to the time he takes or decides to take the action in question. If S is free with respect to that action, then it is causally or naturally possible both that U hold and S *take* (or decide to take) the action, and that U hold and S *refrain* from it.[1] Further, let us say that an action is *morally significant*, for a given person at a given time, if it would be wrong for him to perform the action then but right to refrain, or vice versa. Keeping a promise, for example, would typically be morally significant, as would refusing induction into the army; having an apple for lunch (instead of an orange) would not. And, a person *goes wrong with respect to a morally significant action* if it is wrong for him to perform it and he does, or wrong for him not to and he does not. Still further, suppose we say that a person is *significantly free*, on a given occasion, if he is then free with respect to an action that is morally significant for him. And finally, we must distinguish between *moral* evil and *natural* evil. The former is evil that results from some human being's going wrong with respect to an action that is morally significant for him; any other evil is natural evil.[2] Suffering due to human cruelty—Hitler's treatment of the Jews, for example—would be an example of the former; suffering resulting from an earthquake or tidal wave, an example of the latter. An analogous distinction is made between moral and natural good.

Given these definitions and distinctions, we can make a preliminary statement of the Free Will Defence as follows. A world containing creatures who are sometimes significantly free (and freely perform more good than evil actions) is more valuable, all else being equal, than a world containing no free creatures at all. Now God can create free creatures, but he cannot *cause* or *determine* them to do only what is right. For if he does so, then they are not significantly free after all; they do not

---

[1] Of course it does not follow that if S is free with respect to some of his actions, then what he will do is in principle unpredicable or unknowable.

[2] This distinction is not very precise (how, exactly, are we to construe 'results from'?); but perhaps it will serve our present purposes.

do what is right *freely*. To create creatures capable of *moral good*, therefore, he must create creatures capable of moral evil; and he cannot leave these creatures *free* to perform evil and at the same time prevent them from doing so. God did in fact create significantly free creatures; but some of them went wrong in the exercise of their freedom: this is the source of moral evil. The fact that these free creatures sometimes go wrong, however, counts neither against God's omnipotence nor against his goodness; for he could have forestalled the occurrence of moral evil only by excising the possibility of moral good.

I said earlier that the Free Will Defender tries to find a proposition that is consistent with

(1) God is omniscient, omnipotent, and wholly good

and together with (1) entails that there is evil. According to the Free Will Defence, we must find this proposition somewhere in the above story. The heart of the Free Will Defence is the claim that it is *possible* that God could not have created a universe containing moral good (or as much moral good as this one contains) without creating one containing moral evil.

3. *The Objection*

A formidable objection goes like this. Surely it is logically possible that there be a world containing significantly free creatures who always do what is right. There is certainly no contradiction or inconsistency in this idea. If so, however, there are possible worlds containing moral good but no moral evil. Now the theist says that God is omnipotent—which means, roughly, that there are no non-logical limits to his power. Accordingly, he could have created just any possible world he chose, including those containing moral good but no moral evil. If it is possible that there be a world containing significantly free creatures who never do what is wrong, then it follows that an omnipotent God could have created such a world. If so, however, the Free Will Defence must be mistaken in its insistence upon the possibility that God, though omnipotent, could not have created a world containing moral good without permitting moral evil. As Mackie puts it:

If God has made men such that in their free choices they sometimes prefer what is good and sometimes what is evil, why could he not have made men such that they always freely choose the good? If there is no logical impossibility in a man's freely choosing the good on one, or on several occasions, there cannot be a logical impossibility in his freely choosing the good on every occasion. God was not, then, faced with a choice between making innocent automata and making beings who, in acting freely, would sometimes go wrong; there was open to him the obviously better possibility of making beings who would act freely but always go right. Clearly, his failure to avail himself of this possibility is inconsistent with his being both omnipotent and wholly good.[1]

Was it within the power of an omnipotent God to create just any logically possible world? This is the important question for the Free Will Defence, and a subtle question it is. Leibniz, as you recall, insisted that *this* world, the actual world, must be the best of all possible worlds. His reasoning is as follows. Before God created anything at all, he was confronted with an enormous range of choices; he could have created or actualized any of the myriads of different possible worlds. Being perfectly good, he must have chosen to create the best world he could; being omnipotent, he was able to create just any possible world he pleased. He must, therefore, have chosen the best of all possible worlds; and hence *this* world, the one he did create, must be (despite appearances) the best possible. Now Mackie agrees with Leibniz that God, if omnipotent, could have created just any world he pleased and would have created the best world he could. But while Leibniz draws the conclusion that *this* world must be the best possible, Mackie concludes instead that there is no omnipotent, wholly good God. For, he says, it is obvious enough that this actual world is not the best possible.

The Free Will Defender disagrees with both Leibniz and Mackie. First, we have the question whether *there is* such a thing as the best of all possible worlds, or even *a* best. Perhaps for any world you pick, there is a better. But what is really characteristic and central to the Free Will Defence is the claim that God, though omnipotent, could not have created just any possible world he pleased; and this is the claim we must investigate.

[1] Op. cit., p. 209.

4. *Which Worlds Could God Have Created?*

We speak of God as *creating* the world; yet if it is α of which we speak, what we say is false. For a thing is created only if there is a time before which it does not exist; and this is patently false of α, as it is of any state of affairs. What God has created are the heavens and the earth and all that they contain; he has not created himself, or numbers, propositions, properties, or states of affairs: these have no beginnings. We can say, however, that God *actualizes* states of affairs; his creative activity results in their being or becoming actual. God has *created* Socrates, but *actualized* the state of affairs consisting in the latter's existence. And God is actualizing but not creating α.

Furthermore, while we may properly say that God actualizes α, it does not follow that he actualizes every state of affairs the latter includes. He does not, as previously mentioned, actualize his own existence; that is to say, he does not create himself. Nor does he create his own properties; hence he does not actualize the state of affairs consisting in the existence of such properties as omniscience, omnipotence, moral excellence, and *being the creator of the heavens and the earth*. But the same is really true of other properties too; God no more creates the property of being red than that of omnipotence. Properties are not creatable: to suppose that they have been created is to suppose that although they exist now, there was a time at which they did not; and this seems clearly false. Again, since God did not create numbers, propositions, pure sets, and the like, he did not actualize the states of affairs consisting in the existence of these things. Nor does he actualize such other necessary states of affairs as *7+5's equalling 12*. Necessary states of affairs do not owe their actuality to the creative activity of God. So if we speak of God as actualizing α, we should not think of him as actualizing every state of affairs α includes. But perhaps we may say that he actualizes every *contingent* state of affairs included in α; and perhaps we may say that God *can* actualize a given possible world *W* only if he can actualize every contingent state of affairs *W* includes. And now we can put our question: can an omnipotent being actualize just any possible world he pleases—that is, is every possible world such that an omnipotent being can actualize it?

Here more distinctions are needed. Although there are any number of possible worlds in which Abraham never met Melchizedek, God can actualize none of them. That is, he can no longer actualize any of them; for Abraham in fact *did* meet Melchizedek (let us suppose) and not even an omnipotent being can bring it about that Abraham did *not* meet Melchizedek; it is too late for that. Take any time t; at t there will be any number of worlds God cannot actualize; for there will be any number of worlds in which things go differently before t. So God cannot actualize any world in which Abraham did not meet Melchizedek; but perhaps God *could have* actualized such worlds. Perhaps we should say that God could have actualized a world W if and only if for every contingent state of affairs S included by W, there is a time at which it is (timelessly) within his power to actualize S.[1] And now perhaps the atheologian's claim may be put as follows:

(3) If God is omnipotent, then God could have actualized just any possible world.

But this will not be entirely accurate either—not, at any rate, if God himself is a contingent being. For if he is a contingent being, then there are worlds in which he does not exist; and clearly he could not have actualized any of *these* worlds. Clearly the only worlds within God's power to actualize are those that include his existence. So suppose we restrict our attention to these worlds. (In Chapter X I shall argue that this is no real restriction.) Is it true that

(4) If God is omnipotent, then he could have actualized just any world that includes his existence?

Still more distinctions are needed. In particular, we must look more closely at the idea of *freedom*. According to the Free Will Defender, God thought it good to create free persons. And a person is free with respect to an action A at a time t only if no causal laws and antecedent conditions determine either that he

---

[1] To say that God could have actualized W suggests that there is some time—some past time—such that God could have performed the action of actualizing W at that time. Thus it suggests that actualizing a possible world requires but a moment or at any rate a limited stretch of time. This suggestion must be resisted; perhaps God's actualizing a possible world requires an unlimited span of time; perhaps it requires his action at *every* time, past, present, and future.

performs *A* at *t* or that he refrains from so doing. This is not a comment upon the ordinary use of the word 'free'; that use may or may not coincide with the Free Will Defender's. What God thought good, on this view, was the existence of creatures whose activity is not causally determined—who, like he himself, are centres of creative activity. The freedom of such creatures will no doubt be *limited* by causal laws and antecedent conditions. They will not be free to do just anything; even if I am free, I am not free to run a mile in two minutes. Of course my freedom is also *enhanced* by causal laws; it is only by virtue of such laws that I am free to build a house or walk on the surface of the earth. But if I am free with respect to an action *A*, then causal laws and antecedent conditions determine neither that I take *A* nor that I refrain.

More broadly, if I am free with respect to an action *A*, then God does not *bring it about* or *cause it to be the case* either that I take or that I refrain from this action; he neither causes this to be so through the laws he establishes, nor by direct intervention, nor in any other way. For if he *brings it about* or *causes it to be the case* that I take *A*, then I am not free to *refrain* from *A*, in which case I am not free with respect to *A*. Although of course God may cause it to be the case that I *am* free with respect to *A*, he cannot cause it to be the case either that I freely take or that I freely refrain from this action—and this though he is omnipotent.[1] But then it follows that there are plenty of contingent states of affairs such that it is not within the power of God to bring about their actuality, or cause them to be actual. He cannot cause it to be the case that I freely refrain from an action *A*; for if he does so, he causes it to be the case that I refrain from *A*, in which case I do not do so *freely*.

Now I have been using 'brings it about that' as a rough synonym for 'causes it to be the case that'. Suppose we take the term 'actualize' the same way. Then God can actualize a given state of affairs *S* only if he can cause it to be the case that *S*, cause *S* to be actual. And then there will be many contingent states of affairs *S* such that there is no time at which God can actualize *S*. But we said a page back that

(5) God could have actualized a given possible world *W* if and

---

[1] Just to simplify matters I shall henceforth take it for granted that *if God exists, he is omnipotent* is a necessary truth.

only if for every contingent state of affairs *S* that *W* includes, there is a time at which God can actualize *S*.

Given just the possibility that there are created free agents, it follows that there are any number of possible worlds including God's existence and *also* including a contingent state of affairs *S* such that there is no time at which God can actualize *S*. Hence (contrary to (4) and to the atheologian's claim) there are any number of possible worlds that God could not have actualized, even though they include his existence: all those containing a state of affairs consisting in some creature's freely taking or refraining from some action. Since a world containing moral good is such a world, it follows that God could not have actualized any world containing moral good; *a fortiori* he could not have actualized a world containing moral good but no moral evil.

The atheologian's proper retort, I think, is as follows. Suppose we concede that not even God can cause it to be the case that I freely refrain from *A*. Even so, he *can* cause me to be free with respect to *A*, and to be in some set *S* of circumstances including appropriate laws and antecedent conditions. He may also know, furthermore, that *if* he creates me and causes me to be free in these circumstances, I will refrain from *A*. If so, there is a state of affairs he can actualize, cause to be actual, such that if he does so, then I will freely refrain from *A*. In a broader sense of 'bring about', therefore, he *can* bring it about that I freely refrain from *A*. In the narrower sense there are many contingent state of affairs he cannot bring about; what is relevant to the Free Will Defence, however, is not this narrow sense, but the broader one. For what is really at issue is whether for each possible world there are some actions God could have taken such that if he *had*, then that morally perfect world (one including moral good but no moral evil) would have been actual.

Perhaps we can sharpen this point. The narrow sense of 'bring about' is such that the sentence

(6) If God brings it about that I refrain from *A*, then I do not freely refrain from *A*

expresses a necessary truth. You are free with respect to an action *A* only if God does not bring it about or cause it to be the case that you refrain from *A*. But now suppose God knows that

if he creates you free with respect to A in some set S of circumstances, you will refrain from A; suppose further that he brings
it about (narrow sense) that you *are* free with respect to A in S;
and suppose finally that you do in fact freely refrain from A.
Then in a broader sense of 'bring about' we could properly say
that God has brought it about that you freely refrain from A.
We must make a corresponding distinction, then, between a
stronger and a weaker sense of 'actualize'. In the strong sense,
God can actualize only what he can *cause* to be actual; in that
sense he cannot actualize any state of affairs including the
existence of creatures who freely take some action or other. But
so far we have no reason for supposing that the same holds for
weak actualization. And what the atheologian requires for his
argument, presumably, is not that every possible world (including the existence of God) is one God could have actualized in
the *strong* sense; weak actualization is enough for his purposes.
What is at issue is not the question whether each world is such
that God could have actualized it in the *strong* sense, but
(roughly) whether for each world W there is something he could
have done—some series of actions he could have taken—such
that if he had, W would have been actual. For if God is
wholly good and it *was* within his power thus to secure the
actuality of a perfect world, then presumably he would have
done so. Accordingly the Free Will Defender's claim—that God
could not have actualized a world containing moral good without actualizing one containing moral evil—is either irrelevant
or unsubstantiated: irrelevant if 'actualize' is taken in the strong
sense and unsubstantiated otherwise.

Since it is weak actualization that is relevant, let us henceforth use 'actualize' to mean 'weakly actualize'. And so our
question is this: could God have actualized just any possible
world that includes his existence?

Perhaps we can best proceed by way of an example. Curley
Smith, the mayor of Boston, is opposed to the proposed freeway
route. From the Highway Department's point of view, his
objection is frivolous; he complains that the route would require
destruction of the Old North Church along with some other
antiquated and structurally unsound buildings. The Director of
Highways offers him a bribe of \$35,000 to drop his opposition.
Unwilling to break with the fine old traditions of Bay State

politics, Curley accepts; whereupon the Director spends a sleepless night wondering whether he could have had Curley for $20,000. That is to say, Smedes wonders which of

(7) If Curley had been offered $20,000, he would have accepted the bribe

or

(8) If Curley had been offered $20,000, he would have rejected the bribe

is true.

5. *Counterfactuals*

But here an objection arises. (7) and (8), of course, are *counterfactual conditionals*. Subject to all the difficulty and obscurity of that peculiar breed, they contain traps for the unwary. Here, for example, we seem to be assuming that either (7) or (8) must be true. But what is the justification for that? How do we know that at least one of them *is* true? What leads us to suppose that there is an answer to the question what Curley would have done, had he been offered a bribe of $20,000?

This question can be amplified. According to an interesting proposal[1] a counterfactual conditional such as (7) can be explained as follows. Consider those possible worlds that include its antecedent; and then of these consider that one *W* that is *most similar to* the actual world. (7) is true if and only if its consequent—that is,

(9) Curley took the bribe

is true in *W*. A counterfactual is true if and only if its antecedent is impossible, or its consequent is true in the world most similar to the actual in which its antecedent is.

This intriguing proposal provokes questions. In the first place, the required notion of similarity is in many respects problematic. What does it mean to say that one possible world is more similar to α than another? In this context, is there such a thing as similarity *uberhaupt*, or should we speak only of similarity in given respects? These are good questions; we have no time to linger over them, but let us pause just long enough to note that we do seem to have an intuitive grasp of this notion—the notion

[1] See Robert Stalnaker, "A Theory of Conditionals", in N. Rescher, *Studies in Logical Theory* (*American Philosophical Quarterly*, supplementary monograph, 1968), p. 98.

of similarity between states of affairs. Secondly, the proposal presumes that for each contingently false proposition p there is a possible world including p that is uniquely closest (i.e. most similar) to the actual world. So take any such proposition and any proposition q: on the proposal in question, either *if p then q* or *if p then $\sim q$* will be true. This may seem a bit strong: *if I had red hair, Napoleon would not have lost the Battle of Waterloo* is obviously false, but *if I had red hair Napoleon would have won the Battle of Waterloo* does not seem much better. (*Even if*, perhaps, but not *if*.) Indeed, take any such proposition p: on this view there is some entire possible world W such that the counterfactual *if p had been true, W would have obtained* holds. But is it not unduly extravagant to claim that there is some possible world W such that if I had red hair, W would have been actual? Is there a possible world W^* such that if α had not been actual, W^* would have been? Is there reason to believe that there is a world including the antecedent of (7) and (8) (call it 'A') that is *uniquely closest* to α? Perhaps several worlds include it, each such that none including it is closer.[1] And this leads directly to our question. Perhaps there is a family of closest worlds in which A is true; and perhaps in some of these

(9) Curley accepted the bribe

is true, while in others it is

(10) Curley rejected the bribe

that enjoys that distinction. If so, then perhaps we must conclude that neither (7) nor (8) is true; there is then no such thing as *what Curley would have done* under the envisaged circumstances.

Indeed, perhaps the objector need not rest content with the idle suspicion that there may be such a family of worlds; perhaps he can go further. There are possible worlds W and W^* that include A and are *exactly alike* up to 10.00 a.m., 10 November

---

[1] More radically, perhaps there are no such closest worlds at all; perhaps for any world including A, there is a closer that also includes it. See David Lewis, *Counterfactuals* (Blackwell, 1973), Chapter 1, Section 1.3. According to Lewis, a counterfactual $A \rightarrow B$ is true if and only if either A is impossible or some world W in which A and C hold is more similar to the actual world than any world in which A and $\bar{C}$ hold. In writing this section I have benefited from Lewis's analysis; I am grateful to him for a criticism that triggered substantial improvement in the argument of this chapter.

1973, the time at which Curley makes his response to the bribe offer; in W Curley accepts the bribe and in W^* he does not. If $t = 10.00$ a.m., 10 November 1973, let us say that W and W^* *share an initial segment up to* t. We could call the t-initial segment of W 'S_W^{-t}', the subscript 'W' indicating that S is a segment of W, and the superscript '$-t$' indicating that this segment terminates at t. (S_W^{+t} would be the unending segment of W that begins at t.) And of course $S_W^{-t} = S_{W^*}^{-t}$.

It is not entirely easy to give a rigorous characterization of this notion of an initial segment. It is clear that if W and W^* share an initial segment terminating at t, then for any object x and for any time t^* earlier than t, x exists in W at t^* if and only if x exists in W^* at t^*. But we cannot say that if a thing x has a property P in W at t^*, then x has P in W^* at t^*. For one property Curley has at t^* in W is that of being such at t he will take the bribe; and of course he does not have *that* property in W^* at t^*. Perhaps there is an intuitive notion of a *non-temporal* property under which we could say that if at t^* x has a non-temporal property P in W then x also has P in W^* at t^*. The problem of course is to say just what this notion of a non-temporal property amounts to; and that is by no means easy. Still the idea of a pair of worlds W and W^* sharing an initial segment is fairly clear; roughly, it amounts to saying that the two worlds are the same up to a certain time t. And if there is no time t^* later than t such that $S_W^{-t^*} = S_{W^*}^{-t^*}$, then at t W and W^* *branch*. Of course there will be a large class of worlds sharing S_W^{-t} with W and W^*; and if e is an event that takes place in W but not in W^*, there will be a class of worlds including S_W^{-t} in which e occurs and another class including it in which e does not.

Suppose we concede (or pretend) that we have this notion of an initial segment well in hand. It may then appear that we can construct a convincing argument for the conclusion that neither (7) nor (8) is true. For each of W and W^* are as similar to α, in the relevant respects, as any world including A. But if they share S_W^{-t}, then are they not *equally* similar, in the appropriate ways, to α? Up to t things are just alike in these two worlds. What happens after t seems scarcely relevant to the question of what Curley would have done if offered the bribe. We should conclude, therefore, that W and W^* are equally similar to α; but these two worlds resemble α as much as any others;

hence the closest worlds in which A is true do not speak with a single voice; hence neither (7) nor (8) is true.[1]

What about this argument? In the first place, it proves too much. It gains a specious plausibility from the case we are considering. We do not know, after all, whether Curley would have accepted the bribe—it is a fairly small one and perhaps his pride would have been injured. Let us ask instead whether he would have accepted a bribe of $36,000, everything else being as much as possible like the actual world. Here the answer seems fairly clear: indeed he would have. And this despite the fact that for any possible world W as close as you please to α in which Curley takes the bribe, there is a world W^* that shares the appropriate initial segment with W in which he manfully refuses it.

The argument suffers from another defect, however—one which is more instructive. Suppose we approach it by way of another example. Royal Robbins is climbing the Dihedral Wall of El Capitan. The usual method involving ropes and belays has lost its appeal; he is soloing the Wall unprotected. Just as he reaches Thanksgiving Ledge, some 2500 feet above the Valley floor, one of his hand holds breaks out. He teeters precariously on one foot, regains his balance, and leaps lightly on to the ledge, where he bivouacs; the next day he continues triumphantly to the top. Now suppose we consider

(11) If Robbins had slipped and fallen at Thanksgiving Ledge, he would have been killed.

No doubt we are initially inclined to accept this proposition. But should we? In the actual world Robbins did not fall at Thanksgiving Ledge; instead he nimbly climbed on to it and spent a comfortable night there. Now what happens in the closest worlds in which he falls? Well, there is at least one of these—call it W'—in which he falls at t just as he is reaching the Ledge; at the next moment $t+1$ (as close as you please to t) he shows up exactly where he is in α at $t+1$; and everything else goes just as it does in α. Would W' not be more similar to the actual world than any in which he hurtles down to the Valley floor, thus depriving American rockclimbing of its most eloquent spokesman? And if so, should we not rate (11) false?

---

[1] This argument surfaced in discussion with David Kaplan.

The answer, of course, is that we are neglecting causal or natural *laws*. Our world α contains a number of these, and they are among its more impressive constituents. In particular, there are some implying (together with the relevant antecedent conditions) that anyone who falls unroped and unprotected from a ledge 2500 feet up a vertical cliff, moves with increasing rapidity towards the centre of the earth, finally arriving with considerable impact at its surface. Evidently not all of these laws are present in W', for the latter shares the relevant initial conditions with α but in it Robbins does not fall to the Valley floor—instead, after a brief feint in that direction, he reappears on the cliff. And once we note that these laws do not hold in W', so the claim goes, we shall no longer be tempted to think it very similar to α, where they do hold.

No doubt there is truth in this reply. But the relationship between causal laws and counterfactuals, like that between Guinevere and Sir Lancelot, is both intimate and notorious. A salient feature of the former, indeed, is that (unlike accidental generalizations) they are said to support or entail counterfactuals. So instead of denigrating W' on the grounds that its laws differ from α's, we might as well have complained, in view of the above connection, that W' lacks some of α's counterfactuals. One measure of similarity between worlds involves the question whether they share their counterfactuals.

We should be unduly hasty, I think, if we drew the conclusion that the possible worlds explanation of counter-factuals is viciously circular or of no theoretical interest or importance. But it does follow that we cannot as a rule *discover* the truth value of a counter-factual by asking whether its consequent holds in those worlds most similar to the actual in which its antecedent holds. For one feature determining the similarity of worlds is whether they share their counterfactuals.

And of course this is relevant to the argument we have been examining. As you recall, it went like this. There are worlds W and W^* that share $S_{\overline{W}}^{-!}$; these worlds, therefore, are equally similar to α in the relevant respects. In W, however, Curley takes the bribe; in W^* he refuses. Accordingly, neither (7) nor (8) is such that its consequent is true in the closest worlds to α in which its antecedent is; hence neither (7) nor (8) is true. But now we see that this argument does not settle the matter. For from the fact that W and W^* share the appropriate initial segment, it does not follow that they are equally similar to α. Suppose that (7) *is* true; then W^* does not share that counterfactual with α, and is to that extent less similar to it than W. Here we have a relevant dissimilarity between the two worlds in virtue of which the one may indeed be more similar to the actual world than the other. Accordingly, the argument fails.

A second argument is sometimes given for the conclusion that we have no right to the assumption that either (7) or (8) is true: perhaps the fact is that

(12) If Curley had been offered a bribe of $20,000 and had believed that his decision would be headlined in the *Boston Globe*, he would have rejected the bribe.

If so, then (7) is false. But perhaps it is also true that

(13) If Curley had been offered a bribe of $20,000 and had believed that his venality would remain undetected, he would have accepted the bribe;

in which case (8) would be false. So if (12) and (13) are both true (as they might well be) then neither (7) nor (8) is.

This argument is in error. If we let '$\rightarrow$' represent the counterfactual connective, we see that the crucial inference here is of the form

$$\frac{A \rightarrow C}{\therefore\ A \ \& \ B \rightarrow C}$$

which is clearly fallacious (and invalid on both the Stalnaker and Lewis semantics for counterfactuals). No doubt it is true that

(14) If the Pope were a Protestant, he would be a dissembler;

it does not follow that

(15) If the Pope were a Protestant, had been born in Friesland and been a lifelong member of the Gereformeerde Kerk, he would be a dissembler.

Nor does it follow from (7) that, if Curley had been offered the bribe and had believed his decision would be headlined in the *Globe*, he would have accepted it.

Now of course the failure of these arguments does not guarantee that either (7) or (8) must be true. But suppose we think about a state of affairs that includes Curley's having been offered $20,000, all relevant conditions—Curley's financial situation, his general acquisitive tendencies, his venality—being the same as in fact, in the actual world. Our question is really whether there is something Curley would have done had this state of affairs been actual. Would an omniscient being know what Curley would have done—would he know, that is, either that Curley would have taken the bribe or that he would have rejected it?

The answer, I should think, is obvious and affirmative. There is something Curley would have done, had that state of affairs obtained. But I do not know how to produce a conclusive argument for this supposition, in case you are inclined to dispute it. I do think it is the natural view, the one we take in reflecting on our own moral failures and triumphs. Suppose I have applied for a National Science Foundation Fellowship and have asked you to write me a recommendation. I am eager to get the fellowship, but eminently unqualified to carry out the project I have proposed. Realizing that you know this, I act upon the maxim that every man has his price and offer you $500 to write a glowing, if inaccurate, report. You indignantly refuse, and add moral turpitude to my other disqualifications. Later we reflectively discuss what you would have done had you been offered a bribe of $50,000. One thing we would take for granted, I should think, is that there is a right answer here. We may not know what that answer is; but we would reject out of hand, I should think, the suggestion that there simply is none. Accordingly, I shall temporarily take it for granted, in what follows, that either (7) or (8) is true; as we shall see in Section 6 this assumption, harmless as it no doubt is, can be dispensed with.

6. *Leibniz's Lapse*

Thus armed, let us return to the question that provoked this digression. Was it within God's power, supposing him omnipotent, to actualize just any possible world that includes his existence? No. In a nutshell, the reason is this. There is a possible world W where God strongly actualizes a totality T of states of affairs including Curley's being free with respect to taking the bribe, and where Curley takes the bribe. But there is another possible world W^* where God actualizes the very same states of affairs and where Curley *rejects* the bribe. Now suppose it is true as a matter of fact that if God had actualized T, Curley would have accepted the bribe: then God could not have actualized W. And if, on the other hand, Curley would have rejected the bribe, had God actualized T, then God could not have actualized W^*. So either way there are worlds God could not have actualized.

We can put this argument more fully as follows. Let C be the state of affairs consisting in Curley's being offered a bribe of $20,000 and being free to accept or reject it; let A be Curley's accepting the bribe; and let GC be God's strongly actualizing C. Then by our assumption either

(16) $GC \rightarrow A$

or

(17) $GC \rightarrow \bar{A}$

is true. Suppose, first, that (16) is true. If so, then on the Stalnaker and Lewis semantics there is a possible world W such that GC and A hold in W, and such that A holds in any world as close where GC holds. No doubt in W God strongly actualizes many states of affairs in addition to C; let T be the state of affairs that includes each of these. That is, T is a state of affairs that God strongly actualizes in W; and T includes every state of affairs God strongly actualizes in W. It is evident that if God had strongly actualized T, then Curley would have accepted the bribe, i.e.,

(18) $GT \rightarrow A$.

For GT and A hold in W; by (16), in any world as close as W where GC holds, A holds; but GT includes GC; so, in any world as close as W where GT holds, A holds. Now there is no possible world in which God strongly actualizes A; for A is Curley's *freely* accepting the bribe. But then GT does not include A; for, if it did, any world where God actualizes T would be one where he actualizes A; there are no worlds where he actualizes A; and there are worlds—e.g. W—where he actualizes GT. So there is another possible world W^* where God actualizes the very same states of affairs as he does in W, and in which Curley rejects the bribe. W^* therefore includes GT and $\bar{A}$. That is, in W^* God strongly actualizes T but no state of affairs properly including T; and in W^* $\bar{A}$ holds. And now it is easy to see that God could not have actualized this world W^*.

For suppose he could have. Then there is a state of affairs C^* such that God could have strongly actualized C^* and such that, if he had, W^* would be actual. That is,

(19) $GC^* \rightarrow W^*$.

But W^* includes GT; so

(20) $GC^* \rightarrow GT$.

Now W^* either includes or precludes GC^*; if the latter, GC^* precludes W^*. But in view of (19) GC^* does not preclude W^* unless, contrary to our hypothesis, GC^* is impossible. So W^* includes GC^*. T, furthermore, is the largest state of affairs God actualizes in W^*; T, therefore, includes C^* and GT includes GC^*. Hence the state of affairs GT & GC^* is or is equivalent to GT. By (18), $GT \rightarrow A$; hence

(21) GC^* & $GT \rightarrow A$.

But from (20) and (21) it follows that

(22) $GC^* \rightarrow A$.[1]

But A precludes W^* and hence includes $\overline{W}^*$; so

(23) $GC^* \rightarrow \overline{W}^*$.

(19) and (23), however, are both true only if GC^* is impossible, in which case God could not have actualized C^*. Accordingly, there is no state of affairs C^* such that God could have strongly actualized C^* and such that if he had, W^* would have been actual. If (16) is true, therefore, there are possible worlds including his existence that God could not have actualized: those worlds, namely, where God actualizes T and Curley rejects the bribe. On the other hand, if

(17) $GC \rightarrow \bar{A}$

is true, then by precisely a similar argument there are other possible worlds God could not have actualized. As I have assumed, either (16) or (17) is true; so despite God's omnipotence there are worlds including his existence he could not have actualized.

Now the assumption that either (16) or (17) is true is fairly innocent; but it is also dispensable. For let W be a world

---

[1] The argument form involved here is

$$A \rightarrow B$$
$$A \text{ \& } B \rightarrow C$$
$$\therefore \quad \overline{A \rightarrow C.}$$

This form is intuitively valid and valid on both Stalnaker and Lewis semantics.

where God exists, where Curley is free with respect to the action of taking a \$20,000 bribe, and where he accepts it; and as before, let T be the largest state of affairs God strongly actualizes in W. God's actualizing T (GT) includes neither Curley's accepting the bribe (A) nor his rejecting it $(\bar{A})$; so there is a world W^* where God strongly actualizes T and in which Curley rejects the bribe. Now

(24) $GT \rightarrow A$

is either true or false. If (24) is true, then by the previous argument God could not have actualized W^*.

On the other hand, if (24) is false, then God could not have actualized W. For suppose he could have; then (as before) there would be a state of affairs C such that God could have strongly actualized C and such that, if he had, W would have been actual. That is

(25) $GC \rightarrow W$.

Now if (25) is true, then so is either

(26) GC & $GT \rightarrow W$

or

(27) GC & $\overline{GT} \rightarrow W$.[1]

Both (26) and (27), however, are false if (24) is. Consider (26): if (25) is true, then W includes GC (unless GC is impossible, in which case, contrary to the assumption, God could not have actualized it); but T is the largest state of affairs God strongly actualizes in W; hence GT includes GC. If so, however, GC & GT is equivalent to GT. And, since (24) is false, the same goes for (26).

And now consider (27). Either GC includes GT or it does not. Suppose it does. As we have seen, if GC is possible and (25) is true, then W includes GC; but T includes C; so GT includes GC. So if GC includes GT, then GC and GT are equivalent. But (24) is false; hence so is (25), if GC includes GT. So GC does not include GT; hence GC & $\overline{GT}$ is a possible state of affairs. But W includes GT; hence $\overline{GT}$ includes $\overline{W}$; hence GC & $\overline{GT}$ includes $\overline{W}$; hence (since GC & $\overline{GT}$ is possible) (27) is false.

---

[1] The form of argument involved here, namely

$$\frac{A \rightarrow B}{\therefore \ (A \ \& \ C \rightarrow B) \ \vee \ (A \ \& \ \overline{C} \rightarrow B);}$$

is intuitively valid and valid on both Stalnaker and Lewis semantics.

(24), therefore, is either true or false. And either way there are possible worlds including his existence that God could not have actualized. So there are possible worlds including his existence that God could not have actualized.

If we consider a world in which GT obtains and in which Curley freely rejects the bribe, we see that whether it was within God's power to actualize it depends in part upon what Curley would have done if God had strongly actualized T. Accordingly, there are possible worlds such that it is partly up to Curley whether or not God can actualize them. It is of course up to God whether or not to create Curley, and also up to God whether or not to make him free with respect to the action of taking the bribe at t. But if he creates him, and creates him free with respect to this action, then whether or not he takes it is up to Curley—not God.

Now we can return to the Free Will Defence and the problem of evil. The Free Will Defender, you recall, insists on the possibility that it is not within God's power to create a world containing moral good without creating one containing moral evil. His atheological opponent agrees with Leibniz in claiming that *if* (as the theist holds) God is omnipotent, then *it follows* that he could have created just any possible world (or any such world including his existence) he pleased. We now see that this contention—call it *Leibniz's Lapse*—is a mistake. The atheologian is right in holding that there are many possible worlds containing moral good but no moral evil; his mistake lies in endorsing Leibniz's Lapse. So one of his central contentions—that God, if omnipotent, could have actualized just any world he pleased—is false.

7. *Transworld Depravity*

Now suppose we recapitulate the logic of the situation. The Free Will Defender claims that

(28) God is omnipotent and it was not within his power to create a world containing moral good but no moral evil

is possible. By way of retort the atheologian insists that there are possible worlds containing moral good but no moral evil. He adds that an omnipotent being could have actualized just any possible world he chose. So if God is omnipotent, it follows that he could have actualized a world containing moral good but no moral evil; hence (28) is not possible. What we have seen so far is that his second premiss—Leibniz's Lapse—is false.

Of course this does not settle the issue in the Free Will Defender's favour. Leibniz's Lapse (appropriately enough for a lapse) is false; but this does not show that (28) is possible. To show this latter, we must demonstrate the possibility that among the worlds God could not have actualized are all the worlds containing moral good but no moral evil. How can we approach this question?

Let us return to Curley and his venality. The latter is unbounded; Curley's bribability is utter and absolute. We could put this more exactly as follows. Take any positive integer n. If (1) at t Curley had been offered n dollars by way of a bribe, and (2) he had been free with respect to the action of taking the bribe, and (3) conditions had otherwise been as much as possible like those that did in fact obtain, Curley would have accepted the bribe. But there is worse to come. Significant freedom, obviously, does not *entail* wrongdoing; so there are possible worlds in which God and Curley both exist and in which the latter is significantly free but never goes wrong. But consider W, any one of these worlds. There is a state of affairs T such that God strongly actualizes T in W and T includes every state of affairs God strongly actualizes in W. Furthermore, since Curley is significantly free in W, there are some actions that are morally significant for him in W and with respect to which he is free in W. The sad truth, however, maybe this: among these actions there is one—call it A—such that if God had actualized T, Curley would have gone wrong with respect to A. But then it follows (by the argument of Section 6) that God could not have actualized W. Now W was just any of the worlds in which Curley is significantly free but always does only what is right. It therefore follows that it was not within God's power to actualize a world in which Curley produces moral good but no moral evil. Every world God could have actualized is such that if Curley is significantly free in it, he takes at least one wrong action.

The intuitive idea underlying this argument can be put as follows. Of course God can create Curley in various states of affairs that include his being significantly free with respect to some action A. Furthermore, God knows in advance what

Curley would do if created and placed in these states of affairs. Now take any one of these states of affairs S. Perhaps what God knows is that if he creates Curley, causes him to be free with respect to A, and brings it about that S is actual, then Curley will go wrong with respect to A. But perhaps the same is true for *any other* state of affairs in which God might create Curley and give him significant freedom; that is, perhaps what God knows in advance is that no matter *what* circumstances he places Curley in, so long as he leaves him significantly free, he will take at least one wrong action. And the present claim is not, of course, that Curley or anyone else is *in fact* like this, but only that this story about Curley is *possibly* true.

If it *is* true, however, Curley suffers from what I shall call *transworld depravity*.[1] By way of explicit definition:

(29) A person P *suffers from transworld depravity* if and only if for every world W such that P is significantly free in W and P does only what is right in W, there is a state of affairs T and an action A such that

(1) God strongly actualizes T in W and W includes every state of affairs God strongly actualizes in W,

(2) A is morally significant for P in W,

and

(3) if God had strongly actualized T, P would have gone wrong with respect to A.

What is important about the idea of transworld depravity is that if a person suffers from it, then it was not within God's power to actualize any world in which that person is significantly free but does no wrong—that is, a world in which he produces moral good but no moral evil. But clearly it is possible that everybody suffers from transworld depravity. If this possibility were actual, then God could not have created any of the possible worlds that include the existence and significant freedom of just the persons who do in fact exist, and also contain moral good but no moral evil. For to do so he would have had to create persons who were significantly free but suffered from transworld depravity. And the price for creating a world in

---

[1] I leave as homework the problem of comparing transworld depravity with what Calvinists call "total depravity".

which such persons produce moral good is creating one in which they also produce moral evil.

Now we might think this settles the question in favour of the Free Will Defender. But the fact is it does not. For suppose all the people that exist in α suffer from transworld depravity; it does not follow that God could not have created a world containing moral good without creating one containing moral evil. God could have created *other people*. Instead of creating us, he could have created a world containing people all right, but not containing any of us. And perhaps if he had done that, he could have created a world containing moral good but no moral evil.

Perhaps. But then again, perhaps not. Return to the notion of *essence* or *individual concept* as developed in Chapter V: an essence of Curley is a property he has in every world in which he exists and that is not exemplified in any world by any object distinct from Curley. An essence *simpliciter* is a property P such that there is a world W in which there exists an object x that has P essentially and is such that in no world W^* is there an object that has P and is distinct from x. More briefly, an essence is an encaptic property that is essentially exemplified in some world, where an encaptic property entails either P or $\bar{P}$, for every world-indexed property P.

And now recall that Curley suffers from transworld depravity. This fact implies something interesting about Curleyhood, Curley's essence. Take those worlds W such that *is significantly free in W and never does what is wrong in W* is entailed by Curley's essence. Each of these worlds has an important property, if Curley suffers from transworld depravity; each is such that God could not have actualized it. We can see this as follows. Suppose W^* is some world such that Curley's essence entails the property *is significantly free but never does what is wrong in W^**. That is, W^* is a world in which Curley is significantly free but always does what is right. But of course Curley suffers from transworld depravity. This means (as we have already seen) that God could not have actualized W^*. So if Curley suffers from transworld depravity, then Curley's essence has this property: God could not have actualized any world W such that Curleyhood contains the properties *is significantly free in W* and *always does what is right in W*.

We can use this connection between Curley's transworld depravity and his essence as the basis for a definition of transworld depravity as applied to essences rather than persons. We should note first that if E is a person's essence, then he is the instantiation of E; he is the thing that has (or exemplifies) every property in E. To instantiate an essence, God creates a person who has that essence; and in creating a person he instantiates an essence. Now we can say that

> (30) An essence E *suffers from transworld depravity* if and only if for every world W such that E entails the properties *is significantly free in W* and *always does what is right in W*, there is a state of affairs T and an action A such that
>
>> (1) T is the largest state of affairs God strongly actualizes in W,
>>
>> (2) A is morally significant for E's instantiation in W,
>
> and
>
>> (3) if God had strongly actualized T, E's instantiation would have gone wrong with respect to A.

Note that transworld depravity is an accidental property of those essences and persons it afflicts. For suppose Curley suffers from transworld depravity: then so does his essence. There is a world, however, in which Curley is significantly free but always does what is right. If *that* world had been actual, then of course neither Curley nor his essence would have suffered from transworld depravity. So the latter is essential neither to those persons nor to those essences that exemplify it. But by now it is evident, I take it, that if an essence E *does* suffer from transworld depravity, then it was not within God's power to actualize a possible world W such that E contains the properties *is significantly free in W* and *always does what is right in W*. Hence it was not within God's power to create a world in which E's instantiation is significantly free but always does what is right.

Now the interesting fact here is this: it is possible that every creaturely essence[1] suffers from transworld depravity. But suppose this is true. God can create a world containing moral good only by creating significantly free persons. And, since every person is the instantiation of an essence, he can create significantly free persons only by instantiating some creaturely

---

[1] i.e. every essence entailing *is created by God*.

essences. But if every such essence suffers from transworld depravity, then no matter which essences God instantiated, the resulting persons, if free with respect to morally significant actions, would always perform at least some wrong actions. If every creaturely essence suffers from transworld depravity, then it was beyond the power of God himself to create a world containing moral good but no moral evil. He might have been able to create worlds in which moral evil is very considerably outweighed by moral good; but it was not within the power of omnipotence to create worlds containing moral good but no moral evil. Under these conditions God could have created a world containing no moral evil only by creating one without significantly free persons. But it is possible that every essence suffers from transworld depravity; so it is possible that God could not have created a world containing moral good but no moral evil.

8. *The Free Will Defence Triumphant*

Put formally, you remember, the Free Will Defender's project was to show that

(1) God is omniscient, omnipotent, and wholly good

is consistent with

(2) There is evil

by employing the truth that a pair of propositions p and q are jointly consistent if there is a proposition r whose conjunction with p is consistent and entails q. What we have just seen is that

(31) Every essence suffers from transworld depravity

is consistent with God's omnipotence. But then it is clearly consistent with (1). So we can use it to show that (1) is consistent with (2). For consider the conjunction of (1), (31), and

(32) God actualizes a world containing moral good.

This conjunction is evidently consistent. But it entails

(2) There is evil.

Accordingly (1) is consistent with (2); the Free Will Defence is successful.

Of course the conjunction of (31) with (32) is not the only proposition that can play the role of r in the Free Will Defence.

Perhaps, for example, it was within the power of God to actualize a world including moral good but no moral evil, but not within his power to actualize one including no moral evil and including as much moral good as the actual world contains. So

(33) For any world W, if W contains no moral evil and W includes as much moral good as α contains, then God could not have actualized W

(which is weaker than (31)) could be used in conjunction with

(34) God actualizes a world containing as much moral good as α contains

to show that (1) and (2) are consistent. The essential point of the Free Will Defence is that the creation of a world containing moral good is a co-operative venture; it requires the uncoerced concurrence of significantly free creatures. But then the actualization of a world W containing moral good is not up to God alone; it also depends upon what the significantly free creatures of W would do if God created them and placed them in the situations W contains. Of course it is up to God whether to create free creatures at all; but if he aims to produce moral good, then he must create significantly free creatures upon whose co-operation he must depend. Thus is the power of an omnipotent God limited by the freedom he confers upon his creatures.[1]

9. *God's Existence and the* Amount *of Moral Evil*

The world, after all, contains a *great deal* of moral evil; and what we have seen so far is only that God's existence is compatible with *some* evil. Perhaps the atheologian can regroup, arguing that at any rate God's existence is not consistent with the vast amount and variety of evil the universe actually contains. Of course we cannot measure moral evil—that is, we do not have units like volts or pounds or kilowatts so that we could say "this situation contains about 35 turps of moral evil". Still we can compare situations in terms of evil; we can see that some contain more moral evil than others. And perhaps the atheologian means to maintain that it is at any rate obvious that God, if omnipotent, could have created a *morally better* world—one

---

[1] See William Wainwright, "Freedom and Omnipotence", *Nous*, 2 (1968), 293–301.

containing a better mixture of moral good and evil than α—
one, let us say, that contained as much moral good but less
moral evil.

But is this really obvious? I do not think so. Possibly this was
not within God's power, which is all the Free Will Defender
needs. We can see this as follows. Of course there are many
possible worlds containing as much moral good as α, but less
moral evil. Let W^* be any such world. If W^* had been actual,
there would have been as much moral good (past, present, and
future) as in fact there was, is, and will be; and there would
have been less moral evil in all. Now in W^* a certain set of S of
essences is instantiated. So to actualize W^*, God would have
had to create persons who were the instantiations of these
essences. But perhaps one of these essences would have had an
unco-operative instantiation. That is, possibly

(35) There is a member E of S, a state of affairs T, and an action A
such that

(1) E's instantiation freely performs A in W^*,

(2) T is the largest state of affairs God actualizes in W^*,
and

(3) if God had strongly actualized T, E's instantiation
would not have performed A.

I say it is possible that (35) is true; but clearly *if* it is, then for
reasons by now familiar God could not have actualized W^*.
And the fact is it is possible that every morally better world
is like W in that God could not have actualized it. For it is
possible that for every morally better world there is a member
E of S, an action A, and a state of affairs T that meet the
conditions laid down in (35). But if so, then (1) is compatible
with the existence of as much evil as α does in fact contain.

10. *God's Existence and* Natural *Evil*

But perhaps the atheologian can regroup once more. What
about *natural* evil? Evil that cannot be ascribed to the free
actions of human beings? Suffering due to earthquakes, disease,
and the like? Is the existence of evil of *this sort* compatible with
(1)? Here two lines of thought present themselves. Some people
deal creatively with certain kinds of hardship or suffering, so
acting that on balance the whole state of affairs is valuable.

Perhaps their responses would have been less impressive and the total situations less valuable without the evil. Perhaps some natural evils and some persons are so related that the persons would have produced less moral good if the evils had been absent.[1] But another and more traditional line of thought is pursued by St. Augustine, who attributes much of the evil we find to *Satan*, or to Satan and his cohorts.[2] Satan, so the traditional doctrine goes, is a mighty non-human spirit who, along with many other angels, was created long before God created man. Unlike most of his colleagues, Satan rebelled against God and has since been wreaking whatever havoc he can. The result is natural evil. So the natural evil we find is due to free actions of non-human spirits.

This is a *theodicy*, as opposed to a *defence*.[3] St. Augustine believes that natural evil (except for what can be attributed to God's punishment) is *in fact* to be ascribed to the activity of beings that are free and rational but non-human. The Free Will Defender, on the other hand, need not assert that this is *true*; he says only that it is *possible* (and consistent with (1)). He points to the possibility that natural evil is due to the actions of significantly free but non-human persons. We have noted the possibility that God could not have actualized a world with a better balance of moral good over moral evil than this one displays. Something similar holds here; possibly natural evil is due to the free activity of a set of non-human persons, and perhaps it was not within God's power to create a set of such persons whose free actions produced a greater balance of good over evil. That is to say, it is possible that

(36) All natural evil is due to the free activity of non-human persons; there is a balance of good over evil with respect to the actions of these non-human persons; and there is no world God could have created which contains a more favourable balance of good over evil with respect to the free activity of the non-human persons it contains.

Again, it must be emphasized that (36) is not required to be

[1] As in John Hick's *Soul-making* theodicy; see his *Evil and the God of Love* (London: Macmillan), 1966.

[2] See "The Problem of Free Choice", in *Ancient Christian Writers*, vol. 22 (New York: Paulist / Newman Press), pp. 71 ff.; and *Confessions and Enchiridion*, tr. and ed. by Albert C. Outler (Philadelphia: Westminster Press), pp. 341–6.

[3] I am indebted to Henry Schuurman for this use of these terms.

true for the success of the Free Will Defence; it need only be compatible with (1). And it certainly looks as if it is. If (36) *is* true, furthermore, then *natural* evil significantly resembles *moral* evil in that, like the latter, it is the result of the activity of significantly free persons. In fact both moral and natural evil would then be special cases of what we might call *broadly moral evil*—evil resulting from the free actions of personal beings, whether human or not. (Of course there is a correlative notion of broadly moral good.) To facilitate discussion, furthermore, let us stipulate that the *turp* is the basic unit of evil and that there are 10^{13} turps of evil in the actual world; the total amount of evil (past, present, and future) contained by α is 10^{13} turps. Given these ideas, we can combine (35) and (36) into one compendious statement:

(37) All the evil in the actual world is broadly moral evil; and every world that God could have actualized, and that contains as much broadly moral good as the actual world displays, contains at least 10^{13} turps of evil.

Now (37) appears to be consistent with (1) and

(38) God actualizes a world containing as much broadly moral good as the actual world contains.

But (1), (37), and (38) together entail that there is as much evil as α contains; so (1) is consistent with the proposition that there is as much evil as α contains. I therefore conclude that the Free Will Defence successfully rebuts the charge of inconsistency brought against the theist. If evil is a problem for the believer, it is not that the existence of evil—moral or natural—is inconsistent with the existence of God.

11. *The Probabilistic Argument from Evil*

Not all atheologians who argue that one cannot rationally accept the existence of both God and evil, maintain that there is *inconsistency* here. Another possibility is that the existence of evil, or of the amount of it we find (perhaps coupled with other things we know) makes it *unlikely* or *improbable* that God exists. And of course this could be true even if the existence of God is consistent with that of evil. But *is* it true? Suppose we briefly investigate the matter. Let us say that a proposition *p confirms* a proposition q if q is more probable than not on p alone: if, that is, q would be more probable than not-q, with respect to what we know, if p were the only thing we knew that was relevant to q. And let us say that p *disconfirms* q if p confirms the denial of q. Now recall

(37) All the evil in the world is broadly moral evil; and every world that God could have actualized and that contains as much moral good as the actual world displays, contains at least 10^{13} turps of evil;

or consider (39), which allows for the possibility that not all natural evil is broadly moral:

(39) Every world that God could have actualized and that contains less than 10^{13} turps of evil, contains less broadly moral good and a less favourable over-all balance of good and evil than the actual world contains.

It is evident that

(40) There are 10^{13} turps of moral evil

disconfirms neither (37) nor (39). Nor, then, does it disconfirm either

(41) God is the omnipotent, omniscient, and morally perfect creator of the world; all the evil in the world is broadly moral evil; and every world that God could have actualized and that contains as much moral good as the actual world displays, contains at least 10^{13} turps of evil;

or

(42) God is the omnipotent, omniscient, and morally perfect creator of the world; and every world that God could have actualized and that contains less than 10^{13} turps of evil, contains less broadly moral good and a less favourable over-all balance of good and evil than the actual world contains.

Now if a proposition p confirms a proposition q, then it confirms every proposition q entails. But then it follows that if p *disconfirms* q, p disconfirms every proposition that entails q. (40) does not disconfirm (41) or (42); (41) and (42) each entail (1); therefore, the existence of the amount of evil actually displayed in the world does not render improbable the existence of an omniscient, omnipotent, and wholly good God. So far as this argument goes, of course, there may be *other* things we know such that (41) and/or (42) is improbable with respect to the conjunction of (40) with *them*. It may be that (41) and (42) are improbable with respect to our *total evidence*, the totality of what we know. (41), for example, involves the idea that the evil that is not due to free human agency, is due to the free agency of *other* rational and significantly free creatures. Do we have evidence against this idea? Many people find it preposterous; but that is scarcely evidence against it. Theologians sometimes tell us that this idea is repugnant to "man come of age" or to "modern habits of thought". I am not convinced that this is so; in any case it does not come to much as evidence. The mere fact that a belief is unpopular at present (or at some other time) is interesting, no doubt, from a sociological point of view; it is evidentially irrelevant. Perhaps we do have evidence against this belief; but if we do, I do not know what it is.

At any rate, I cannot see that our total evidence disconfirms the idea that natural evil results from the activity of rational and significantly free creatures. Of course our total evidence is vast and amorphous; its bearing on the idea in question is not easy to assess. So I conclude, not that our total evidence does not disconfirm (41), but that I have no reason to suppose it does. And the same holds for (42); here too I can see no reason for supposing that our total evidence disconfirms it. So I see no reason to think that the existence of the amount of evil the world contains, taken either by itself or in connection with other things we know, makes God's existence improbable.

The upshot, I believe, is that there is no good atheological argument from evil. The existence of God is neither precluded nor rendered improbable by the existence of evil. Of course suffering and misfortune may none the less constitute a *problem* for one who believes in God; but the problem is not that presented by holding beliefs that are logically or probabilistically incompatible. He may find a *religious* problem in evil; in the presence of his own suffering or that of someone near to him, he may fail to maintain a right attitude towards God. Faced with great personal suffering or misfortune, he may be tempted to rebel against God, to shake his fist in God's face, to curse God. He may despair of God's goodness, or even give up belief in God altogether. But this is a problem of a different dimension. Such a problem calls for pastoral rather than philosophical counsel.

X

GOD AND NECESSITY

ALTHOUGH the subject of this chapter—the Ontological
Argument for the existence of God—looks, at first sight,
like a verbal sleight of hand or a piece of word magic, it
has fascinated philosophers ever since St. Anselm had the good
fortune to formulate it. Nearly every major philosopher from
that time to this has had his say about it. Such comment,
furthermore, has been by no means exclusively adverse; the
argument has a long and illustrious line of defenders extending
to the present and at the moment including, among others,
Professors Charles Hartshorne and Norman Malcolm. What
accounts for this fascination? First, many of the most knotty and
difficult problems in philosophy meet in this argument: is
existence a property? Are existential propositions ever necessarily true? Are existential propositions about what they seem
to be about? How are we to understand negative existentials?
Are there, in any respectable sense of 'are', some objects that do
not exist? If so, do they have any properties? Can they be compared with things that do exist? These issues and a score of
others arise in connection with St. Anselm's argument.

Second: we noted that the argument has about it an air of
egregious unsoundness or perhaps even trumpery and deceit;
yet it is profoundly difficult to say exactly where it goes wrong.
The fact, I think, is that no philosopher has ever given a really
convincing, conclusive, and *general* refutation—one relevant to
all or most of the myriad forms the argument takes.[1] Too often
philosophers are content to remark that Kant refuted St. Anselm
by showing that "existence is not a predicate" and that "one
cannot build bridges from the conceptual realm to the real
world". But Kant never specified a sense of 'is a predicate' such
that, in that sense, it is clear both that existence is *not* a predicate
and that St. Anselm's argument requires it to be one.[1] Nor are

---

[1] See *God and Other Minds*, Chapter 2.

the mere claims that no existential propositions are necessary (or the above comment about bridge building) impressive as refutations of St. Anselm—after all, he claims to have an *argument* for the necessity of at least one existential proposition. In this chapter I shall take a fresh look at this argument—this time from the perspective of what (as I hopefully take it) we have learned about possible worlds. These ideas permit a much clearer understanding of the argument; and they may enable us to see (as I shall claim) that at least one version of the argument is sound.

1. *The Anselmian Statement*

And so, Lord, do thou, who dost give understanding to faith, give me, so far as thou knowest it to be profitable, to understand that thou art as we believe; and that thou art that which we believe. And indeed, we believe that thou art a being than which nothing greater can be conceived. Or is there no such nature, since the fool hath said in his heart, there is no God? . . . But, at any rate, this very fool, when he hears of this being of which I speak—a being than which nothing greater can be conceived—understands what he hears, and what he understands is in his understanding, although he does not understand it to exist.

For, it is one thing for an object to be in the understanding, and another to understand that the object exists. When a painter first conceives of what he will afterwards perform, he has it in his understanding, but he does not yet understand it to be, because he has not yet performed it. But after he has made the painting, he both has it in his understanding, and he understands that it exists, because he has made it.

Hence, even the fool is convinced that something exists in the understanding, at least, than which nothing greater can be conceived. For, when he hears of this, he understands it. And whatever is understood, exists in the understanding. And assuredly that, than which nothing greater can be conceived, cannot exist in the understanding alone; for suppose it exists in the understanding alone; then it can be conceived to exist in reality; which is greater.

Therefore, if that, than which nothing greater can be conceived, exists in the understanding alone, the very being, than which nothing greater can be conceived, is one, than which a greater can be conceived. But obviously this is impossible. Hence, there is no doubt that there exists a being, than which nothing greater can be conceived, and it exists both in the understanding and in reality.[1]

Thus St. Anselm. I think we may best understand him as giving a *reductio ad absurdum* argument; postulate the non-existence of God and show that this supposition leads to absurdity or contradiction. Let us use the term 'God' as an abbreviation for the phrase 'the being than which nothing greater can be conceived'. Then, sticking as closely as possible to Anselm's wording, we may put his argument more explicitly as follows: suppose

(1) God exists in the understanding but not in reality.

(2) Existence in reality is greater than existence in the understanding alone.

(3) God's existence in reality is conceivable.

(4) If God did exist in reality, then he would be greater than he is (from (1) and (2)).

(5) It is conceivable that there be a being greater than God is ((3) and (4)).

(6) It is conceivable that there be a being greater than the being than which nothing greater can be conceived ((5), by the definition of 'God').

But surely

(7) It is false that it is conceivable that there be a being greater than the being than which none greater can be conceived.

Since (6) and (7) contradict each other, we may conclude that

(8) It is false that God exists in the understanding but not in reality.

So if God exists in the understanding, he also exists in reality; but clearly enough he does exist in the understanding, as even the fool will testify; therefore he exists in reality as well.

2. *The Argument Restated*

First, a couple of preliminary comments. When St. Anselm says that a being *exists in the understanding* we may take him, I think, as saying that someone has thought of or conceived of that

[1] *Proslogion*, Chapter 2.

being. When he says that something *exists in reality*, on the other hand, he means to say what we would mean by saying simply that the thing in question exists. And when he says that a certain state of affairs is *conceivable* he means to say (or so, at any rate, I shall take him)[1] that it is a logically possible state of affairs— possible in our broadly logical sense. So, for example, step (3) in the above argument is more clearly put as

(3′) It is possible that God exists in reality;

and step (7) may be put as

(7′) It is false that it is possible that there is a being greater than the being than which it is not possible that there be a greater.

In the argument as I outlined it, we have step (1) as the assumption to be reduced to absurdity, steps (2), (3), and (7) as premises in the argument, and the remaining steps as consequences of these premises. I think it is fair to say that it is step (2)—the assertion that existence in reality is greater than existence in the understanding alone—that is the troublemaker here. What could St. Anselm have meant? He takes it for granted that some beings are greater than others. A man who displays such qualities as wisdom and courage is greater, so far forth, than one who does not. Furthermore, a cat, let us say, is not as great a being as a man, in that the latter has properties of intelligence and knowledge that the former lacks. Such qualities as life, consciousness, knowledge, wisdom, moral excellence, power, courage, and the like are what we might call 'great-making' properties; the more of these properties a being has and the greater the degree to which it has them, the greater, all else being equal, it is. Of course there will be appropriate weightings; perhaps the modest degree of wisdom displayed by your average candidate for public office counts for more than the cheetah's singular locomotive swiftness; and no doubt moral excellence outweighs power. Further, there may be cases where comparison with respect to greatness is difficult or impossible; how shall we compare a really splendid inanimate object—the Grand Teton, let us say—with a fairly undistinguished living

---

[1] My concern throughout will be less with fidelity to St. Anselm's actual intentions than with the various arguments his words suggest. For a determined attempt to get at what St. Anselm himself most probably had in mind, see D. P. Henry, *Medieval Logic and Metaphysics* (London: Hutchinson & Co. Ltd., 1972), pp. 101–18.

thing—an earthworm, perhaps? Or how compare the latter with a number? Perhaps these items cannot be compared with respect to greatness; perhaps the relation *is at least as great as* is not connected. But St. Anselm need not suppose that it is. Of course he *is* committed to the claim that there is or could be a being bearing this relation to everything; he need not add that for any beings A and B, A bears it to B or B bears it to A.

Furthermore, a given object may have more greatness in one possible state of affairs than in another. In the actual world, for example, Raquel Welch has many impressive assets; in some other world she may be fifty pounds overweight and mousy. In this world, Leibniz is a very great man; he discovered the calculus, made some contributions to biology and optics, wrote some great philosophy and did all this in his spare time. Things could have gone differently, however; suppose he had joined Captain Cook on a voyage of exploration, visited the Islands of the South Seas, became enamoured of their climate and inhabitants, eschewed the life of the mind, and never been heard of again. Then, by certain standards, at least, he would not have been as great a man as he was in fact.

There may be some problems with St. Anselm's conception of greatness; still, I think we can see roughly, at any rate, what he had in mind. But in step (2) St. Anselm suggests that *existence* is a great-making property. And how, exactly, are we to understand that? In Chapter VIII, I argued that there are no possible but unactual objects, no possible things that do not exist. Step (2) and indeed St. Anselm's entire argument receives a smoother and more intelligible formulation, however, if we concede or pretend that there *are* such objects. So suppose we temporarily go along with this idea; later we shall see what happens if we reject it. The relation *being at least as great as*, then, is to be thought of as relating merely possible objects as well as actual objects; and it may relate some of the former to some of the latter. This notion in mind, we may find it tempting to take step (2) as suggesting a comparison between existing beings and things like Pegasus or Superman that do not exist; he seems to be suggesting that an existing being has the advantage, so far forth, over a nonexistent being. C. D. Broad reads him thus: St. Anselm's argument, he says, "presupposes that . . . there is sense in talking of a comparison between a nonexistent term and an existent term; and it produces the impression that this is like comparing two existing terms, e.g. a corpse and a living organism, one of which lacks life and the other of which has it". But this, he says, "is nonsensical verbiage".[1] In *God and Other Minds*, I took step (2) as something like

(2a) If A has every property B has (except for nonexistence and any property entailing it) and A exists and B does not, then A is greater than B.[2]

Like Broad, I believed that St. Anselm's fundamental idea involved a comparison of *different* beings, one of them existent and the other not. And for reasons we need not enter here, this makes the argument exceedingly difficult to state.[3]

Now perhaps St. Anselm did mean to suggest something like (2a). Another look at his argument, however, shows that at the least he also meant to suggest something else.[4] As he puts it,

. . . that than which nothing greater can be conceived does not exist in the understanding alone. For, suppose it exists in the understanding alone; then it can be conceived to exist in reality; which is greater.

Here his idea is pretty clearly this: if this being *did* exist in reality, it would be greater than it is. St. Anselm means to be speaking of just one object; and he says of *that* thing, supposed for the moment not to exist, that it would be greater if it *did* exist. He means to compare the greatness it has in *one* state of affairs with the greatness it has in some other state of affairs; he means to suggest that this object is greater in the worlds in which it exists than it is in this one, where it does not. More generally, perhaps St. Anselm means to suggest that if an object x exists in a world W and does not exist in a world W', then its greatness in W exceeds its greatness in W'. But given this premiss, we can restate the ontological argument as follows. Let us concede that there is just one possible being than which it is not possible that there be a greater; and suppose again we use the term 'God' to abbreviate the description 'the being than which it is not possible that there be a greater'. The argument

---

[1] *Religion, Philosophy and Psychical Research* (London, 1953), p. 182.
[2] p. 67.
[3] pp. 66 ff.
[4] As David Lewis points out in his "Anselm and Actuality", *Nous*, 5 (1970), p. 178.

then aims to show that this being must be actual as well as possible. For suppose

(9) God does not exist in the actual world.

(10) For any worlds W and W' and object x, if x exists in W and x does not exist in W', then the greatness of x in W exceeds the greatness of x in W'.

(11) It is possible that God exists.

(12) So there is a possible world W such that God exists in W (from (11)).

(13) God exists in W and God does not exist in the actual world (from (9) and (12)).

(14) If God exists in W and God does not exist in the actual world, then the greatness of God in W exceeds the greatness of God in the actual world (from (10)).

(15) So the greatness of God in W exceeds the greatness of God in the actual world ((13) and (14)).

(16) So there is a possible being x and a world W such that the greatness of x in W exceeds the greatness of God in actuality (15).

(17) So it is possible that there be a being greater than God is (16).

(18) Hence it is possible that there be a being greater than the being than which it is not possible that there be a greater (from (17) by definition of 'God').

Our supposition at step (9), therefore, with the help of the premisses expressed by (10) and (11), implies a false statement; for surely

(19) It is not possible that there be a being greater than the being than which it is not possible that there be a greater.

Step (9) accordingly must be false and the existence of God established.

3. *The Argument Examined*

Now where, if anywhere, can we fault this argument? Step (9), of course, is the hypothesis for a *reductio* argument and is thus entirely above reproach. Steps (12) to (18) appear to follow quite properly from the items they are said to follow from. (19) certainly seems correct on the face of things; is it not contradictory to suppose that there is a being greater than the being than which it is not possible that there be a greater? So that leaves only the premisses. Step (11) is just our supposition that there is a possible being than which it is not possible that there be a greater; but what about step (10)? Well, is (10) not plausible? A being that does not even *exist* in a given world certainly cannot have much by way of greatness in *that* world, however good its credentials in other worlds. But in fact a vastly weaker premiss than (10) will serve in the argument; we can replace (10) by

(10′) For any world W and object x, if x does not exist in W, then there is a world W' such that the greatness of x in W' exceeds the greatness of x in W.

(10′) does not assert that a being is greater in all the worlds in which it exists than it is in any of the worlds in which it does not; it says merely that for any world W in which a thing does not exist, there is at least one world in which it has more greatness than it has in W. This is compatible, of course, with the existence of a pair of worlds W and W' such that x exists in W and does not exist in W', but is none the less greater in W' than in W. What (10′) says is only that a thing does not attain its *greatest* greatness in any world in which it does not exist; and this seems eminently plausible.

But now suppose we think a bit more about the being than which it is not possible that there be a greater. This being possesses a maximal degree of greatness; a degree of greatness that is nowhere excelled. That is to say, its greatness is not exceeded by the greatness of any being in any possible world. But *which* greatness of this being are we speaking of?[1] We said earlier that a being may have different degrees of greatness in different worlds; in which world does the being in question possess the degree of greatness in question? All we know so far, really, is that there is *some world or other* where it has this greatness; what step (11) really tells us is that among the possible beings there is one that in some world or other has a degree of greatness that is nowhere excelled; this being has a degree of greatness, in some world W, so impressive that there is no being

[1] See Lewis, op. cit., p. 179. My criticism (pp. 202–5) of this version of St. Anselm's argument substantially follows Lewis.

x and world W' such that x has a greater degree of greatness in W'. So when the argument speaks of the being than which it is not possible that there be a greater, we should take it that this phrase is meant to denote the possible being whose greatness *in some world or other* is nowhere exceeded. And then step (12) should be read as

> (12') There is a possible world W such that the being whose greatness in some world is nowhere exceeded, exists in W.

This certainly follows from (11). Further, all the steps of the argument through (16) seem right. (17) and (18) also follow quite properly from preceding steps; we can see that this is so if we restate (18) as

> (18') There is a possible world W and a possible being x such that the greatness of x in W exceeds the greatness of God in the actual world;

W is any world in which God exists (and where his greatness is maximal) and x is God himself. But what about (19), according to which it is impossible that there be a being that is greater than the being than which it is not possible that there be a greater? Initially this sounds convincing; but does it really have the solid ring of truth? Let W be any world in which God exists and achieves maximum greatness. It is certainly not possible that there be a being with a degree of greatness that exceeds that enjoyed by God in W; and if this is what (19) said, then (19) would be true. Unfortunately, if this is what is said, it would not follow that (18') is false, and the *reductio* argument would fall to pieces. (19) is of use in the argument only if it contradicts (18'). But understood in the above fashion—that is, as

> (19') There is no possible world W' and being x such that the greatness of x in W' exceeds the greatness of God in W

it is not inconsistent with (18'), which says that God's greatness in the *actual* world, is somewhere exceeded; this is quite compatible with saying, as (19') does, that God's greatness in that world W is nowhere exceeded. For so far, of course, we have no reason to think that W is the actual world. If, on the other hand, we take (19) as

> (19") There is no possible world W and being x such that the

greatness of x in W exceeds the greatness of God *in the actual world*

then indeed it contradicts (18'); but then we have no reason to think that it is true. What we know about this being, about God, is that *in some world or other* his greatness is at an absolute maximum; in some world or other he enjoys a degree of greatness that is not excelled by any being in any world. What (19") says, however, is that the *actual world* is a world in which the greatness of this being is at such a high pitch; and so far we have no reason at all for supposing that true. This version of the argument therefore fails; (19') is clearly true but contributes nothing to the argument; (19") contributes mightily to the argument, but we have no reason at all for supposing it true.

4. *A Mistaken Modal Version*

But is it not *possibly* true at any rate? Is it not possible that the actual world is one of the worlds in which God's greatness is maximal? Or to put the same thing differently, is it not possible that one of the worlds in which his greatness is at a maximum, is actual? Of course; *every* world is possibly actual; and so, therefore, are those worlds in which God's greatness is at a maximum. But perhaps we can use this fact to revise the argument. Let us suppose as before that the term 'God' simply abbreviates the longer phrase 'the being whose greatness in some world or other is nowhere exceeded'. And let us take as our first premiss the statement that possibly God exists—that is

(20) There is just one possible being whose greatness in some world W is unexceeded by the greatness of any being in any world.

Further, suppose we add a premiss that corresponds to step (10) and (10') but is a bit weaker and hence even more plausible:

(21) If a possible being x does not exist in a world W, then there is a possible being y and a world W' such that the greatness of y in W' exceeds the greatness of x in W.

What (21) says is that if a being does not exist, then it is possible that there be a being greater than it is. Now we know that God exists in some world where his greatness is maximal. Let W be any such world and suppose that

(22) W obtains.

If so, then

(23) W is the actual world.

But God's greatness in W is nowhere exceeded; so God's greatness in the actual world is nowhere exceeded. That is to say, for any possible object x and world W, the greatness of God in the actual world equals or exceeds the greatness of x in W. Suppose we give a name to the property a possible object has if there is no world in which its greatness exceeds that enjoyed by God in the actual world: call this property 'P'. What follows from (22), therefore, is

(24) Every possible being has P.

But

(25) Possibly W obtains.

Hence

(26) Possibly everything (every possible being) has P.

Now this property P has a certain interesting peculiarity. For many properties Q there are objects x such that x has Q in some worlds, but has its complement $\bar{Q}$ in others. Snubnosedness, for example, characterizes Socrates in this world; but clearly enough there are plenty of possible worlds in which he has its complement. *Other* properties, however, are not like that. Consider now, not snubnosedness, but the world-indexed property *being-snubnosed-in-α*. As we have seen (Chapter IV, Section 11) if Socrates has this property, then there is no world in which he has its complement. Let us say that a property is a *universal* property if it resembles the property of *being-snubnosed-in-α* in that if an object has it in any world, then there is no world in which it has its complement. That is to say, let us adopt the following definition:

D_1 A property P is a universal property if and only if it is impossible that there be an object that has P in one world and $\bar{P}$ in some other world.

Clearly enough, world-indexed properties will be universal. And now consider this property of nowhere exceeding the greatness of God in the actual world. That too, surely, is a universal property; if in a given world W, it is true of x that in no world does its greatness exceed that enjoyed by God in the actual world, then (see Chapter IV, Section 6) there will be no world in which x has the property of being such that in some world its greatness *does* exceed that of God in the actual world. So

(27) P is a universal property.

But if there is a world in which everything, that is every possible object, has a given universal property, then obviously there is no world in which there is a possible object that has the complement of that property; hence

(28) If there is at least one world in which everything has P, then in no world is there something that has $\bar{P}$.

Now (26) tells us that there is a world in which everything has P; hence

(29) In no world is there anything that has $\bar{P}$.

But if so, then nothing has $\bar{P}$ in the actual world; that is to say, it is in fact true that nothing anywhere exceeds the greatness of God in the actual world. Now from (21) it follows that

(30) If God does not exist in the actual world, then there is a possible being x and a world W such that the greatness of x in W exceeds the greatness of God in the actual world;

But (29) tells us that there is no such possible being and world W; it follows, therefore, that God exists in the actual world.

What shall we say about this argument?

Unfortunately it suffers from a serious defect: it rests upon confusion. Subtle confusion, no doubt, but confusion none the less. Consider again the alleged fact (alleged by step (27)) that P is a universal property. This means that if there is any world at all in which a thing has P, then there is no world in which that thing has $\bar{P}$. Now is this really true? Let W be one of the worlds in which God's greatness is at a maximum. *God* has this property *P* in *W*; for if *W* has obtained, *W* would have been the actual world; hence

(31) Nothing anywhere exceeds the greatness of God in the actual world

is a true statement in *W*. Had *W* obtained, *it* would have been the actual world, and nothing anywhere exceeds the greatness of God in *W*; so if *W* had obtained, (31) would have been a true statement. But if (31) is true in *W*, then everything, including God, has *P* in *W*; so God has the property *P* in *W*.

But now consider a world *W** in which God does not exist. Does God have *P* in *that* world? He does not exist in that world; so his greatness there is inferior to his greatness in *W*. So if *W** had been the actual world, then there would have been a world —i.e. *W*—where his greatness exceeded that of God in the actual world. But if so, then in *W** God has the complement of *P*; so it looks as if *P* is not a universal property after all. God has it in some worlds and has its complement is others—this is true, at any rate, if there are worlds in which God does not exist. So we can say that *P* is a universal property only if we already know that God exists in every world—which, after all, is what the argument was supposed to prove.

But if this is so, what initially led us to suppose that *P is* a universal property? The answer is that we were treating the phrase 'the actual world' as a *proper name* or like a proper name of a certain possible world—the one which happens to be actual. We were supposing that in using the phrase 'the actual world' we would be talking about α, even if we were reasoning about what things would have been like had some world other than α had the distinction of obtaining. We were thinking of the phrase, 'the property of nowhere exceeding the greatness of God in the actual world' as meaning the same thing as the phrase 'the property of nowhere exceeding the greatness of God in α'. And the latter phrase *does* denote a universal property. But can we not use the phrase 'the actual world' in that way if we wish? Can we not use it to mean the same as 'α', so that even if some other world had obtained, that world would not have been the actual world? Of course; but suppose we do use it in that way; then look again at the inference of

(23) *W* is the actual world

from

(22) *W* obtains.

If we are using 'the actual world' as a name like 'α', then this inference is equivalent to inferring

(23') *W* is α

from (22); and this inference is manifestly fallacious. From the supposition that *W* obtains—*W* being one of the worlds in which God's greatness is at a maximum—we cannot properly infer that α obtains; we do not know that α is one of those worlds. So if we use this phrase as a name like 'α' then the proof fails because (23) does not follow from (22); if we use it in such a way that (23) follows from (22), then we have no right to the premiss that *P* is a universal property. We may put the same point another way. On the one hand we might take *P* to be the property a thing has if and only if its greatness nowhere exceeds that of God in α. Then *P* is a universal property, but

(24) Every possible being has *P*

does not follow from the supposition that *W*, a world in which God's greatness is maximal, obtains. On the other hand, *P* might be the property of nowhere exceeding God in the actual world, where we understand that phrase in such a way that if some other world *W* had obtained, then *W* rather than α would have enjoyed the distinction of being the actual world. But then we have no right to suppose that *P* is a universal property.

5. *The Argument Without Possible Objects*

These versions of the argument, therefore, are based upon confusion. Both involve, furthermore, the idea that there are or could have been possible but nonexistent objects. What happens if (as is entirely right and proper according to Chapter VIII) we reject this assumption? Suppose we briefly examine the first formulation from this point of view. The name 'God' was taken as short for the phrase 'the being than which it is not possible that there be a greater'. And the attempt was to deduce an absurdity from

(9) God does not exist in the actual world

> (10) For any worlds W and W' and any object x, if x exists in W but not in W' then the greatness of x in W exceeds the greatness of x in W'

and

> (11) It is possible that God exists.

Here (9) was taken to be a singular statement about a being that is at any rate possible; (10) was taken as quantifying over merely possible as well as actual objects, and (11) credited the being referred to in (9) with existence in some world or other. The argument then proceeded by plausibly confusing the property of having maximal greatness with that of having maximal greatness in some world or other.

Now if we are unwilling to concede that there are possible but unactual beings, we shall have to read (9) not as the claim that a certain being lacks existence, but instead as the proposition that there is no being with maximal greatness—equivalently, that maximal greatness is not exemplified. (11) must then be construed not as the claim that the being mentioned in (9) *does* exist in some world, but instead as the proposition that there is a possible world in which maximal greatness is exemplified. But it is not quite so easy to reconstrue (10). If there are no possible objects, then an object that does not exist in a given world W does not have any greatness at all in W—at any rate there is no property of having such-and-such a degree of greatness that this object has in W. It then seems at the least peculiar and misleading to say that Leibniz, for example, has more greatness in α than he does in a world in which he does not exist; for there is no degree of greatness at all such that he would have had *that* degree of greatness if he had not existed. But presumably all the argument really requires is that Leibniz *fail* to have the *maximal* degree of greatness in a world where he does not exist; and if we recall the distinction between predicative and impredicative propositions (Chapter VIII, Section 1) we see that his failing to have the maximal degree of greatness in such worlds does not entail that there is some *other* degree of greatness he *does* have in those worlds. We may therefore regard (10) as the claim that any object failing to exist in a world W does not have maximal greatness there. So stated, of course, the claim is just about objects that do exist; but we may add that there could not have been objects for which this claim is false. (10) therefore becomes

(10′) Necessarily, for any object x and world W, if x does not exist in W, then x does not have maximal greatness in W.

And this seems plainly true.

So we have

(9′) There is no maximally great being

(10′) Necessarily, for any object x and world W, if x does not exist in W, then x does not have maximal greatness in W,

and

(11′) There is a world in which there exists a maximally great being.

But we cannot plausibly proceed much further. There is a world W in which there exists a being that has maximal greatness there but does not exist here in α. So if W had been actual, there would have been a maximally great being with the properties of failing to exist in α and (by (10′)) failing to have maximal greatness in α. But here we do not have the appearance of contradiction to which the first version appealed. On the earlier formulation, the illusion of paradox arose in that the phrase 'the being than which it is not possible that there be a greater' was used confusingly; it was not initially clear whether it was supposed to denote a possible being that has maximal greatness *in fact*, or one that has that property *in some world or other*; and the argument proceeded to make capital of that confusion. But this illusion is dispelled when we state the argument without reference to possibles.

Here, perhaps, we have a way of so construing Kant's *dictum* —that existence is not a real predicate or property—that it becomes relevant to many versions of the Ontological Argument. In many formulations the argument begins with the claim that there is a certain being—the greatest possible being—that is at any rate *possible* even if it does not exist. This being is denoted by the phrase, 'the being than which it is not possible that there be a greater': and the hypothesis to be reduced to absurdity—that this being does not exist—is construed as a singular proposition predicating nonexistence of the being in question. The argument then goes on to claim that this very being is such that if it *did* exist, it would be greater than it *is*.

But if we reject possible but nonexistent objects, we see that the initial hypothesis—that the greatest possible being does not exist—cannot coherently be construed as a singular proposition unless we already know that there is, that is, exists, such a being. And if, as the initial hypothesis rightly construed asserts, there is *no* such being, then there is nothing of which we can coherently claim that it would be greater if it did exist. Perhaps we may read Kant as suggesting this observation; or perhaps it is only that reading Kant suggests the observation.

6. *The Hartshorne–Malcolm Version*

But of course there are many other versions of the argument. (And I wish to remark parenthetically that the existence of many importantly different versions makes most of the 'refutations' one finds in textbooks look pretty silly.) Professors Charles Hartshorne[1] and Norman Malcolm,[2] for example, find two quite distinct versions of the argument in St. Anselm's writings. In the first of these St. Anselm holds that *existence* is a perfection; he holds some version of the view that a being is greater in a world in which it exists than it is in a world in which it does not. But in the second version, say Malcolm and Hartshorne, it is *necessary* existence that is said to be a perfection. What does *that* mean? Take a world like α and consider two things, A and B that exist in it, where A exists not only in α but in every other world as well while B exists in some but not all worlds. According to the doctrine under consideration, A is so far forth greater in α than B is. Of course B may have some other properties—properties that make for greatness—that A lacks. It may be that on balance it is B that is greater in α. For example, the number 7 exists necessarily and Socrates does not; but it would be peculiar indeed to conclude that the number seven is therefore greater, in α, than Socrates is. The point is only that necessary existence is a great-making quality—it is one of the qualities that must be considered in comparing a pair of beings with respect to greatness. But then it is plausible to suppose that the maximum degree of greatness includes necessary existence— that is to say, a possible being has the maximum degree of

[1] *Man's Vision of God* (Harper & Row, Inc.), 1941.
[2] "Anselm's Ontological Arguments", *Philosophical Review*, 69 (1960).

greatness in a given world only if it exists in that world and furthermore exists in every other world as well. The argument may accordingly be stated as follows:

(32) There is a world W in which there exists a being with maximal greatness,

and

(33) A being has maximal greatness in a world only if it exists in every world.

W, therefore, includes the existence of a being with maximal greatness who exists in every world. So there is an essence E, exemplified in W, that entails the property *exists in every world*. So it is impossible in W that E not be exemplified. But what is impossible does not vary from world to world (Chapter IV, Section 6). Hence E is exemplified, and necessarily exemplified, in *this* world. So there is a greatest possible being, and it exists necessarily.

What this argument shows is that if it is even *possible* that God, so conceived, exists, then it is true that he does, and, indeed, necessarily true that he does. As it is stated, however, there is one fairly impressive flaw: even if an essence entailing *is maximally great in W* is exemplified, it does not so far follow that this essence entails *is maximally great in α*. For all we have shown so far, this being might be at a maximum in some world W, but be pretty insignificant in α, our world. So the argument does not show that there is a being that enjoys maximal greatness in fact; it shows at most that there is a being that in some world or other has maximal greatness.

7. *A Victorious Modal Version*

Is there a way to remove this flaw? Perhaps. Why, after all, should we think that necessary existence is a perfection or great-making quality? Because the greatness of a being in a world W depends not merely upon the qualities it has in W; what it is like in other worlds is also relevant. In the course of an attempt to *disprove* God's existence J. N. Findlay puts this point as follows:

Not only is it contrary to the demands and claims inherent in religious attitudes that their object should *exist* "accidentally"; it is also contrary to these demands that it should *possess its various excellences* in some merely adventitious manner. It would be quite unsatisfactory from the religious stand point, if an object merely *happened* to be wise, good, powerful, and so forth, even to a superlative degree. . . . And so we are led on irresistibly, by the demands inherent in religious reverence, to hold that an adequate object of our worship must possess its various excellence in some necessary manner.[1]

I think there is sense in what Findlay says. His point is that the greatness of a being in a world *W* does not depend merely upon its qualities and attributes in *W*; what it is like in other worlds is also to the point. Those who worship God do not think of him as a being that happens to be of surpassing excellence in *this* world but who in some other worlds is powerless or uninformed or of dubious moral character. We might make a distinction here between *greatness* and *excellence*; we might say that the *excellence* of a being in a given world *W* depends only upon its (non world-indexed) properties in *W*, while its greatness in *W* depends not merely upon its excellence in *W*, but also upon its excellence in other worlds. The limiting degree of greatness, therefore, would be enjoyed in a given world *W* only by a being who had maximal excellence in *W* and in every other possible world as well. And now perhaps we do not need the supposition that necessary existence is a perfection; for (as I argued in Chapter VIII) a being has no properties at all and *a fortiori* no excellent-making properties in a world in which it does not exist. So existence and necessary existence are not themselves perfections, but necessary conditions of perfection.

We may state this argument more fully as follows.

(34) The property *has maximal greatness* entails[2] the property *has maximal excellence in every possible world.*

(35) *Maximal excellence* entails *omniscience, omnipotence,* and *moral perfection.*

(36) *Maximal greatness* is possibly exemplified.

But for any property *P*, if *P* is possibly exemplified, then there

[1] "Can God's Existence be Disproved?", *Mind*, 57 (1948), pp. 108–18.

[2] Where, we recall, a property *P* entails a property *Q* if there is no world in which there exists an object *x* that has *P* but lacks *Q*.

is world W and an essence E such that E is exemplified in W, and E entails *has P in W*. So

(37) There is a world W^* and an essence E^* such that E^* is exemplified in W^* and E^* entails *has maximal greatness in W**.

If W^* had been actual, therefore, E^* would have been exemplified by an object that had maximal greatness and hence (by (34)) had maximal excellence in every possible world. So if W^* had been actual, E^* would have been exemplified by a being that for any world W had the property *has maximal excellence in W*. But every world-indexed property of an object is entailed by its essence (Chapter IV, Section 11). Hence if W^* had been actual, E^* would have entailed, for every world W, the property *has maximal excellence in W*; hence it would have entailed the property *has maximal excellence in every possible world*. That is, if W^* had been actual, the proposition

(38) For any object x, if x exemplifies E^*, then x exemplifies the property *has maximal excellence in every possible world*

would have been necessarily true. But what is necessarily true does not vary from world to world. Hence (38) is necessary in every world and is therefore necessary. So

(39) E^* entails the property *has maximal excellence in every possible world*.

Now (as we have learned from Chapter VIII) a being has a property in a world W only if it exists in that world. So E^* entails the property *exist in every possible world*. E^* is exemplified in W^*; hence if W^* had been actual, E^* would have been exemplified by something that existed and exemplified it in every possible world. Hence

(40) If W^* had been actual, it would have been impossible that E^* fail to be exemplified.

But again, what is impossible does not vary from world to world; hence it is *in fact* impossible that E^* fail to be exemplified; so E^* is exemplified; so

(41) There exists a being that has maximal excellence in every world.

That is, there actually exists a being that is omniscient,

omnipotent, and morally perfect; and that exists and has these properties in every possible world. This being is God.

A similar but simpler version of the argument could go as follows. Let us say that *unsurpassable greatness* is equivalent to *maximal excellence in every possible world*. Then

(42) There is a possible world in which unsurpassable greatness is exemplified.

(43) The proposition *a thing has unsurpassable greatness if and only if it has maximal excellence in every possible world* is necessarily true.

(44) The proposition *whatever has maximal excellence is omnipotent, omniscient, and morally perfect* is necessarily true.

Now here we should notice the following interesting fact about properties. Some, like *is a human person*, are instantiated in some but not all worlds. On the other hand, however, there are such properties as *is a person in every world*. By the principle that what is necessary or impossible does not vary from world to world, this property cannot be instantiated in some worlds but not in others. Either it is instantiated in *every* world or it is not instantiated at all. Using the term 'universal property' in a way slightly different from the way we used it before, we might say that

D$_2$ *P* is a universal property if and only if *P* is instantiated in *every* world or in *no* world.

But clearly the property *possesses unsurpassable greatness* is universal in this sense, for this property is equivalent to the property of having maximal excellence in every world; since the latter is universal, so is the former.

From (42) and (43), therefore, it follows that

(45) *Possesses unsurpassable greatness* is instantiated in every world.

But if so, it is instantiated in this world; hence there actually exists a being who is omnipotent, omniscient, and morally perfect and who exists and has these properties in every world.

What shall we say of these arguments? Clearly they are valid; and hence they show that if it is even possible that God, so thought of, exists, then it is true and necessarily true that he does. The only question of interest, it seems to me, is whether its main premiss—that indeed unsurpassable greatness is possibly exemplified, that there is an essence entailing unsurpassable greatness—is *true*. I think this premiss is indeed true. Accordingly, I think this version of the Ontological Argument is sound.

8. *Final Objections and Reflections*

Now some philosophers do not take kindly to the Ontological Argument; the claim that it or some version of it is sound is often met with puzzled outrage or even baffled rage. One objection I have heard is that the formulation of the last section (call it Argument A) may be valid, but is clearly *circular* or *question-begging*. Sometimes this *caveat* has no more substance than the recognition that the argument is indeed valid and that its premiss could not be true unless its conclusion were—which, of course, does not come to much as an objection. But suppose we briefly look into the complaint. What is it for an argument to be circular? In the paradigm case, one argues for a proposition A_1 on the basis of A_2, for A_2 on the basis of A_3, ..., for A_{n-1} on the basis of A_n, and for A_n on the basis of A_1. Whatever the merits of such a procedure, Argument A is clearly not an example of it; to conform to this pattern one who offered Argument A would be obliged to produce in turn an argument for its main premiss—an argument that involved as premiss the conclusion of A or some other proposition such that A's conclusion was proximately or ultimately offered as evidence for it.

So the argument is not obviously circular. Is it question-begging? Although surely some arguments *are* question-begging, it is by no means easy to say what this fault consists in or how it is related to circularity. But perhaps we can get at the objector's dissatisfaction by means of an example. Consider Argument B:

(46) Either $7+5 = 13$ or God exists.

(47) $7+5 \neq 13$.

Therefore

(48) God exists.

This argument is valid. Since I accept its conclusion and therefore its first premiss, I believe it to be sound as well. Still, I could scarcely claim much for it as a piece of Natural Theology. Probably it will never rank with Aquinas's Third Way, or even his much less impressive Fourth Way. And the reason is that indeed this argument is in some way question begging, or at least dialectically deficient. For presumably a person would not come to believe (46) unless he already believed (48). Not that the alternative is *impossible*—it *could* happen, I suppose, that someone inexplicably find himself with the belief that (46) (and (47)) is true, and then go on to conclude that the same holds for (48). But that certainly would not be the general case. Most people who believe (46) do so only because they already believe (48) and infer the former from the latter. But how do these considerations apply to Argument A? It is by no means obvious that anyone who accepts its main premiss does so only because he infers it from the conclusion. If anyone *did* do that, then for him the argument is dialectically deficient in the way B is; but surely Argument A need not be thus dialectically deficient for one who accepts it.

A second objection: there are plenty of properties that are *non-compossible* with maximal greatness; that is, their possibility is incompatible with that of the latter. Consider, for example, the property of *near-maximality*, enjoyed by a being if and only if it does not exist in every possible world but has a degree of greatness not exceeded by that of any being in any world. This property is possibly exemplified only if there is a world W in which there exists a being who does not exist in every world and whose greatness could not be exceeded. And clearly near-maximality is possibly exemplified only if maximal greatness is *not* possibly exemplified. Or more simply, consider the property of no-maximality, the property of being such that there is no maximally great being. If this property is possible, then maximal greatness is not. But, so claims the objector, these properties are every bit as plausibly possible as maximal greatness. So if Argument A is sound, so is Argument C:

(49) Near-maximality is possibly exemplified

(50) If near-maximality is possible, then maximal greatness is not

therefore

(51) Maximal greatness is impossible.

Since A and C cannot both be sound, he continues, we must conclude that neither is.

But of course here there is confusion. Agreed: A and C cannot both be sound; but why conclude that *neither* is? Consider Argument D:

(52) No-maximality is possibly exemplified

(53) If no-maximality is possibly exemplified, then maximal greatness is impossible.

Therefore

(54) Maximal greatness is impossible.

Logic tells us that A and D cannot both be sound; but it also tells us they cannot both be *un*sound; one is sound and the other is not.

I have also heard the following rider to the last objection. There are vast numbers of properties not compossible with maximal greatness. There are near-maximality and no-maximality, as we have seen, but any numbers of others as well. For example, there is the intersection of no-maximality with such a property as *being Socrates*; this is a property exemplified by something only in the event that that thing is Socrates and there is no maximally great being. Clearly there are as many properties of this sort as you please; for each it seems fairly plausible, initially, at least, to claim that it is possibly exemplified; but each is non-compossible with maximal greatness. So in all probability the latter is impossible; granted, it does not initially *look* impossible, but its claims are outweighed by the claims of the indefinitely many non-compossible properties that look as possible as it.

This argument has little to recommend it. Indeed there are any number of fairly plausible properties that are not compossible with maximal greatness; but there are just as many (and just as plausible) whose possibility *entails* that of the latter: *being a maximally great creator of Socrates, being a maximally great creator of Plato*, etc. For any number *n* there is the property of being maximally great and creating just *n* persons; and the possibility of each of these properties will be precisely as plausible as that of maximal greatness itself.

It must be conceded, however, that Argument A is not a successful piece of natural theology. For the latter typically draws its premisses from the stock of propositions accepted by nearly every sane man, or perhaps nearly every rational man. So, for example, each of St. Thomas's Five Ways begins by appealing to a premiss few would be willing to contest: such propositions as that some things are in motion; or that things change; or that there are contingent beings. And (36), the central premiss of Argument A, is not of this sort; a sane and rational man who thought it through and understood it might none the less reject it, remaining agnostic or even accepting instead the possibility of no-maximality.

Well then, why accept this premiss? Is there not something improper, unreasonable, irrational about so doing? I cannot see why. Philosophers sometimes suggest that certain scientific theories—quantum mechanics, perhaps—require us to give up certain laws of logic—the Principle of Distribution,[1] for example. If we can accept the denial of the Distributive Law in the interests of simplifying physical theory, we should be able to accept (36) in order to do the same for Theology. More seriously, suppose we consider analogous situations. In Chapter VIII, I examined the question whether

(55) There are or could be possible but unactual objects

is true. This proposition resembles (36) in that if it is *possible*, it is true and indeed necessarily true. The same goes for its denial. Furthermore, there are plenty of initially plausible propositions that are not compossible with (55); and plenty more that are not compossible with its denial. There seems to be no argument against this proposition that need compel a determined advocate; and, as Chapter VIII shows, there are none for it. Shall we conclude that it is improper or irrational or philosophically irresponsible to accept (55) or its negation? Surely not. Or consider Leibniz's Law:

(56) For any objects x and y and property P, if $x = y$, then x has P if and only if y has P.

Some philosophers reject (56);[2] various counterexamples have been alleged; various restrictions have been proposed. None of these 'counterexamples' are genuine in my view; but there seems to be no compelling argument for (56) that does not at

---

[1] See Hilary Putnam's "Is Logic Empirical?", in *Boston Studies in Philosophy of Science*, Vol. 5 (Dordrecht: D. Riedel, 1969), pp. 216–41.

[2] Geach and Grice, for example.

some point invoke that very principle. Must we conclude that it is improper to accept it, or to employ it as a premiss? No indeed. The same goes for any number of philosophical claims and ideas. Indeed, philosophy contains little else. Were we to believe only what is uncontested or for which there are incontestable arguments from uncontested premises, we should find ourselves with a pretty slim and pretty dull philosophy. Perhaps we should have *Modus Ponens*; certainly not much more. The policy of accepting only the incontestable promises security but little else.

So if we carefully ponder Leibniz's Law and the alleged objections, if we consider its connections with other propositions we accept or reject and still find it compelling, we are within our rights in accepting it—and this whether or not we can convince others. But then the same goes for (36). Hence our verdict on these reformulated versions of St. Anselm's argument must be as follows. They cannot, perhaps, be said to *prove* or *establish* their conclusion. But since it is rational to accept their central premiss, they do show that it is rational to *accept* that conclusion. And perhaps that is all that can be expected of any such argument.

APPENDIX

QUINE'S OBJECTION TO QUANTIFIED MODAL LOGIC

1. *The Objection Initially Stated*

FOR animadversions on quantified modal logic, we naturally look to the writings of W. V. Quine. Nor are we disappointed; in the revised edition of "Reference and Modality",[1] the most recent in a series of powerful strictures on such systems of logic, Quine introduces his attack by setting out what by now we may call the Classical Objection:

> Now the difficulty recurs when we try to apply existential generalization to modal statements. The apparent consequences
>
> (30) (Ex) (x is necessarily greater than 7)
>
> (31) (Ex) (necessarily, if there is life on the Evening Star then there is life on x)
>
> of
>
> (15) [9 is necessarily greater than 7][2]
>
> and
>
> (16) [Necessarily, if there is life on the Evening Star, then there is life on the Evening Star]
>
> raise the same questions as did
>
> (29) Something is such that Philip is unaware that it denounced Cataline.
>
> What is the number which, according to (30), is necessarily greater than 7? According to (15), from which (30) was inferred, it was 9, that is the number of planets; but to suppose this would conflict with the fact that
>
> (18) the number of planets is necessarily greater than 7
>
> is false. In a word, to be necessarily greater than 7 is not a trait of a number but depends on the manner of referring to the number.   (148)

How are we to understand 'necessarily' here? What sort of modal

---

[1] In *From a Logical Point of View* (hereafter FLPV) (New York: Harper & Row, 1961), p. 147.

[2] Throughout this passage Quine appears to use (15) as a stylistic variant of 'Necessarily, 9 is greater than 7'.

statement is it that is not properly subject to existential generalization?

> The subject under discussion [says Quine] is the so-called *modal* contexts 'Necessarily . . .' and 'Possibly . . .' at least when these are given the sense of *strict* necessity and possibility as in Lewis's modal logic. A statement of the form 'Necessarily . . .' is true if and only if the component statement which 'necessarily' governs is analytic, and a statement of the form 'Possibly . . .' is false if and only if the negation of the component statement which 'possibly' governs is analytic.   (143)

Quine's objection, then, arises at the semantical level; it is modal logic as *interpreted* that draws his fire—more specifically modal logic so interpreted that the operators express modality *de dicto*.[1] And indeed when the modal logician explains the ideas he aims to study and explore, he typically does so in *de dicto* terms. Thus Lewis:

> Self-consistency or possibility: $\Diamond p$. This may be read "*p* is self-consistent" or "*p* is possible" or "It is possible that *p* be true." . . . "$\Diamond p$" is equivalent to "It is false that *p* implies its own negation." . . .[2]

More recently, Hughes and Cresswell:

> Among true propositions we can distinguish between those which merely *happen* to be true and those which are *bound* to be true (or which could not be false). . . . A proposition which is bound to be true we call a *necessarily* true proposition . . .; one which is bound to be false, we call an *impossible* proposition; . . . Given any proposition, *p*, we can of course form the proposition that *p* is necessary, i.e. the proposition we express as 'It is necessary that *p*'. This proposition will be *true* when *p* itself is necessary, and false when *p* is *not* necessary.
>   We shall introduce the symbols *L* and *M* as monadic operators . . . with the intention of interpreting them as 'It is necessary that' and 'It is possible that' . . . In view of the intended interpretation we shall call *L* the *necessity operator* and *M* the *possibility operator*.[3]

We must note, of course, that 'necessarily' and '□' are semantical *operators* attaching to sentences to form sentences. They are not (as the quotation from Lewis suggests) *predicates* that attach to expressions denoting sentences or propositions:

(1)   □ All men are mortal

therefore, is to be read as 'necessarily all men are mortal'—not as 'the proposition (or sentence) *all men are mortal* is necessarily true'.[4]

[1] See Chapter I, Section 2.
[2] Lewis and Langford, *Symbolic Logic* (New York, 1932; reprinted New York: Dover, 1951), p. 123.
[3] *An Introduction to Modal Logic* (London: Methuen, 1968), pp. 22–4.
[4] Indeed, if we extend the usual modal logics by adding names for sentences,

Nevertheless, where S is a sentence expressing a proposition, $\Box S$, under the usual interpretation, will be true if and only if S (or the proposition it expresses) is necessarily true.

So explained, therefore, the modal operators express modality *de dicto*; sentences in which they figure are to be understood as equivalent to sentences predicating modal properties—necessity, possibility, contingency—of sentences. And Quine's objection is that a *de dicto* sentence such as

(2) Necessarily, 9 is composite

does not properly yield

(3) $(\exists x)$ necessarily x is composite

by way of existential generalization—or, for that matter, by way of anything else; for (3) makes no clear sense. The objection is not, of course, to the existential generalization of a *de re* modal statement— one predicating of a given object the necessary or essential possession of a given property; Quine has his doubts about *de re* modal statements, but given their propriety, the appropriate quantified statements would indeed be forthcoming. If there is some property P such that some object—the number nine, let us say—has P essentially, then there is at least one thing that has that property essentially; and it is no part of Quine's programme to assert otherwise.

2. *Sizeability is not a property*

But what, exactly, is objectionable about the inference of (3) from (2)? Just how does the objection go? If we are to understand Quine here, we must pay careful attention to his claims that "to be necessarily greater than 7 is not a trait of a number, but depends upon the manner of referring to the number", and "being necessarily or possibly thus and so is in general not a trait of the object concerned, but depends on the manner of referring to the object". What do these assertions mean? "to be necessarily greater than 7 is not a trait of a number"; how are we to understand this? An appealing and straightforward way is to construe him here as holding that such a context as

(4) Necessarily, ____ is greater than 7

(where the blank is to be filled by a singular term) *does not express a trait (or property)*. Here we meet an initial anomaly, however; Quine

a necessity predicate 'N' and the rules: $\Box p$ / ∴ NB, and NB / ∴ $\Box p$ (where B denotes p), we quickly generate paradox; see R. Montague, "Syntactical Treatments of Modality, with Corollaries on Reflexion Principles and Finite Axiomatizability", *Acta Philosophica Fennica*, fasc. xvi (1963), pp. 153–68.

elsewhere voices considerable scepticism of properties, attributes, or traits. Still, Quine is willing to avail himself of such locutions as 'property' or 'attribute' when he can produce an acceptable paraphrase, or if he can 'reduce' the entities purportedly denoted to a more domesticated variety. Presumably it is thus that he here uses 'trait'. Our present interpretation of Quine, therefore, will itself require further paraphrase from his point of view;[1] meanwhile those of us who find no problems with traits and properties, qualities and attributes, can accept it as it stands.

Quine's claim, then, is that (4) does not express a trait or property. In this regard, it contrasts with

(5) ____ is greater than 7

which does. But what, exactly, does this mean? With what distinction do we credit (5) when we say that it *does* express a property or trait? The basic idea is as follows: in the standard case, a singular context expresses a property if the result of filling its blank with a singular term α is a sentence typically used to make an assertion about α's denotation, if any. More specifically, a singular context C expresses a property only if there is a trait or property P such that the result of filling C's blank by a singular term α predicates P of the denotation (if any) of α. To put it a bit differently, C expresses a property only if the truth value of an instance of C—the result of filling its blank by a singular term α—is to be assessed by determining whether the denotation (if any) of α has P. In the typical case, furthermore, C expresses a property only if its *existential closure*—the result of filling its blank with a variable and prefixing an appropriate quantifier—says that at least one object has P; its universal closure typically adds that everything has P.

And now Quine's claim is that

(4) Necessarily, ____ is greater than 7

does not in this sense express a property or trait. But how could such a context fail to express a property? And how could an instance of (4)—

(6) Necessarily, 9 is greater than 7

for example—fail to say something about or predicate a property of 9? Perhaps an example in the Quinian spirit can help us see how. Let us introduce and explain the context '____ has sizeability' as follows:

(7) ____ has sizeability = def. ♯ ____ ♯ contains more than six letters.

[1] I shall also speak of a sentence's expressing a proposition; this too, of course, requires paraphrase on Quine's view.

This is a schema enabling us to eliminate any sentence or phrase of the form '____ has sizeability' (where the blank is to be filled by a singular term) in favour of a synonymous sentence or phrase that does not contain the word 'sizeability': the sharps indicate that the second blank in the schema is to be filled by the quotation of whatever fills the first blank. So, for example,

(8) The Grand Teton has sizeability

is to be understood as

(9) 'The Grand Teton' contains more than six letters

and is accordingly true;

(10) El Cap has sizeability,

on the other hand, falsely predicates *having more than six letters* of 'El Cap'.

We may plausibly suppose that the expression '____ has sizeability', thus understood, does not express a property or trait. For it is plausible to suppose that a singular context expresses a property P only if the result of filling its blank with a singular term t predicates P of t's denotation (if any)—only if, at any rate, this holds for some range of standard cases.[1] Here this condition is apparently unsatisfied. (8), for example, is the result of filling the blank of '____ has sizeability' by a singular term: 'the Grand Teton'. And while (8) predicates a property (*having more than six letters*) of that *term*, it does not predicate that property of the term's denotation; if it did, it would be false. So this context does not express the property *having more than six letters*. Does it perhaps express some other property? The property of *bearing at least one name containing more than six letters*, for example? No. For suppose it did. Then (10) would predicate that property of El Cap and would accordingly be true, in view of El Cap's possessing the longer name 'El Capitan'. In fact, however, (10) is false, implausibly claiming, as it does, that 'El Cap' contains more than six letters.

Further, suppose '____ has sizeability' did express a property. If so, then presumably each of (10) and

(11) El Capitan has sizeability

predicate that property of El Capitan. (10), however, is true and (11) is false; hence this property, whatever it is, is apparently had by El Capitan but lacked by El Cap—and this, alarmingly enough, despite the identity of the former with the latter. Such an outcome flagrantly conflicts with Leibniz's Law, according to which a property is had by

[1] See below, p. 229.

any object identical with anything that has it. If the context '___
has sizeability' *did* express a property, that property would fail to
meet this condition. Hence it is hard to escape the conclusion that
this context does not express a property. And Quine's claim is that
the context 'Necessarily, ___ is composite' resembles '___ has
sizeability' in just this respect.

But how is this relevant to Quine's conclusion that

(2) Necessarily, 9 is composite

does not properly yield

(3) (∃x) necessarily, x is composite

by existential generalization? The answer, of course, is that on the
standard objectual[1] understanding of quantification there is an intimate connection between a context's expressing a property and its
instances being subject to existential generalization. Roughly and
briefly, the existential generalization of a singular sentence says that
something has the property that sentence (or the proposition thereby
expressed) predicates of the denotation of its singular term. Thus

Something is pink

follows by this form of argument from

The Taj Mahal is pink.

But where, as with '___ is sizeable', a context expresses no property
at all, its substitution instances do not in general predicate a property
of the denotations of their singular terms; and existential generalization thus misfires. From the truth that

(12) Dietrich of Dordtrecht is sizeable

we cannot soundly conclude that

(13) (∃x) x is sizeable;

counting 'x' as a singular term, (13) (by (7)) is short for

(∃x) 'x' contains more than six letters

which, given usual conventions, is a vacuous quantification of an
outrageous falsehood. So (13) does not claim that something has the
property (12) predicates of Dietrich; there is no such property.

Accordingly, if Quine is right in holding that the context 'Necessarily, ___ greater than 7' does not express a property, then there
is reason indeed to insist that existential generalization misfires if
applied to its instances.

---

[1] As opposed to Mrs. Marcus's "substitutional" reading; see her "Interpreting
Quantification", *Inquiry*, 5 (1962), 252–9; see also J. M. Dunn and N. Belnap, Jr.,
"The Substitutional Interpretation of the Quantifiers", *Nous*, 2 (1968), 177–85.

3. *The Objection Restated*

So suppose we irenically concede that (2) is subject to existential generalization only if

(14) Necessarily _____ is composite

expresses a property. Quine adds, of course, that it does not. Why not? In 'Reference and Modality' and elsewhere Quine displays a strong inclination towards the claim that quantification and *substitutivity* go together. Suppose we call this *Quine's Thesis*. What it means, in the present context, is that a singular sentence S is subject to existential generalization only if the singular term to be generalized *has referential position*—only if, that is, any other singular term denoting the same object can replace it in S *salva veritate*. But what (apart from a pardonable penchant for accepting his own theses) might lead Quine to accept Quine's Thesis? Why suppose that a singular sentence is properly generalized only if its singular term has referential position?

Here perhaps the reasoning is as follows. We have already agreed that a singular sentence is subject to existential generalization only if the context of which it is an instance expresses a property. But it is natural to think that a context C expresses a property only if there is some property P such that instances of C predicate P of the denotation of their singular terms—that is,

(15) A singular context C expresses a property only if there is some property P such that an instance $C\alpha$ of C is true if and only if the denotation (if any) of α has P.

Now suppose C expresses a property and let $C\alpha$ and $C\beta$ be among its instances; suppose furthermore α and β denote the same object. Then $C\alpha$ will be true if and only if the denotation of α has P, i.e. if and only if the denotation of β has P. So $C\alpha$ will be true if and only if $C\beta$ is. If C expresses a property, therefore, then in any instance $C\alpha$ of C, α has referential position. We might put this by saying that C's blank has referential position. Accordingly a singular context expresses a property only if its blank has referential position. Given that a singular sentence is subject to existential generalization only if its context expresses a property, Quine's thesis is clearly true if (15) is. So

(14) Necessarily _____ is composite

expresses a property only if its blank has referential position; and of course it does not, according to Quine. Why not? At bottom, because, as Quine initially assumes, the operator 'necessarily' expresses modality *de dicto*, i.e. because

(16) *Necessarily* S is true if and only if S is necessarily true.[1]

Given (16),

(2) Necessarily 9 is composite

is true while

(17) Necessarily the number of planets is composite

is not, in spite of '9' 's being coreferential with 'the number of planets'.

In essence, then, Quine's argument goes as follows. A singular sentence such as (2) is subject to existential generalization only if its context expresses a property. But a singular context expresses a property only if its blank has referential position. The context

(14) Necessarily ＿＿＿ is composite

does not meet this condition; hence (2) is not properly subject to existential generalization. And the essential premises of this argument are

(15) a singular context C expresses a property only if there is some property P such that an instance $C\alpha$ of C is true if and only if the denotation of α (if any) has P

and

(16) *Necessarily* S is true if and only if S is necessarily true.

4. *The Objection Examined*

What about these premises? (16) seems initially plausible in that it merely makes specific the modal logician's original explanation of his modal operator; 'necessarily' (or '$\square$') expresses modality *de dicto*. But (15) bears further examination. Why, after all, should we suppose that *every* instance of a context expressing a property P must predicate P of the denotation (if any) of its singular term? Is it not sufficient that some large and systematically identifiable range of its instances do so? Let C be a singular context such that some large and systematically identifiable range of its instances predicate a property P of the denotations of their singular terms—and such that its existential and universal closures express, respectively, the propositions that something and everything have P. Then it seems fair to say that C would

---

[1] Where a sentence is necessarily true if it expresses a necessarily true proposition. To avoid certain versions of the liar paradox we may add that S ranges over sentences that are true or false, i.e. express propositions.

express a property; it does not follow that its blank has referential position. For perhaps among its substitution instances there are some that do *not* predicate P of the denotation of their singular terms. If so, there might well be instances S and S' of C, containing distinct singular terms t and t' denoting the same object, such that S but not S' predicates P of the denotation of t and t'. Then there is no reason why S and S' should not differ in truth value; and if they did, then C would express a property despite the irreferential position of its blank.

Consider, by way of example, the context '____ is smurdley'. This context is just like '____ is wise' except that when a singular term containing an odd number of letters fills its blank, the result expresses any false proposition you please—let us say, for definiteness, *7 plus 5 equals 13*. That is, the result of filling the blank of '____ is smurdley' by a name containing an even number of letters predicates wisdom of the bearer of that name; 'something is smurdley', furthermore, and 'everything is smurdley' express respectively the propositions *something is wise* and *everything is wise*. But the result of filling the blank by an odd numbered singular term expresses the proposition that 7 plus 5 equals 13. Thus in the true sentence

(18) Socrates is smurdley

'Socrates' will occur irreferentially in that

the teacher of Plato is smurdley

express an arithmetical absurdity. Nevertheless (18) predicates wisdom of Socrates and properly yields (by existential generalization)

Something is smurdley

which says simply that something is wise. So '____ is smurdley' expresses a property although its blank does not have referential position. Accordingly (15) does not seem to be true—not, at least, if a property-expressing context can have some instances that do not predicate that property of the denotations of their singular terms.

But what happens if we resolutely insist that *every* instance of a context C that expresses a property must predicate that property of the object, if any, denoted by its singular term? Then it becomes difficult to see that or why a singular sentence is properly generalized only if it is a substitution instance of a context that expresses a property. For even if *some* instances of C did not predicate a property of the denotation of their singular terms, others might; and if they did (and if C's existential closure expressed the right proposition) why should we not accept them as successful candidates for existential generalization?

A. *The Hintikka Response*

So (15) is not compelling; and its failure to convince may be exploited by the modal logician. Some of Hintikka's work suggests just this sort of response to Quine.[1] According to this line of response, a sentence of the form □*S* predicates necessity of *S*, thus expressing modality *de dicto*. Nothing prevents it, however, from expressing modality *de re* as well; and some sentences of this form do exactly that.

(2) □9 is composite

and

(19) ◇9 is prime,

for example, are assertions of modality *de dicto*; the first predicates necessity and the second possibility of the contained sentences. But they are also *de re*; each also predicates a property of 9—the properties expressed by the contexts '◇ ___ is prime' and '□ ___ is composite' respectively. So such contexts as '□ ___ is composite' and '◇ ___ is prime' express properties. But some of their substitution instances do *not* predicate this property of the denotation of their singular term; all depends upon the nature of that term.

(17) □ the number of planets is composite,

for example, is false in virtue of the contingency of the contained sentence; but the denotation of its singular term—the number nine —does have the property expressed by '□ ___ is composite'. Similarly,

(20) ◇ the number of planets is prime

is true; but the number of planets does not have the property expressed by '◇ ___ is prime'. (17) and (20) are *de dicto* assertions about statements; they venture no direct comment on the number of planets.

Accordingly, a context like '□ ___ is composite' expresses a property; nevertheless only some of its substitution instances predicate this property of the denotations of their singular terms. And the difference is a matter of the singular terms involved. Some singular terms—'9' for example—are such that the result of inserting them in the blank of '□ ___ is composite' predicates the property that context expresses of the term's denotation (if any); other singular terms ('the number of planets', for example) do not meet this condition. According to the Hintikka response, this distinction turns on the fact that such singular terms as '9' "denote the same object in every possible

---

[1] See, for example, "The Modes of Modality", *Acta Philosophica Fennica*, fasc. xvi (1963), pp. 65–82.

world".[1] Others—'the number of planets', for example—denote different objects in different worlds; the term in question denotes in a given world the object that (in that world) numbers the planets, and in some worlds that number will not be nine.

This distinction among singular terms, then, is crucial to the Hintikka response. All instances of

(4) □ ____ is composite

express modality *de dicto* by virtue of the truth of (16). But some of its instances also predicate a property of the denotations of their singular terms: those whose singular terms "denote the same object in every possible world". These instances, then, express both modality *de re* and modality *de dicto*.

B. *The Smullyan Reply*

The Hintikka response to Quine's argument rejects (15); another reply (one plausibly associated with Arthur Smullyan's work)[2] rejects

(16) □S is true if and only if S is necessarily true.

Consider once more

(17) □ the number of planets is composite.

Since, as Smullyan points out, we can give the description 'the number of planets' either wide or narrow scope, this sentence is ambiguous between

(17') (∃x) (x numbers the planets and (y) (if y numbers the planets then y is identical with x) and □(x is composite))

and

(17″) □ (∃x) (x numbers the planets and (y) (if y numbers the planets then y is identical with x) and x is composite).

Smullyan rates (17″) as false (since the proposition of which it predicates necessity would have been false had there been just 7 planets); (17'), on the other hand, is in his view true; it properly predicates of the number of planets the property expressed by

(4) □ ____ is composite.

(17') is a true statement of modality *de re*; (17″) is a false statement of modality *de dicto*.

---

[1] "The Modes of Modality", p. 73. See above, Chapter V, Section 3.

[2] "Modality and Description", *Journal of Symbolic Logic*, 13, 1 (1948), 31–7. Reprinted in Leonard Linsky, *Reference and Modality* (Oxford: Oxford University Press, 1971), pp. 88–100. See also Frederick B. Fitch, "The Problem of the Morning Star and the Evening Star", *Philosophy of Science*, 17 (1949), 137–40.

Now of course the ambiguity of (17) can be resolved by appropriate scope indication.¹ If we take this course (as Smullyan himself does) then we must join Hintikka in rejecting (15); for (4) expresses a property despite the fact that an instance of (4) containing a narrow scope description ((17) taken as (17″), for example) may fail to predicate that property of what its singular term denotes. But we must also reject (16); (17) with its description given wide scope predicates a property of the number of planets but says nothing about the modal properties of

(21) the number of planets is composite.

Alternatively, however, we could accept (15) by adopting the general policy of giving the description wide scope—i.e. the policy of reading such items as (17) on the model of (17′). Then '9' and 'the number of planets' will be intersubstitutible in

(4) □ ____ is composite;

that context's blank will now have referential position. (16), of course, remains false; for (17) is now true although it is the result of attaching '□' to the contingent (21). On either policy a scope distinction arises only with respect to descriptions; it is irrelevant to an item like

(2) □9 is composite

where the contained singular term is a proper name. The Smullyan reply, therefore, resembles the Hintikka response in that a distinction among singular terms is crucial to it. On either version of the Smullyan reply, a statement of modality *de dicto* like (2) is properly subject to existential generalization only because it is also *de re*; and those substitution instances of (4) that express both modality *de dicto* and modality *de re* are just the ones whose singular terms are proper names, not definite descriptions.

5. *Proper Terms and Aristotelian Essentialism*

The Smullyan reply and the Hintikka response unite in holding that some substitution instances of '□ ____ is composite' are both *de re* and *de dicto* while others are one or the other but not both; they differ in that on the former approach (2nd version) each substitution instance of this context is *de re*, some being also *de dicto*, while on the latter each is *de dicto*, some being also *de re*. According to the former approach, furthermore, the context in question contains a referentially occurring blank, but does not always express modality *de dicto*.

---

¹ See R. Thomason and R. Stalnaker, "Modality and Reference", *Nous*, 2 (1968), 359–72.

On the latter, it always expresses modality *de dicto*, but its blank has irreferential occurrence. On either approach a statement like

(2) □9 is composite,

performs at least two distinct functions. It predicates necessity of

(22) 9 is composite;

but since it yields

(3) (∃x) (□x is composite)

by way of existential generalization, it must also predicate a property of 9—the property (3) says something has. (Call this 'the property of being necessarily composite'.) (2), therefore, on these two approaches, expresses both modality *de dicto* and modality *de re*; and only because of this dual role is a *de dicto* item like (2) subject to existential generalization.

But the complexity of such contexts as '□ ____ is composite' and '◇ ____ is prime', on the Smullyan and Hintikka alternatives, does not stop here. For while (2) plays the dual role of predicating necessity of (22) and a property of nine, such items as

(17) □ the number of planets is composite

and

(20) ◇ the number of planets is prime

cannot as gracefully express both modality *de dicto* and modality *de re*. The dual role of (2) is acceptable because the propositions expressed by

nine is composite is necessary

and

nine has the property of being necessarily composite

are equivalent in a very strong sense, if indeed there are two distinct propositions here. But (17) and (20) cannot thus smoothly play both *de dicto* and *de re* roles, the former expressing something equivalent to each of

(17′) *The number of planets is composite* is necessary

and

(17″) The number of planets has the property of being necessarily composite

and the latter doing the same for

(20′) *The number of planets is prime* is possible

and

(20″) The number of planets has the property of being possibly prime.

The reason, of course, is that (17′) and (17″) differ in truth value. The former is false; but the number of planets has the property of being necessarily composite if nine does, and nine has it if (2) yields (3) by existential generalization. And of course a similar difference in truth value characterizes (20′) and (20″). The Hintikka response and the Smullyan reply (2nd version) accordingly diverge at this point, the former reading (17) as (17′) and the latter reading it as (17″).

On each of these approaches, (2) is subject to existential generalization and (3) makes sense only because

(4) _____ is composite

plays this complex and devious role; some of its substitution instances —(2), for example—express both modality *de re* and modality *de dicto*, while others—(17), for example—perform only one of these functions. And on each of these approaches the difference is referred to a difference between the contained singular terms. On the first approach, '9' but not 'the number of planets' "denotes the same object in every possible world"; on this approach a substitution instance of (4) expresses both modality *de dicto* and modality *de re* only if its singular term resembles '9' in this respect. On the Smullyan approach a substitution instance of (4) plays this dual role only if scope considerations do not arise—i.e. only if the contained singular term is a name, not a description. Suppose we say that a singular term is *proper* if and only if the result of inserting it in the blank of

(4) □ _____ is composite

expresses both modality *de re* and modality *de dicto*. In holding that some *de dicto* modal sentences are subject to existential generalization, the Hintikka and Smullyan approaches must distinguish proper from improper singular terms. These proper terms are ones in which *de re* greets *de dicto*.

Both of these approaches, then, provide a way to reason from such a proposition as (2) to its existential generalization—a way that does not display the absurdities of which Quine initially speaks. But each pays a price—the *same* price: each is obliged to distinguish proper from improper terms.

6. *Modal Logic and Essentialism*

If these are replies to Quine's objection to quantified modal logic, what, in turn, is Quine's response? The answer, in a word (or two) is ARISTOTELIAN ESSENTIALISM. Quine does not, if I have him right, mean finally to insist that '□ ___ is composite' does not express a property. His ultimate criticism, instead, is that one who so takes it will lose his way in the jungles of Aristotelian Essentialism, the doctrine

> that some of the attributes of a thing (quite independently of the language in which the thing is referred to, if at all) may be essential to the thing and others accidental. E.g., a man or talking animal, or featherless biped (for they are all in fact the same *things*) is essentially rational and accidentally two legged and talkative, not merely *qua* man but *qua* itself.[1]   (FLPV 21)

But why, exactly? The argument here has two interconnected strands. We noted that the Smullyan reply and the Hintikka response unite in making a distinction between proper and improper singular terms. But to each singular term t there corresponds a singular condition. This distinction among singular terms, therefore, is mirrored by a distinction among singular conditions; for example, the conditions

(32) $x = \sqrt{x} + \sqrt{x} + \sqrt{x} \neq x^2$

and

(33) there are exactly x planets

correspond respectively to proper and improper singular terms denoting the same number (FLPV 149). But making this distinction, says Quine, commits one to Aristotelian Essentialism:

> Nevertheless, the only hope of sustaining quantified modal logic lies in adopting a course that resembles Smullyan's rather than Church and Carnap, in this way: it must overrule my objection. It must consist in arguing or deciding that quantification into modal contexts makes sense even though any value of the variable of such a quantification be determinable by conditions that are not analytically equivalent to each other. The only hope lies in accepting the situation illustrated by (32) and (33) and insisting, despite it, that the object x in question is necessarily greater than 7. This means adopting an invidious attitude toward certain ways of uniquely specifying x, for example (33), and favoring other ways, for example (32), as somehow better revealing the "essence" of the object. Consequences of (32) can, from such a point of view, be looked upon as necessarily true of the object which is 9 (and is the number of planets), while some consequences of (33) are rated still as only contingently true of that object.

[1] This doctrine may or may not have a great deal to do with Aristotle. Quine himself remarks that "one attributes it to Aristotle, subject, of course, to contradiction by scholars, such being the penalty for attributions to Aristotle". 'Aristotelian Essentialism', as Quine uses the term, is meant to be a suggestive label rather than a historically accurate description; whether Aristotle accepted Aristotelian Essentialism is not central to Quine's concerns.

Evidently this reversion to Aristotelian Essentialism is required if quantification into modal contexts is to be insisted on. An object, of itself and by whatever name or none, must be seen as having some of its traits necessarily and others contingently, despite the fact that the latter traits follow just as analytically from some ways of specifying the object as the former traits do from other ways of specifying it. (FLPV 154–5)

So apparently this distinction among singular terms or conditions, crucial to the two approaches mentioned above, constitutes a reversion to essentialism, a doctrine of which Quine does not speak kindly: "To defend Aristotelian Essentialism, however, is no part of my plan. Such a philosophy is as unreasonable by my lights as it is by Carnap's or Lewis's. And in conclusion I say, as Carnap and Lewis have not: so much the worse for quantified modal logic." (FLPV 156)

But this same conclusion may be reached by a different and more direct route. Smullyan and Hintikka hold that '□ ____ is composite' express a property that

(3) (Ex) □x is composite

says at least one thing has. It is of fundamental importance to see the following point. Given the *de dicto* understanding of '□'—the only explanation offered by Lewis, Hughes, and Cresswell, *et al.*[1]—given this explanation and the usual objectual reading of the quantifier we do not as yet have the ghost of an explanation of '□' in (3). This point is central. In (3), '□' does not express modality *de dicto*; it does not serve to predicate necessary truth of the proposition expressed by the sentence it governs, there being no such sentence and proposition. Armed only with the usual *de dicto* explanation of '□', we do not have truth conditions for this sentence. We do not know the conditions under which an object satisfies

(4) □ ____ is composite

or what property this context expresses. If y is an object denoted by some singular term, y satisfies such a context as '—— is red' if some result of filling the blank by a singular term denoting y is a true sentence; y fails to satisfy this context if some such result is false. But of course this fails here; for, given no more than the *de dicto* understanding of '□', we find that

(17) □ the number of planets is composite

and

(2) □9 is composite

differ in truth value. So how do we tell when an object satisfies (4)?

---

[1] See above, p. 223.

Learning the difference between necessary and contingent propositions is of no help here. What we need to know, of course, is what property (4) expresses and (3) says something has; and Quine's contention, as I understand him, is that we cannot give an interpretation or explanation of this sentence and this context without committing ourselves to Aristotelian Essentialism. The point is not, I think, the correct but trivial observation that if we quantify into a modal context such as (4) we must take that context to express a property that an object has, if at all, under every description, by whatever name or none. This much follows from Leibniz's Law and our objectual reading of the quantifier. The point is rather this. Given just the usual *de dicto* reading of '□', we have not been told *what property it is* that (4) expresses; and we do not know how to read such a formula as (3). We do know, of course, that whatever property (4) does express will obey Leibniz's Law, that being a condition of propertyhood; but we do not know what property that might be. And Quine's suggestion, if I understand him, is that a natural or standard interpretation of quantified modal logic (thereby explaining what property it is that (4) expresses) will involve essentialism: under interpretation such characteristic formulas as (3) will be no more intelligible than this ancient distinction between essential and accidental properties of objects.

7. *Quine's Charge and Professor Marcus*

Is he right?

Professor Marcus[1] says he is, but remains unimpressed. She agrees that quantified modal logic is essentialist; the essentialism to which it is committed, however, is in her judgement merely trivial, and hence not such as properly to be boggled at. She takes as representative a quantified S_5 that contains individual constants (but no definite descriptions) and includes notation for abstraction as well as the axiom schema

(23) $x \in \hat{y}A \equiv B$, where B is the result of replacing each free occurrence of y in A by x.

Call this theory QM. Abstracts receive a natural interpretation as denoting attributes; every QM sentence, therefore, that contains a name of some object x is equivalent in QM to one or more sentences predicating an attribute of x.

$$\square(Aa \vee {\sim}Aa)$$

for example, is equivalent by (23) to

$$a \in \hat{y}\square(Ay \vee {\sim}Ay)$$

[1] "Essentialism in Modal Logic", *Nous*, 1 (1967), 91.

which predicates of a the attribute denoted by '$\hat{y}\Box(Ay \lor {\sim}Ay)$', an attribute plausibly identified, says Mrs. Marcus, with the property an object x has if and only if it had the attribute $\hat{y}(Ay \lor {\sim}Ay)$ *necessarily* or *essentially* (ibid., p. 92).

Mrs. Marcus characterizes a theory T as *weakly essentialist* if there is some attribute $\hat{y}Ay$ such that

(24) $(\exists x)(\exists z)(\Box(x \in \hat{y}Ay) \cdot{\sim}\Box(z \in \hat{y}Ay))$

is a theorem of T; it is strongly essentialist if there is an attribute such that

(25) $(\exists x)(\exists z)(\Box(x \in \hat{y}Ay) \cdot z \in \hat{y}Ay \cdot{\sim}\Box(z \in \hat{y}Ay))$

is a theorem. Notice that a theory may be essentialist in Quine's sense (above, p. 236) without counting as either weakly or strongly essentialist in Mrs. Marcus's sense. Suppose an extension of QM contains the assertion that

$$Fb \text{ and } {\sim}\Box Fb$$

along with

$$\Box(Bb \lor {\sim}Bb).$$

It will follow that

$$b \in \hat{x}Fx \cdot {\sim}\Box b \in \hat{x}Fx$$

and

(26) $\Box b \in \hat{x}(Bx \lor {\sim}Bx)$;

that is, b has some of its attributes essentially and others merely accidentally. A theory such as this is essentialist in Quine's sense but need be neither weakly nor strongly essentialist in Mrs. Marcus's sense.

This is as it should be. For what disturbs Quine about essentialism? He argues as follows for the 'meaninglessness' of

(31) $(\text{E}x)$ x is necessarily greater than 7:

Whatever is greater than 7 is a number, and any given number x greater than 7 can be uniquely determined by any of various conditions, some of which have '$x > 7$' as a *necessary* consequence and some of which do not. One and the same number x is uniquely determined by the condition:

(32) $x = \sqrt{x} + \sqrt{x} + \sqrt{x} \neq x$

and by the condition:

(33) There are exactly x planets,

but (32) has '$x > 7$' as a necessary consequence while (33) does not. *Necessary* greaterness than 7 makes no sense as applied to a *number x*; necessity attaches only to the connection between '$x > 7$' and the particular method (32), as opposed to (33) of specifying x. (FLPV 149)

But a condition like '$Fx \lor \sim Fx$' is a consequence of *every* way of specifying x; claiming that x has essentially the attribute expressed by this condition ought therefore to occasion no Quinian qualms. Accordingly a theory that confines its essentialist attributions to such items as (26) should be innocent enough, even from a Quinian point of view. An essentialist theory is objectionable, from that point of view, only if it insists that some objects have essentially some attributes that others have accidentally if at all. Hence Mrs. Marcus's characterization of weak and strong essentialism.

Given her characterization, then, it is immediately evident that QM (or rather a trivial extension of it) is weakly essentialist. For suppose we add the assumption that there are at least two individuals and suppose that we have names 'a' and 'b' for them: then among the theorems we shall have

$$\Box a \in \hat{y}(y = a)$$

and

$$\sim \Box b \in \hat{y}(y = a).$$

Accordingly there is an attribute—$\hat{y}(y = a)$—such that

$$(\exists x)(\exists z)(\Box(x \in \hat{y}(y = a)) \cdot \sim \Box(z \in \hat{y}(y = a))).$$

Since this is an instance of (24), QM is shown to be weakly essentialist. Now suppose we add '$\Box a \neq b$' (in QM this will presumably follow from '$a \neq b$'), along with the assumption that there is at least one property b has, but does not have essentially: represent this last by

$$Fb \cdot \sim \Box Fb.$$

The resulting theory is easily seen to be strongly essentialist. We have

$$\Box(a = a \lor Fa) \cdot (b = a \lor Fb) \cdot \sim \Box(b = a \lor Fb)$$

and hence

$$\Box a \in \hat{y}(y = a \lor Fy) \cdot b \in \hat{y}(y = a \lor Fy) \cdot \sim \Box b \in y(y = a \lor Fy)$$

which obviously yields the appropriate substitution instance of (24).

QM, therefore (or a trivial extension of it), is both weakly and strongly essentialist. Well then, is Quine's contention not shown to be true? According to Mrs. Marcus, Quine's claim is true but trivial. How so, exactly? Suppose we agree, she says,

> that an attribute is non-referential with respect to an object a if it represented by an abstract which does not mention a. Otherwise it is referential with respect to a. Now, [(23)], the axiom over abstraction, tells us that although a proposition may be assigning a plurality of attributes to a, these assignments are strictly equivalent. For example
>
> $$\mathbf{a} \in \hat{x}(xIx) \equiv \mathbf{a} \in \hat{x}(aIx).$$

From the substitution principle for strict equivalence, it follows that all statements containing referential attributes can be replaced by statements containing non-referential attributes in QM. This suggests that there is an additional sense in which provably essential attributes are trivial in QM. . . . since any statement which contains a referential attribute can by [(23)] be replaced by an equivalent one which does not contain a referential attribute, such essential attributes are trivialized in QM.

I think we may understand this as follows. Suppose we say that an attribute $\hat{y}Ay$ is QM essentialist if

(24) $(\exists x)(\exists z)(\square x \in \hat{y}Ay \cdot \sim \square z \in \hat{y}Ay)$

is a theorem of QM. Mrs. Marcus means to endorse

(27) Any QM-provable sentence of the form $\square x \in \hat{y}Ay$, where $\hat{y}Ay$ is QM essentialist, is QM-equivalent to another sentence of that form in which the attribute represented is not QM essentialist.

Perhaps the argument for (27) may be construed as follows. If $\hat{y}Ay$ is a QM essentialist attribute and S is any provable sentence of the form $\square x \in \hat{y}Ay$, then $\hat{y}Ay$ will be referential with respect to x. So, for example,

(28) $\square a \in \hat{y}(y = a)$

is QM provable, and the attribute it predicates of a is referential with respect to a. But any sentence S predicating of x an attribute referential with respect to x is QM-equivalent to some sentence predicating of x an attribute which is non-referential with respect to it: simply replace each occurrence of the name of x in S by a variable and apply abstraction. S is therefore equivalent to a sentence of the form $\square x \in \hat{y}By$ where $\hat{y}By$ is not QM essentialist. (28), for example, is QM equivalent to

$$\square a \in \hat{y}(y = y);$$

and of course $\hat{y}(y = y)$ is not referential with respect to a.

Now (27) seems plausible; suppose we concede its truth. Mrs. Marcus apparently thinks it follows that QM, though essentialist, is only *trivially* essentialist. She apparently means to suggest something like

(29) A theory T in which every theorem predicating of an object x the essential possession of a T-essentialist attribute, is equivalent to some sentence predicating of x the essential possession of some attribute that is not T-essentialist, is, if essentialist at all, only trivially so.

It is not easy to see that or why this should be so. First of all, in a theory T which (like QM) contains (23), a sentence like

$$\square a \in \hat{x}Fx$$

will be equivalent to

$$\Box Fa$$

and hence to

$$a \in \hat{x}\Box Fa.$$

The attribute $\hat{x}\Box Fa$, however, is not T-essentialist in that everything, according to T, has it. So let a QM-like theory contain the most blatantly non-trivial essentialist assertion you please:

  $\Box$ Paul Y. Zwier $\in \hat{x}(x$ is a clever conversationalist$)$

for example. Such an assertion will be equivalent, in the theory, to one *not* predicating an essentialist attribute of the object in question —in this case to

  Paul Y. Zwier $\in \hat{x}\Box$(Paul Y. Zwier is a clever conversationalist)

where the attribute represented is not essentialist and hence the theory in question will be, by (29), only trivially essentialist. But surely if *any* theory is non-trivially essentialist, this one about Paul Zwier is.

  Of course, this defect in (29) is easily remedied; we can narrow the class of attributes under discussion to those whose abstracts are of the form $\hat{y}A$ where y occurs free in A. (29) thus revised claims that a QM-like theory T is at most trivially essentialist if every theorem predicating a T-essentialist attribute of any object x is T-equivalent to one that predicates of x a non-essentialist attribute whose abstract meets the condition just mentioned. But the principle thus modified is still dubious at best. Let us extend QM by adding names of numbers, the predicate 'Cx' (for 'x is composite'), and '$\Box$C9'. We then have

  (30) $\Box 9 \in \hat{y}Cy$

equivalent to each of

$$\Box C9,\ \Box 9 = 9, \text{ and } \Box 9 \in \hat{y}(y = y).$$

(30), therefore, is equivalent in the theory to

$$\Box 9 \in \hat{y}(y \in y)$$

which latter, of course, predicates of 9 an attribute that is not essentialist and meets the condition mentioned in the revision of (29). The claim that on this account our theory is only trivially essentialist, however, is at best exceedingly implausible. (29), therefore (or its revision), gives us no good reason to believe that QM is at most trivially essentialist. We might as well argue that a standard propositional modal logic is committed to modality *de dicto* in at most a trivial way, since every statement of the form $\Box S$, provable in the theory, is provably equivalent to $p \vee \sim p$, which contains no modal operators at all.

Seen in broader perspective, the idea underlying (29) seems to be this. If a theory or person commits himself to a proposition P predicating of an object x the essential possession of an essentialist attribute (an attribute that only some things have essentially) and if P is equivalent in some strong sense to a statement predicating of x an attribute that is not essentialist in this sense, then, so far forth, the essentialism embraced is harmless and merely trivial. Now perhaps such an essentialism is indeed harmless, but it scarcely seems trivial. An essentialist who accepts

(31) Socrates is essentially a non-number

and

(31*) Socrates is essentially a person

is likely to hold that Socrates has a property P essentially just in case Socrates has P and there is no possible world in which he has its complement.[1] He is likely to hold further that (31) and (31*) are strongly equivalent in the sense that they are true in the very same worlds. More generally, he is likely to hold that if p and q are any true statements each of which predicates of Socrates the essential possession of some property, then p and q are equivalent in this sense. The attributes *being self-identical* and *being-coloured-if-red* will be essential to Socrates, so that a statement predicating either of him will be equivalent to (31) and (31*). But these two attributes are essential to everything else as well; hence they are not essentialist attributes. Accordingly, such an essentialist will hold that any proposition predicating the essential possession of an essentialist attribute of an object, is equivalent to some statement that predicates a non-essentialist attribute of that same object. But could such an essentialist protest, by way of a genial effort to quiet Quinian qualms, that this equivalence shows his theory to be at most *trivially* essentialist? This would be ill-conceived at best; it would be hard indeed to see what he might mean by 'trivial'.

8 . *Quine's Charge and Professor Parsons*

Terrence Parsons[2] agrees that what perplexes Quine is not the mere suggestion that some properties—*being coloured if red*, for example—are essential to their owners; this is harmless enough. Essentialism

[1] See above, Chapter IV, Section 8.

[2] "Essentialism and Quantified Modal Logic", *Philosophical Review*, 78 (1969), 35–52. Reprinted in L. Linsky (ed.), *Reference and Modality* (Oxford University Press, 1971). Page references are to this volume.

becomes troublesome, he says, when it goes on to add that there are some properties had essentially by some objects and accidentally or not at all by others. Proposing to look for a syntactical criterion of this troublesome version of essentialism—a formula such that if a theory endorses an instance of it, that theory is thereby shown to be committed to essentialism of this sort—Parsons first considers

(32) $(\exists x_1)...(\exists x_n)\Box F \cdot (\exists x_1)...(\exists x_n)\sim\Box F$;

However, he rejects (32) on the grounds that some of its instances are "untroublesome"; for example

(33) $(\exists x)(\exists y)\Box(Fx \vee \sim Fy) \cdot (\exists x)(\exists y)\sim\Box(Fx \vee \sim Fy)$

and

(34) $(\exists x)(\exists y)\Box(x = y) \cdot (\exists x)(\exists y)\sim\Box(x = y)$.[1]

Accordingly he moves to

(35) $(\exists x_1)...(\exists x_n)(\pi_n x_n \cdot \Box F) \cdot (\exists x_1)...(\exists x_n)(\pi_n x_n \cdot \sim\Box F)$

where F is an open formula whose free variables are included among the x_i and where $\pi_n x_n$ is a conjunction of formulas of the form $x_i = x_j$ or $x_i \neq x_j$ for every $1 \leqslant i \leqslant j \leqslant n$, but not including both $x_i = x_j$ and $x_i \neq x_j$ for any i, j. (77)

A theory is essentialist, therefore, if it embraces an instance of (35). But how could a theory do a thing like that? If either (1) some instance of (35) is a theorem, or (2) the addition to the theory of an "obvious and uncontrovertible non-modal fact" yields such a sentence, or (3) the theory permits the formulation of some such essential sentence (p. 78). So is quantified modal logic committed in these senses to essentialism? Obviously the answer depends on which modal logic we are talking about; and Parsons proposes to treat the class of systems whose semantics is examined by Saul Kripke.[2] What Parsons shows is that for the Kripke systems there exist *maximal* models—that is, models in which (essentially) $\mathscr{U}$ is non-empty, and in which for every subset $\mathscr{U}^*$ of $\mathscr{U}$ and every function χ mapping the predicate letters P^n on to subsets of $\mathscr{U}^n$, there is a world W in K such that $\Psi(W) = \mathscr{U}^*$ and $\Phi(P^n, W) = \chi(P^n)$, for all P^n other than '$=$'. Intuitively, we may think of a maximal model as one in which for each object x in $\mathscr{U}$, and for each predicate P^1, there is a world in which x exists and P^1 is true of it, and one in which it exists but P^1 is false of it (and similarly, of course, for n-tuples from $\mathscr{U}$ and n-adic predicates).

What is significant about a maximal model is that in it no essential

---

[1] See below, p. 249.
[2] For a brief account of Kripke semantics, see Chapter VII, Section 2.

sentence is true in any world. It follows, of course, that no essential sentence is a theorem of any of these systems; hence Kripke-style modal logic is not committed to essentialism in sense (1). A further consequence is that no set of non-modal sentences of the system together with the theorems of the system imply (by ordinary predicate logic) an essential sentence; Parsons takes this (p. 79) to show that Kripke-style modal logic is not committed to essentialism in sense (2) either. On the other hand, such a modal logic is obviously committed to essentialism in sense (3), since clearly enough any number of essential sentences are formulable in it. This commitment, however, is not to be boggled at, for "Suppose that the modal logician disbelieves all essential sentences. He then has a simple means of assigning determinate (and natural) truth conditions to all essential sentences. That is to make them false in all possible worlds. In other words, freedom of commitment to essentialism in the first two senses *allows* a freedom of any objectionable commitment in the third sense" (85). Parsons's point, so far as I understand him here, is that while the modal logician is committed to the *meaningfulness* of essentialist sentences, freedom of commitment in the first two senses gives him freedom to assign truth conditions to these sentences in any way he pleases. For example, he can simply declare them necessarily false, making an appropriate addition to the axioms and to the semantical evaluation rules.

Now of course it is modal logic as *applied* that is the focus of Quine's concern; what he finds particularly disconcerting is that the addition to the axioms of a relatively unproblematic statement of modality *de dicto*—for example

(36) □9 is greater than 7

yields a statement

(37) (∃x) □x is greater than 7

that apparently commits us to essentialism. Parsons's response here is to suggest that (36) can be formulated as

(36′) □(∃x)(∃y) (x is nine and y is seven and x is greater than y)

rather than

(36″) (∃x)(∃y) □(x is nine and y is seven and x is greater than y).

(Here 'nine' and 'seven' are not thought of as singular terms but simply as components of the predicates 'is nine' and 'is seven'.) The latter is true only if there are a pair of objects x and y such that x is nine and y is seven in every possible world, and, in every world, x is greater than y—clearly an essentialist contention. The former, on the other hand, does not yield (37) and does not commit us to essentialism, since it requires only that in each world there be a pair of objects one of which is nine, the other being seven and less than the first. Of course it does not follow that the same objects are nine and seven in every world; and hence the essentialist result is not forthcoming.

Is Parsons right? We can accept and apply quantified modal logic and its semantics, he says, while disavowing essentialism by construing statements like (36) on the model of (36′) instead of (36″), holding the latter to be false. But can we do this with any show of plausibility? What, after all, does 'is nine' mean? What property does it express? Presumably this predicate is true of an object just in case that object is the number nine, is identical with nine. To suppose (36″) false, therefore, we must suppose that there is a possible world in which the thing that is in fact (in this world) identical with nine, either is not identical with nine or else is not greater than seven. We shall have to suppose, further, that this thing—the thing that is in fact nine—is in some world identical with the number seventeen— otherwise *not being seventeen* will be essential to it, but not to seventeen, and we shall be back at troublesome essentialism. Indeed, we shall have to suppose that there is a world in which this thing is not a number at all, and one in which it is a tricycle—otherwise *being a number* and *not being a tricycle* will be essential to it but not to everything. But are these suppositions sensible? If we accept the semantical scheme but reject essentialism we shall have to accept them. As for me and my house, however, we find it incredible that there should be possible states of affairs such that had they obtained, the thing that *is* the number nine *would have been* the number 17, or the Taj Mahal, or a tricycle.

The suggested expedient of reading (36) as (36′) rather than (36″), declaring the latter to be false, may gain a certain undeserved plausibility from the familiar claim that number theory can be 'reduced' to set theory in various ways.[1] According to this claim, we can preserve arithmetic while, for example, identifying zero with the null set and a given non-zero number n with the unit set of its predecessor. Or we could take each non-zero number to be the set of its predecessors. Or we could, if we wished, identify the natural numbers with objects of quite a different sort; all that is really required is a countably infinite set of objects together with a relation under which they form a sequence or progression. And since practically anything you please is the tenth element in some progression, any object can be 'identified', in this sense, with nine. It could be tempting to see in this fact justification or evidence for such a claim as that

(38) the number nine could have been a tricycle;

[1] See above, Chapter II, Section 2.

for there is a reduction of number theory in which nine is identified with a tricycle.

It is a mistake, I think, to argue for (38) along the suggested lines. In Chapter II we saw that nine can be identified, in the present sense, with a tricycle or with the unit set of eight; it does not follow that nine is possibly a tricycle or, for that matter, possibly a set.[1] But let us turn instead to the objects with which one customarily identifies numbers—such items, for example, as the unit set of the null set. Could *that* have been a tricycle, or Quine's maiden aunt? Here the answer seems to me both obvious and negative. Suppose therefore we aim to apply our modal logic to such statements as

☐ the unit set of the null set has just one member

or

☐ the unit set of the null set is not a tricycle;

if we wish to follow Parsons's method for eschewing essentialism we shall have to swallow the notion that in some possible world the thing that *is* (in this world) the unit set of the null set has more than one member or is not a set at all but a tricycle. The point is that Parsons's way of avoiding commitment to essentialism exacts a pretty heavy price. We can accept and apply modal logic while avoiding essentialism in the way he suggests only if we are prepared to make these bizarre suppositions.

More important, perhaps, is the fact that this procedure cannot be expected to dispel Quinian qualms about modal logic. In essence, these qualms turn on Quine's belief that in applying this logic we shall have to commit ourselves to such statements as that the number nine is in fact composite and furthermore could not, under any possible circumstances, have been prime—to the supposition that is, that there is no possible state of affairs or possible world such that if it had obtained, nine would have been prime. Quine's claim, of course, is not that such a supposition is tolerably clear but clearly false; he thinks (rightly or wrongly) that statements such as these are incoherent or deficient in sense. Surely these strictures, if sound, will extend with equal force to the suppositions Parsons asks us, as modal logicians intent on eschewing essentialism, to make—such suppositions, e.g., as that there is a possible state of affairs such that, had it obtained, what is in fact nine would have been a tricycle or the number 17 or the Grand Teton. *If*, as Quine contends, it makes no sense to say that nine (but not everything) is composite in every possible world, the same, presumably, will hold for the claim that for

[1] Section 2.

any (consistent) property you care to mention, there is a possible world in which 9 has it.

9. *Essentialism and Applied Semantics*

What is central and most important here, however, is the following. No doubt Parsons is right in holding that no essential sentence is a theorem of the Kripke systems or consistent extensions reached by adding modal free axioms. But this is less than decisive for the question whether Kripke-style quantified modal logic is committed to essentialism. For why, after all, should Parsons think that a theory containing an essentialist theorem *is* committed to essentialism? Well, he apparently takes Kripke semantics in what seems an eminently straightforward and sensible way—as, among other things, a way of giving a meaning or interpretation to the formulae of modal logic. It does so by interpreting

(3) (E*x*) □(*x* is composite),

for example, as expressing the assertion that there exists an object that has the property of being composite in every world. So taken, the semantics involves the ideas that there are such things as possible worlds—"possible states of affairs or ways the world could have been" as Parsons puts it (p. 78). It also involves the idea that a given individual exists in some (but perhaps not all) of these worlds, and that individuals have properties in these worlds. Under this interpretation, an essential sentence expresses a proposition which is true only if there exist objects *x* and *y* and a property *P* such that *P* characterizes *x* but not *y* in every possible world. But if *x* has *P* in every possible world, then it is not possible that *x* should have lacked *P*; i.e. *x* has *P* essentially. A theory with an essential sentence as a theorem, therefore, is committed to the claim that some properties are essential to some but not all objects; it is therefore committed to essentialism in Parsons's sense.

Now to take Kripke semantics in this way—as thus interpreting a sentence like (3)—is of course to take it as *applied* semantics, not *pure* semantics.[1] Strictly speaking, what Kripke presents is a pure semantics. A model structure, for example, is just any triple (G, K, R) where G is a member of K and R is reflexive on K. K could be a set of cities, for example, with G being the largest. In particular K need not be a set of possible worlds. And $\Psi(W)$, the other element in a model structure, is just any function from K to sets of objects. The pure semantics as such is committed to no philosophical doctrine at all.

---

[1] For the distinction between pure and applied semantics, see above, Chapter VII, Section 4.

Of course the pure semantics also fails to give us a meaning or interpretation for '□'; it does not tell us what such an item as

(3) (Ex) □x is composite

might mean. For that we must invoke an appropriate *applied* semantics. Parsons turns to the applied semantics one naturally associates with Kripke pure semantics. K will now be a set of possible worlds. Objects exist in these worlds; that is, at least some possible worlds are such that if they had obtained, there would have existed some objects; α, clearly enough, is such a world. And Ψ'(W) will assign to each world W the set of objects existing in W—the set of objects that would have existed had W been actual.[1] Furthermore, the members of 𝒰 have *properties* (alternatively: are such that predicates are true of them) in these worlds—the same object quite possibly having different properties in different possible worlds.

The applied semantics, of course, gives us a meaning for (3) and other items; (3) is now the claim that there exists an object that has the property of being composite in each possible world. But by the same token the semantics, so taken, is committed to essentialism. Consider, first of all, a formula like

(39) $(\exists x)(\exists y)\Box(x = y) \cdot (\exists x)(\exists y)\sim\Box(x = y),$

a formula Parsons does not find troublesomely essentialist. (39) is a theorem of trivial extensions of the systems under consideration. Interpreted in accordance with the applied semantics, (39) will be true only if there exists a pair of objects—call them 'a' and 'b'—such that a but not b has the property of being identical with a in every possible world—i.e. essentially. (39) so interpreted therefore implies essentialism. True, as Parsons points out, (39) will be "true in any domain of more than one object" and will be true there because "the two quantifiers in the first conjunct can range over the same objects" (p. 76). No doubt this is so: but how does it absolve (39) from its essentialist commitments? What it shows, indeed, is that one need add no more than the proposition that there exist at least two objects in order to achieve the essentialist conclusion. (39) will be true only if there are objects a and b in Ψ'(G) such that (a,a) but not (b,a) is assigned to '=' in every world—i.e. only if there exists an object that in every world has the property of being identical with a and another object that does not have this property in every world. But if so, then essentialism is true; and any theory thus interpreted that has (39) as a theorem is clearly committed to essentialism in the sense

---

[1] So taken, this semantics involves the idea that there are or could have been objects that do not exist; see above, Chapter VII, Section 5.

that the theory is true, under this interpretation, only if essentialism is.

Furthermore, consider such world indexed-properties[1] as *having-P-in-α* or *having-P-in-G*. On the applied semantics, an object that has *P* in fact will have the property *having-P-in-G* and will have it in every world—that is, essentially. So if we accept the applied semantics and add some trivial truths, we are committed to essentialism. For example, if we add the truth that there are several things existing in the actual world, some but not all of which have the property of being wise, we shall have to suppose that some objects have the property *being wise in G* essentially while others do not. In any world, Socrates will have the property *teaches Plato in G*; most other members of Ψ(G) lack this distinction. So Socrates but not everything has that property essentially. Of course it might be argued that such properties as *being identical with Socrates* or *being snubnosed in G* are not "ordinary" or "natural" properties.[2] No doubt these properties are not among these in which, in the day-to-day conduct of our affairs, we have an overwhelming interest. Still there are such properties, maverick and unstylish though they be; and we do not alter this fact by sneering at them or casting aspersions on their ancestry. Parsons's question is whether Kripke semantics for quantified modal logic is committed to essentialism. The answer is that Kripke *pure* semantics commits itself in no way to essentialism; but it also gives us no meaning or interpretation for such sentences as (3). For that we must turn, as Parsons does, to an *applied* semantics; and the applied semantics naturally associated with Kripke pure semantics is indeed committed to essentialism.

Of course it is possible to associate a very different applied semantics with the Kripke pure semantics; one might in consequence take talk of possible worlds to be a mere *façon de parler* or a heuristic device to aid the imagination. One is then obliged to give meaning to '□' and to sentences like (3) in some other way—possibly in terms of speakers of natural languages (or some favourite segment of them) and their linguistic commitments.[3] Here many interesting questions arise; whether such an interpretation can be worked out and defended in detail remains to be seen. But so far the upshot seems to be this. Quine's initial complaint is that such characteristic contexts of quantified modal logic as '□*x* is composite' do not express properties; hence their instances cannot properly sustain existential

---

[1] See Chapter IV, Section 11.

[2] See R. Marcus, "Essential Attribution", *Journal of Philosophy*, 68 (1971), p. 195; and see above, p. 64.

[3] See B. van Fraassen, "Meaning Relations among Predicates", *Nous*, 1 (1967), 161–79, and "Meaning Relations and Modalities", *Nous*, 3 (1969), 155–67.

quantification. This contention is by no means obviously true and Quine himself does not mean to insist upon it. Instead, he moves to the charge that the result of interpreting and applying quantified modal logic presupposes what he calls Aristotelian Essentialism. Here Quine seems to be right, at least in so far as the applied semantics most naturally associated with the dominant variety of pure semantics clearly does imply the truth of that ancient doctrine. Whether we should join Quine in declaring "So much the worse for quantified modal logic" is of course another question. I hope the above chapters show there is no need to do so.

INDEX

DATE DUE